DATE DUE

PRINTED IN U.S.A.

try

nthology

◇

◇

◇

Gwynn

r University

HarperCollins *CollegePublishers*

APR   '76   RIVERSIDE C C LIBRARY

Acquisitions Editor: Lisa Moore
Cover Design: Lucy Krikorian
Production Administrator: Kewal Sharma
Compositors: Mark Gerrard & Pearl Klein
Printer and Binder: R. R. Donnelley & Sons Company
Cover Printer: The Lehigh Press, Inc.

For permission to use copyrighted material, grateful acknowledgment is made to the copyright holders on page 351 which is hereby made part of the copyright page.

Poetry: A HarperCollins Pocket Anthology
Copyright © 1993 by HarperCollins College Publishers

All rights reserved. Printed in the United States of America. No part of this book may be used or reproduced in any manner whatsoever without written permission, except in the case of brief quotations embodied in critical articles and reviews. For information address HarperCollins College Publishers, 10 East 53rd Street, New York, NY 10022.

ISBN: 0-06-501463-4
        96   9 8 7

Contents

✦

✦

✦

Introduction

✦ ✦ ✦

A Collection of Poetry

✦ ✦ ✦

Foreword

The HarperCollins Pocket Anthology series was born of a need we hear almost daily for brief, inexpensive anthologies. Professors tell us they are concerned that anthologies seem to grow larger and larger and that their students feel cheated when less than a third of the selections are actually taught in the course. To meet this demand, we have published three new titles: *POETRY: A HarperCollins Pocket Anthology; DRAMA: A HarperCollins Pocket Anthology*; and *FICTION: A HarperCollins Pocket Anthology*. The three can be used together in an introductory literature class as a replacement for the big textbook anthology that covers all three genres, or they can be used individually for courses that focus specifically on one of the genres. They are easy to supplement with novels or collections of works by single authors as well.

These brief, inexpensive anthologies can easily be carried to class and offer a student real value at a reasonable price. They are designed to offer the most teachable blend of classic and contemporary selections with only the most essential information on each genre so that choice is provided but more of the book is actually used. To determine which selections to include—and whether this idea was hitting a responsive chord among professors—we surveyed numerous professors to ask what they want in an anthology. Our survey helped us determine which poems and poets professors want to teach, so we provided a broad historical range of work, a wide variety of poetic forms, and major writers—including works by women throughout history—along with the diversity of voices that make up the current poetry scene. The suggestions from the professors we surveyed were critical in creating a solid selection that would effectively introduce students to the poetic tradition in English.

It is our hope that these books will respond to the needs of students and professors who are looking for comprehensive, but affordable, alternatives to the big book anthology. We particularly want to thank R.S. Gwynn, whose teaching experience, expert practice in his own poetry, and knowledge of literature were the foundation for the **HarperCollins Pocket Anthology** series. We are also grateful to all those poetry and introductory literature professors whose advice guided us in making selections and putting together the essential introductory material that their students would find useful in POETRY: A HarperCollins Pocket Anthology: Marsha Aldrich, Michigan State University; Herman L. Asarnow, University of Portland; Lea Baechler, Columbia University; Paul Bodmer, Bismark State College; Peggy F. Broder, Cleveland State University; William Covino, University of Chicago; Dwight Eddins, University of Alabama; Wil Gehne, State university of New York, Binghampton; Cheryl Glenn, Oregon State University; Julia Hamilton, Inver Hills Community College; Jennie Harrison, North Harris College; Mary Hojnacki, University of Massachusetts, Lowell; Jim Holte, East Carolina University; Aija Hoover, Odessa College; John Morris, Cameron University; Lee Patterson, Duke University; Marco Portales, Texas A & M University; Lawrence Rainey, Yale University; Kim Roberts, University of Maryland; Danny Robinson, Bloomsburg University; Pam Schirmeister, New York University; James Schuttemeyer, Thomas More College; Shirley Simpson, Nicolls State University; Michael Steinman, Nassau Community College; Kathleen Thornton, State University of New York, Albany; and Clifford Dale Whitman, Southern Arkansas University.

Lisa Moore
Literature Editor

Introduction

An Anecdote: Where Poetry Starts

The room is not particularly grand, a large lecture hall in one of the old build-
ings on the college campus, and the small group of first-year students whose liter-
ature class has been dismissed so that they can attend the poetry reading have taken
seats near the back of the room. They have been encouraged to come for several
weeks by their instructor, and when she enters she looks around the room and nods
in their direction, smiling.

The seats gradually fill. The crowd is a mixed one—several men and women
known by sight as senior faculty members; a scattering of visitors, many of them
apparently from the community; a large contingent of instructors and graduate
students from the English Department sitting on the front rows; and small clus-
ters of undergraduates scattered throughout the room.

One of the students scans the crowd, wondering aloud which is the poet. On
the walk to the reading, the class's consensus has been that the poet, a cadaverous
grey-haired man wrapped in a black cloak, would recite his poems in a resonant
monotone, preferably with a strong breeze tossing his hair. Speculating on how
the wind effect might be managed inside a lecture hall made them laugh.

Now the crowd grows quiet as their instructor steps to the podium and
adjusts the microphone. She makes a few complimentary remarks about the strong
turnout and thanks several benefactors for their financial support of poetry at the
university. Then she introduces the guest. Her students know most of this infor-
mation, for they have studied several of his poems in class that week, but they are
still slightly surprised when he rises to polite applause and takes the lectern. The
balding middle-aged man wearing a chambray shirt and knit tie could be taken
for an associate professor in any campus department, and when he adjusts his
glasses and clears his throat, blinking at the audience, there is little about him
that would fit anyone's romantic stereotype of the poet.

Surprisingly, he does not begin with a poem. Instead, in a relaxed voice he
tells an anecdote about his younger daughter and an overdue science project. When
he moves from the background story into the poem itself, there is little change in
his volume level, and his tone remains conversational. The students find that the

1

poem, which they had discussed in class only a couple of days before, takes on new meaning when its origins are explained by the poet himself. They find themselves listening attentively to his words, even laughing out loud several times. The hour goes quickly, and at its end their applause, like that of the rest of the audience, is long and sincere.

At the next class meeting the instructor asks for reactions to the reading. While some of the class members are slightly critical, faulting the speaker for his informal manner and his failure to maintain eye contact with the room, most of the remarks are positive. The comments that surface most often have to do with how much more meaningful the poems in the textbook become when the poet explains how he came to write them, how one poem is actually spoken in the voice of his dead father, how another is addressed to a friend who was paralyzed in an automobile accident. While these things could perhaps be inferred from the poems alone, the students are unanimous that knowing the details beforehand adds a great deal to the first impression a poem makes. As one student puts it, "It's just that a poem makes a lot more sense when you know who's talking and when and where it's supposed to be taking place."

"It always helps to know where poetry starts," adds one of her classmates.

Speaker, Listener, and Context

The situation described above is hardly unique. Instructors have long been encouraging, even begging their students to attend events like this one, and the college poetry reading has become, for many Americans, the closest encounter they can have with this complex and often perplexing art form. But what students often find at such readings, to their amazement, is that poetry need not be intimidating or obscure; a gentle reminder that the roots of poetry, like those of all literature, were originally part of the **oral tradition,** stories and poems that were passed down from generation to generation in ancient societies and were recited for audiences that included all members of the tribe, from the wizened elders to the youngest children. For most of its long history poetry has been a popular art form designed for presentation to live *audiences* (the word, from the Latin *audio,* literally means hearers), and it is only recently that its most visible signs of life are to be found on college campuses. The reasons for this academic retreat are too complicated to go into here, but it is perhaps worth noting that we are exposed daily to a great deal of poetry in oral form, for the most part through the medium of recorded song lyrics, and that the unique qualities of poetry throughout the ages—its ability to tell stories or summarize complicated emotions in a few well-chosen words—are demonstrated whenever we memorize or sing the lines of a popular song.

Of course, poetry written for the page is usually more demanding than song lyrics. Writers of popular songs aim at a wide commercial audience, and this simple fact of economics, added to the fact that the lyrics are not intended primarily for publication but for being recorded with all the resources of studio technology, tends to make many song lyrics relatively uninteresting when they appear in print. A poem, on the other hand, will primarily exist as a printed text, though certainly its effect may be enhanced greatly through a skillful oral performance in which the poet can also explain the background of the poem, its setting and speaker, and the circumstances under which it was written. In general, these details, so crucial to understanding a poem yet so often only implied when the poem appears in print, are called the **dramatic situation** of a poem. Reduced to its simplest formulation, dramatic situation can be summed up by a question: *Who is speaking to whom under what circumstances?* If the poet fails to provide us with clues or if we are careless in picking up the information that is provided, then we may begin reading with no sense of reference and, thus, may go far astray. Even such words as "on," "upon," or "to" in titles can be crucial to our understanding of dramatic situation, and can tell us something about an event or object that has provided the stimulus for the poem or about the identity of the "you" addressed in the poem.

An illustration may be helpful. Suppose we look at what is unquestionably the most widely known poem ever written by an American. It is a poem which virtually all Americans can recite in part and, in fact, do so by the millions every week. Yet if we were told that this poem is unusual in that its best known section is a long, unanswered question addressed by the speaker to a companion about whether or not the object named in the title even exists, then it is likely that most of us would be confused. Before going further, let's look at the poem.

The Star-Spangled Banner

O say, can you see, by the dawn's early light,
    What so proudly we hailed at the twilight's last gleaming?
Whose broad stripes and bright stars through the perilous fight,
    O'er the ramparts we watched, were so gallantly streaming!
And the rockets' red glare, the bombs bursting in air,
    Gave proof through the night that our flag was still there:
O say, does that star-spangled banner yet wave
    O'er the land of the free and the home of the brave?

On the shore, dimly seen through the mists of the deep,
    Where the foe's haughty host in dread silence reposes,
What is that which the breeze, o'er the towering steep,
    As it fitfully blows, now conceals, now discloses?
Now it catches the gleam of the morning's first beam,
    In full glory reflected now shines on the stream:
'Tis the star-spangled banner! O long may it wave
    O'er the land of the free and the home of the brave!

And where is that band who so vauntingly swore
    That the havoc of war and the battle's confusion
A home and a country should leave us no more?
    Their blood has washed out their foul footsteps' pollution.
No refuge could save the hireling and slave
    From the terror of flight, or the gloom of the grave:
And the star-spangled banner in triumph doth wave
    O'er the land of the free and the home of the brave!

Oh! thus be it ever, when freemen shall stand
    Between their loved homes and the war's desolation!

Blest with victory and peace, may the heaven-rescued land
  Praise the Power that hath made and preserved us a nation.
Then conquer we must, when our cause it is just,
  And this be our motto: "In God is our trust."
And the star-spangled banner in triumph shall wave
  O'er the land of the free and the home of the brave!

"Now wait a minute!" you may be wondering. "'The Star-Spangled Banner'
is a *song*, not a poem. And what's this question business? Don't we always sing it
while facing the flag? Besides, it's just a patriotic song. Nobody really worries
about what it *means*."

In answer to the first comment, "The Star-Spangled Banner" *was* in fact writ-
ten as a poem and set to music only after its composition. Most of us will proba-
bly agree that the words are not particularly well suited to the melody (which was
taken, curiously, from a popular British barroom ballad) and the song remains
notoriously difficult to sing well, even for professional performers. Garth
Brooks, the popular country singer, once remarked before attempting it at a Super
Bowl that it "is one of the hardest songs to sing." In its original form, "The Star-
Spangled Banner" (or "The Defense of Fort McHenry," the title under which it
was first published) is an example of **occasional verse,** a poem that is written
about or for an important event (or occasion), sometimes private but usually of
some public significance. While poems of this type are not often printed on the
front pages of newspapers as they once were, they are still being written. Enough
poems appeared after the assassination of President John F. Kennedy in 1963 to
fill a book, *Of Poetry and Power*, and the *Challenger* disaster of 1985 stimulated
a similar outpouring of occasional poems, one of them by Howard Nemerov,
who served as poet laureate of the United States. Most recently, Maya Angelou
recited "On the Pulse of Morning" at the inauguration of President Clinton.
The author of "The Star-Spangled Banner," Francis Scott Key (1779-1843), wrote
poetry as an avocation. Like many men and women who are not professional writ-
ers, Key was so deeply moved by an event that he witnessed that poetry was the only
medium through which he could express his feelings.

Now let's go back to our question about dramatic situation, taking it one
part at a time: *Who is speaking?* A technical word that is often used to designate
the speaker of a poem is **persona** (plural: **personae**), a word that meant "mask" in
ancient Greek. Even though the persona of "The Star-Spangled Banner" never uses
the word "I" in the poem, the speaker seems to be Key himself, a fact that can be
verified by biographical research. Still, it is probably safer to look at poems
carefully to see if they give any evidence that the speaker is someone other than the
poet. Poems like "Ulysses" by Alfred, Lord Tennyson or "Porphyria's Lover" by
Robert Browning have titles that identify personae who are, respectively, a charac-
ter from ancient epic poetry and an unnamed man who is confessing the murder of
his lover, Porphyria. In neither case is the persona to be identified with the poet
himself. Other poems may be somewhat more problematical. Edgar Allan Poe's
"The Raven," like many of Poe's short stories, is spoken by a persona who is not to
be identified with the author, even though he shares many of the same morbid
preoccupations of Poe's other characters; even Sylvia Plath, a poet usually associ-
ated with an extremely candid form of autobiographical poetry known as **confes-**

sional poetry, identified the persona of her masterpiece "Daddy" as an invented character, "a girl with an Electra complex." Sometimes poems have more than one personae, which is the case with Thomas Hardy's "The Ruined Maid" and Robert Frost's "Home Burial," two poems which consist almost entirely of dialogue. In other poems, the speaker may simply be a third-person **narrator** such as we might find in a short story or novel. While it is perhaps true that many poems (including the majority of those included here) are in fact spoken by the poet out of his or her most private feelings, it is not a good idea to leap too quickly to the assumption that the persona of a poem is identical to the poet and shares his or her views. Conclusions about the degree to which a poem is autobiographical can only be verified by research and familiarity with a poet's other works.

To return to our question: Who is speaking *to whom?* Another useful term is **auditor,** the person or persons spoken to in a poem. Some poems identify no auditor; others clearly do specify an auditor or auditors, in most cases identified by name or by the second-person pronoun "you" (or "thee/thou" in older poetry). Again, the title may give clues: Poe's "To Helen" is addressed to the famous beauty of Homeric legend; Robert Herrick's "To the Virgins, to Make Much of Time" is addressed to a group of young women; William Cullen Bryant's "To a Waterfowl" is addressed to, yes, a *duck.* (The figure of speech **apostrophe** is used when a nonhuman, inanimate, or abstract thing is addressed directly). Relatively few poems are addressed directly to the reader, so when we read the opening of William Shakespeare's Sonnet 18 ("Shall I compare thee to a summer's day?") we should keep in mind that he is not addressing us but another individual, in this case a young friend who is referred to in many of the sonnets. A powerful poem like Claude McKay's "If We Must Die" begins in this manner:

> If we must die, let it not be like hogs
> Hunted and penned in an inglorious spot,
> While round us bark the mad and hungry dogs,
> Making their mock at our accursed lot.

Later in the poem McKay identifies his auditors as "Kinsmen." Without outside help, all we can say with certainty at first glance is that the poet seems to be addressing a group of companions who share his desperate situation. When we learn, through research, that McKay was a black American poet of the 1920s, the symbolic nature of his exhortation becomes clearer.

Now the final part of the question: Who is speaking to whom *under what circumstances?* First, we might ask if there is a relationship, either implied or stated, between persona and auditor. Obviously many love poems take the form of verbal transactions between two parties, and, since relationships have their ups and downs, these shifts of mood are reflected in the poetry. One famous example is Michael Drayton's sonnet "Since There's No Help," which begins with the persona threatening to end the relationship with the auditor but which ends with an apparent reconciliation. Such "courtship ritual" poems as John Donne's "The Flea" and Andrew Marvell's "To His Coy Mistress" are witty arguments in favor of the couple's engaging in sexual intercourse—no more, no less. Another example from love poetry is Matthew Arnold's "Dover Beach," which ends with the plea "Ah, love, let us be true / To one another" as the only hope for stability the persona can find in a world filled with uncertainty and fear. Even an age disparity between persona and auditor can lend meaning to a poem, which is the case with the Herrick poem mentioned above and a dialogue poem like John Crowe Ransom's "Piazza Piece," a classic example of the debate between innocence and experience.

Other questions relating to circumstances of the dramatic situation might concern the poem's physical setting (if any), time (of day, year, historical era), even such matters as weather. Thomas Hardy's "Neutral Tones" provides a good example of a poem in which the setting, a gray winter day in a barren outdoor place, reinforces symbolically the persona's memory of the bitter end of a love affair. The shift in setting from the springtime idyll to the "cold hillside" in John Keats's "La Belle Dame Sans Merci" cannot be overlooked when discussing the persona's disillusionment. Of course, many poems are explicitly occasional and may even contain an **epigraph,** a brief explanatory statement or quotation, or a **dedication** which explains the setting. Sometimes footnotes or even outside research may be necessary. John Milton's "On the Late Massacre in Piedmont" will make little sense to readers if they do not know that the poet is reacting to the massacre of a group of Protestants by Roman Catholic soldiers and that Milton, an English Puritan, uses the occasion to attack the Papacy as a "triple tyrant" and the "Babylonian woe."

To return, then, one final time to "The Star-Spangled Banner," let's apply our question to the poem. We have already determined that Key is the persona. Who is the "you" mentioned four words into the poem? It seems clear that Key is addressing an auditor standing close to him, either a single individual or a group, as he asks the auditor if he can see the flag that they both observed for the last time the previous day at sundown. Key tells us that it is now just at the moment of dawn, and that even though the flag could be glimpsed periodically in the "rockets' red glare" of the bombardment throughout the night, it cannot be clearly seen now. It is a crucial question, for if the flag is no longer flying "o'er the ramparts" it will mean that the fort has fallen to the enemy. The tension mounts and moves into the second stanza, where at last, "thro' the mists of the deep," the flag can be discerned, "dimly seen" at first, then clearly as it "catches the gleam" of the full sunlight.

The full story of how Key came to write the poem is fairly well known and supports this reading. The events which the poem describes took place on September 13 and 14, 1814, during the War of 1812. A lawyer, Key came aboard a British warship anchored off Baltimore to argue for the release of a client and friend who had been taken hostage by the British. After granting the release, the British captain, fearing that Key might reveal information he had learned on board, kept Key overnight, releasing Key and his client in the morning. It was during that night that Key witnessed the bombardment and, with it, the failure of the British to take Baltimore. The final half of the poem celebrates this victory and offers a hopeful prayer that God will continue to smile on America "when our cause it is just." One might well argue that Key's phrase "conquer we must" contradicts the spirit of the earlier parts of the poem, but few people would assert that "The Star-Spangled Banner" is a great poem. It is, however, an effective piece of patriotic verse that has a few moments of real drama, expressed in a vivid manner that lets readers become eyewitnesses to an incident from American history.

Lyric, Narrative, Dramatic

The starting point for all literary criticism in Western civilization is Aristotle's *Poetics,* a work dating from the fourth century B.C. While Aristotle's remarks on drama, tragedy in particular, are more complete that his analysis of other types of literature, he does mention three main types of poetry: lyric, epic, and dithyrambic. In doing so, Aristotle outlines for the first time a theory of literature based on **genres,** or separate categories delineated by distinct style, form, and content. This three-fold division remains useful today, though in two cases different terminology is employed. The first genre, **lyrical poetry,** originally comprised brief poems that were meant to be sung or chanted. Today we still use the word "lyrics" in a specialized sense when referring to the words of a song, but lyrical poetry has become such a large category that it includes virtually all poems that are primarily *about* a subject and contain little narrative content. The subject of a lyrical poem may be the poet's emotions, an abstract idea, a satirical insight, or a description of a person or place. The persona in a lyric is usually closely identified with the poet himself or herself; since we tend to identify the essence of poetry with personal, subjective expression of feelings or ideas, lyrical poetry remains the largest genre, with a number of subtypes. Among them are the **epigram,** a short, satirical lyric usually aimed at a specific person; the **elegy,** a lyric on the occasion of a death; the **ode,** a long lyrical poem in elevated language on a serious theme.

Aristotle's second genre, the epic, has been expanded to include all types of **narrative poetry,** that is, poetry whose main function is to tell a story. Like prose fiction, narrative poems have plots, characters, settings, and points-of-view, and may be discussed in much the same way as, say, a short story. An **epic** is a long narrative poem about the exploits of a hero. **Folk epics** like *The Iliad* or *Beowulf* were originally intended for public recitation and existed in oral form centuries before they were transcribed. Little or nothing is known about the authors of folk epics. **Literary epics,** like Virgil's *Aeneid* or Henry Wadsworth Longfellow's *The Song of Hiawatha*, differ in that they are the products of known authors who wrote primarily for publication. **Ballads** are generally shorter narratives with songlike qualities which often include rhyme and repeated refrains. **Folk ballads,** like folk epics, come from the oral tradition and are usually published anonymously; "Bonny Barbara Allen" and "Sir Patrick Spens" are typical examples. **Art or literary ballads,** on the other hand, are conscious imitations of the ballad style by later poets and are generally somewhat more sophisticated than folk ballads in their techniques. Examples of this popular genre include Keats's "La Belle Dame Sans Merci" and Marilyn Nelson Waniek's recent "Ballad of Aunt Geneva." There are also other types of narrative poetry that have been popular through the centuries. **Metrical romances,** verse tales of the exploits of knights, were a popular genre of the Middle Ages and Renaissance; Edmund Spenser's "The Faery Queen" is one of the most ambitious examples of the type. At the opposite extreme are **mock-heroic narratives** like John Dryden's "MacFlecknoe" or Lord Byron's "Don Juan," which spoof the conventions of epic poetry for comic or satirical effect. **Realistic narratives** of medium length (under one thousand lines) like Wordsworth's "Michael," a story of the dissolution of a shepherd's family, or Robert Frost's "Home Burial" have been popular since the beginning of the nineteenth century and are sometimes discussed as "poetic novels" or "short stories in verse."

There is no exact contemporary analogue for Aristotle's third category, **dithyrambic poetry.** This type of poem was composed to be chanted at religious rituals by a chorus and is the forerunner of tragedy. Today the third type is usually called **dramatic poetry,** since it has perhaps as much in common with the separate genre of drama than with lyrical and narrative poetry. In general, the persona in a dramatic poem is an invented character or characters not to be identified with the poet. The poem is presented as a speech or dialogue that might be acted out like a soliloquy or scene from a play. The **dramatic monologue** is a speech for a single character, usually delivered to a silent auditor. Notable examples are Tennyson's "Ulysses" and Browning's "My Last Duchess." A dramatic monologue sometimes implies, through the words of its persona, a distinct setting and interplay between persona and auditor. At the close of "Ulysses," the aged hero urges his gathered "mariners" to listen closely and to observe the ship in the harbor waiting to take them off on their final voyage. Dramatic poetry can also take the form of **dialogue poetry,** in which two personae speak alternately. Examples are Christina Rossetti's "Uphill" and Thomas Hardy's "The Ruined Maid." A popular type of dialogue poem in the past was the **débat,** or mock-debate, in which two characters, usually personified abstractions such as the Soul and the Body, argued their respective merits.

While it is easy enough to find examples of "pure" lyrics, narratives, and dramatic monologues, sometimes the distinction between the three major types can become blurred, even in the same poem. "The Star-Spangled Banner," for example, contains elements of all three genres. The opening stanza, with its vivid recreation of a question asked at dawn, is closest to dramatic poetry. The second and third stanzas, which tell of the outcome of the battle, are primarily narrative. The final stanza, with its patriotic effusion and religious sentiment, is lyrical. Still, the three-fold division is useful in discussing an author's varied ways of dealing with subjects or in comparing examples of one type by separate authors. To cite three poems by the same poet in this collection, we might look at William Blake's "The Tyger," "A Poison Tree," and "The Little Black Boy." The first of these is a descriptive lyric, focusing for the most part on the symbolic meaning of the tiger's appearance; the second is a narrative that relates, in the allegorical manner of a parable, the events leading up to a murder; the third is a dramatic monologue spoken by the persona identified in the title.

The Language of Poetry

One of the most persistent myths about poetry is that its language is artificial, "flowery," and essentially different from the language that people speak in their daily lives. While these beliefs may be true of *some* poetry, one can easily find numerous examples that reveal the opposite side of the coin. It is impossible to characterize poetic language narrowly, for poetry, which is after all the *art* of language, covers the widest possible range of linguistic possibilities. For example, here are several passages from different poets, all describing birds:

> Hail to thee, blithe Spirit!
> Bird thou never wert—

That from Heaven, or near it,
　　Pourest thy full heart
In profuse strains of unpremeditated art.

　Higher still and higher
　　From the earth thou springest
Like a cloud of fire;
　　The blue deep thou wingest,
And singing still dost soar, and soaring ever singest.
Percy Bysshe Shelley, "To a Skylark"

I caught this morning morning's minion, kingdom of daylight's
　　dauphin, dapple-dawn-drawn Falcon, in his riding
Of the rolling level underneath him steady air, and striding
High there, how he rung upon the rein of a wimpling wing
In his ecstacy!
Gerard Manley Hopkins, "The Windhover"

When the lilac-scent was in the air and Fifth-month grass was growing,
Up this seashore in some briers,
Two feather'd guests from Alabama, two together,
And their nest, and four light-green eggs spotted with brown,
And every day the he-bird to and fro near at hand,
And every day the she-bird crouch'd on her nest, silent, with bright eyes,
And every day I, a curious boy, never too close, never disturbing them,
Cautiously peering, absorbing, translating.
Walt Whitman, "Out of the Cradle Endlessly Rocking"

At once a voice arose among
　　The bleak twigs overhead
In a full-hearted evensong
　　Of joy illimited;
An aged thrush, frail, gaunt, and small,
　　In blast-beruffled plume,
Had chosen thus to fling his soul
　　Upon the growing gloom.
Thomas Hardy, "The Darkling Thrush"

There is a singer everyone has heard,
Loud, a mid-summer and a mid-wood bird,
Who makes the solid tree trunks sound again.
He says that leaves are old and that for flowers
Mid-summer is to spring as one to ten.
Robert Frost, "The Oven Bird"

　Of these quotes only the oldest, from the early nineteenth century, possesses the stereotypical characteristics of what we mean when we use the term "poetic" in a negative sense. Poetry, like any other art form, follows fashions that change over the years; by Shelley's day, the use of "thee" and "thou" and their related verb forms ("wert" and "wingest") had come full circle from their original use as a familiar form of the second person employed to address intimates and servants, to an artificially heightened grammatical form reserved for prayers and poetry. Hopkins's language, from a poem of the 1870s, is artificial in an entirely different way; here the poet's **idiom,** the personal use of words that marks his poetry, is highly idiosyncratic; indeed, it would be hard to mistake a poem by Hopkins with one by any other poet. Whitman, on the other hand, should present few difficulties; the only oddity expressed here is "Fifth-month" instead of "May," a linguistic inheritance, perhaps, from Whitman's Quaker mother. Of course, one might argue that Whitman's "naturalness" results from his use of his free verse, but both Hardy and Frost, who wrote rhymed, metrical verse, are hardly less natural. When we move to the contemporary period, we can find little difference between the language of many poems and conversational speech.

Still, in reading a poem, particularly one from the past, we should be aware of certain problems that may impede our understanding. **Diction** refers to the individual words in a poem and may be classified in several ways. A poem's **level of diction** can range from slang at one extreme to formal usage at the other, though in an age in which most poems use a level of diction that stays in the middle of the scale, ranging between conversational and standard levels, these distinctions are useful only when a poet is being self-consciously formal (perhaps for ironic effect) or going to the opposite extreme to imitate the language of the streets. In past eras the term **poetic diction** was used to indicate a level of speech somehow refined above ordinary usage and, thus, somehow superior to it; today the same term would most likely be used as a way of condemning a poet's language. We should keep in mind that the slang of one era is the standard usage of another, okay?

A good dictionary is useful in many ways, particularly in dealing with **archaisms** (words no longer commonly in use) and other words that may not be familiar to the reader. Take, for example, the opening lines of Edgar Allan Poe's "To Helen":

> Helen, thy beauty is to me
>   Like those Nicean barks of yore,
> That gently, o'er a perfumed sea,
>   The weary, way-worn wanderer bore
>   To his own native shore.

There are several words here that may prove troublesome to the reader. First, "o'er," like "ne'er" or similar words like "falt'ring" and "glimm'ring," is simply a contraction; this dropping of letter, called **syncope,** is done for the sake of rhythm. "Barks of yore" will probably send most of us to the dictionary since our sense of "bark" as either the outer surface of a tree or the noise that a dog makes does not fit here; likewise, "yore" is unfamiliar, possibly archaic. Looking up the literal sense of a word in a dictionary discloses its **denotation,** or literal meaning. Thus, we find that "barks" are small sailing ships and that "yore" refers to the distant past. Of course, Poe could have said "ships of the past" or a similar phrase, but his word choice was perhaps dictated by **connotation,** the implied meaning or *feel* that some words have acquired; it may be that even in Poe's day "barks of yore" had a remote, exotic quality that somehow evoked ancient Greece. But what are we to make of "Nicean," a proper adjective that sounds geographical but does not appear in either the dictionary or gazetteer. In this case we have encountered an example of a **coinage** or **neologism,** a word made up by the poet. Speculation on the source of "Nicean" has ranged from Nice, in the South of France, to Phoenician, but it is likely that Poe simply coined the word. Similarly, we might note that the phrase "weary, way-worn wanderer" contains words that seem to have been chosen primarily for their sounds.

When we put a poem into our own words, we **paraphrase** it, a practice that is often useful when passages are hard to understand. Other than diction, **syntax,** the order of words in a sentence, may also give us problems. Syntax in poetry, particularly in poems that use rhyme, is likely to be different from both that of speech and prose. If a poet decides to rhyme in a certain pattern, he or she must modify word order to fit the formal design, and this may present difficulties to readers in understanding the grammar of a passage. Here is the opening of a familiar piece of American patriotic verse: "My country, 'tis of thee, / Sweet land of liberty, / Of thee I sing." What is the subject of this sentence? Would you be surprised to learn that the subject is *it* (contained in the contraction *'tis)?* The passage from Poe presents few difficulties of this order but does contain one example of **inversion,** words that fall out of their expected order. A related syntactical problem lies in **ellipsis,** words that are consciously omitted by the poet. If we do not allow for this, we are likely to be confused by "the weary, way-worn wanderer bore / To his own native shore." The wanderer bore *what?* A quick mental sentence diagram shows that "wanderer" is the direct object of "bore," not its subject. A good paraphrase should simplify both diction and syntax: "Helen, to me your beauty is like those Nicean (?) ships of the ancient past that carried the weary, travel-worn wanderer gently over a perfumed sea to his own native land." In paraphrasing, only the potentially troublesome words and phrases should be substituted, leaving as much of the original language intact as possible. Paraphrasing is a useful first step toward unfolding a poem's literal sense, but it obviously takes few of a poet's specific nuances of language into account.

Several other matters relevant to poetic language are worth mentioning. **Etymology,** the study of the sources of words, is a particularly rewarding topic in English since our language has such an unusually rich history. Old English (or Anglo-Saxon), the original language of the British Isles, was part of the Germanic family of languages. When the Norman French successfully invaded the British Isles in 1066 they brought with them their own language, part of the Romance language family (all originally derived from Latin). By the time of Chaucer's death in 1400 these two linguistic traditions had merged into a single language, Middle English, that can be read today, despite its differences in spelling, pronunciation, and vocabulary. We can still, however, distinguish the words that show their Germanic heritage from those of Latinate origin, and despite the fact that English is rich in synonyms, the Germanic and Latinate words often have different connotations. "Smart" is not quite the same as "intelligent," and a "mapmaker" is subtly different from a "cartographer." A poet's preference for words of a certain origin is not always immediately clear, but we can readily distinguish the wide gulf that separates a statement like "I live in a house with my folks" from "I abide in a residence with my parents."

A final type of tension exists in poems between their use of **concrete diction** and **abstract diction.** Concrete words denote that which can be perceived by the senses, and the vividness of a poem's language resides primarily in the way it uses **imagery,** sensory details denoting specific details of experience. Since it is the most important of the five senses, visual imagery ("a dim light"; "a dirty rag"; "a golden daffodil") predominates in poems, but we should also be aware of striking examples of the other types of imagery: auditory ("a pounding surf"), tactile ("a rough floor"), olfactory ("the scent of apple blossoms"), and gustatory ("the bitter tang of gin"). Abstract words are likewise important since they carry the burden of a poem's overall meaning or theme. William Butler Yeats's "Leda and the Swan" provides a good example of how concrete and abstract words coexist in a poem. Reading this account of the myth in which Zeus, in the form of a swan, impregnates a human woman and thus sets in action the chain of events that leads to the Trojan War (Leda was the mother of Helen of Troy), we will probably be struck at first by the way that tactile imagery ("a sudden blow"; fingers attempting to "push / The feathered glory" away; "A shudder in the loins") is used to describe an act of sexual violence. Even though some abstract words ("terrified"; "vague"; "glory"; "strange") appear in the first eight lines of the poem they are all linked closely to concrete words like "fingers," "feathered," and "heart." In the last two lines of the poem, Yeats uses three large abstractions, "knowledge," "power," and "indifferent," to state his theme (or at least ask the crucial question about the meaning of the myth). More often than not, one can expect to encounter the largest number of abstract words near the conclusions of poems. Probably the most famous abstract statement in English poetry—John Keats's "'Beauty is truth, truth beauty,'—that is all / Ye know on earth, and all ye need to know."—appears in the last two lines of a fifty-line poem.

Two final devices aid poets in determining the best choice of words. **Onomatopoeia** refers to individual words like "splash" or "thud" whose meanings are closely related to their sounds. Auditory imagery in a poem can often be enhanced by the use of onomatopoeic words. In some cases, however, an entire line can be called onomatopoeic, even if it contains no single word that illustrates the device. Thomas Hardy uses this line to describe the pounding of distant surf: "Where hill-hid tides throb, throe on throe." Here the repetition of similar sounds helps to imitate the sound of the ocean. A second device is the **pun,** the use of one word to imply the additional meaning of a similar sounding word (the formal term is **paronomasia**). Thus, when Anne Bradstreet is comparing her first book to an illegitimate child, she addresses the book in this manner: "If for thy Father asked, say thou had'st none; / And for thy Mother, she alas is poor, / Which caused her thus to send thee out of door." The closeness of the interjection "alas" to the article and noun "a lass" is hardly coincidental. Poets in Bradstreet's day considered the pun a staple of their repertoire, even in serious poetry, but contemporary poets are more likely to use it primarily for comic effect:

> They have a dozen children; it's their diet,
> For they have bread too often. Please don't try it.

More often than not, puns like these will elicit a groan from the audience, a response that may be exactly what the poet intends.

Figurative Language

We use figurative language in everyday speech without thinking of the poetic functions of the same devices. We can always relate experience in a purely literal fashion: "His table manners were deplorable. Mother scolded him severely, and Dad said some angry words to him. He left the table embarrassed and with his feelings hurt." But a more vivid way of saying the same thing might employ language used not in the literal but in the figurative sense. Thus, another version might run, "His table manners were swinish. Mother jumped on his back about them, and Dad scorched his ears. You should have seen him slink off like a scolded puppy." At least four comparisons are made here in an attempt to describe one character's table manners, his mother's scolding, his father's words, and the manner in which the character retreated from the table. In every case, the thing being described, what is called the **tenor** of the figure of speech, is linked with a concrete image or **vehicle.** All of the types of figurative language, what are called **figures of speech** or **tropes,** involve some kind of comparison, either explicit or implied. Thus, two of the figures in the above example specifically compare aspects of the character's behavior to animal behavior. The other two imply parental words that were delivered with strong physical force or were extremely angry.

Some of the most common figures of speech are:

Metaphor: a direct comparison between two dissimilar things. Metaphors may take several forms.

> His words were sharp knives.
> The sharp knife of his words cut through the silence.
> He spoke sharp, cutting words with his knife edged-voice.
> His words knifed through the still air.
> "I will speak daggers to her . . ." (William Shakespeare, *Hamlet*)

Implied metaphor: a metaphor in which either the tenor or vehicle is implied, not stated.

> The running back gathered steam and chugged toward the goal. (Compares the player to a steam locomotive without naming it explicitly.)
> "While smoke on its chin, that slithering gun / Coiled back from its windowsill." (X.J. Kennedy)

Simile: a comparison using *like, as,* or *than* as a connective device.

> "My love is like a red, red rose." (Robert Burns)
> My love smells as sweet as a rose.
> My love looks fresher than a newly budded rose.

Conceit: an extended or far-fetched metaphor, in most cases comparing things that have almost nothing in common.

> "Make me, O Lord, thy spinning wheel compleat . . ." (Edward Taylor) (The poem draws an analogy between the process of salvation and the manufacture of cloth, ending with the persona attired in "Holy Robes.")

The **Petrarchan conceit,** named perhaps unfairly after the first great master of the sonnet, is a clichéd comparison usually relating to a woman's beauty (see

Thomas Campion's "There Is a Garden in Her Face"; Shakespeare's sonnet 130 parodies this type of trope). The **Metaphysical conceit** refers to the extended comparisons favored by poets like John Donne, George Herbert, and Edward Taylor. The conceit in the final three stanzas of Donne's "Valediction: Forbidding Mourning" compares the poet and his wife to a pair of drafting compasses.

Hyperbole: overstatement, a comparison using conscious exaggeration.

> He threw the ball so fast it caught the catcher's mitt on fire.
> "And I will love thee still, my dear, / Till a' the seas gang dry." (Robert Burns)

Understatement: the opposite of hyperbole.

> I had to spend a moment or two filling out my tax forms before I mailed them to the IRS.
> "The space between [birth and death] is but an hour, / The frail duration of a flower." (Phillip Freneau)

Allusion: metaphor making a direct comparison to a historical or literary event or character, a myth, a biblical reference, and so on.

> He is a Samson of strength but a Judas of duplicity.
> "He dreamed of Thebes and Camelot, / And Priam's neighbors." (Edwin Arlington Robinson)

Metonymy: use of a related object to stand for the thing actually being talked about.

> It's a white-collar street in a blue-collar town.
> "And O ye high-flown quills [literary critics] that soar the skies, / And ever with your prey still catch your praise." (Anne Bradstreet)

Synecdoche: use of a part for the whole, or vice-versa.

> The crowned heads of Europe were in attendance.
> "Before the indifferent beak could let her drop." (William Butler Yeats)

Personification: giving human characteristics to nonhuman things or to abstractions.

> Justice weighs the evidence in her golden scales.
> The ocean cursed and spat at us.
> "Of all her train, the hands of Spring / First plant thee [a yellow violet] in the watery mould." (William Cullen Bryant)

Apostrophe: variety of personification in which a nonhuman thing, abstraction, or person not physically present is directly addressed as if it could respond.

> "Milton! Thou shouldst be living at this hour." (William Wordsworth)
> "Is it, O man, with such discordant noises, / With such accursed instruments as these, / Thou drownest Nature's sweet and kindly voices, / And jarrest the celestial harmonies?" (Henry Wadsworth Longfellow)

Paradox: an apparent contradiction or illogical statement.

> I'll never forget old what's-his-name.

> "His [God's] hand hath made this noble work [the universe] which
> Stands, / His Glorious Handywork not made by hands." (Edward
> Taylor)

Oxymoron: a short paradox, usually consisting of an adjective and noun with
conflicting meanings.
> The touch of her lips was sweet agony.
> "Progress is a comfortable disease." (e.e. cummings)

Synesthesia: a conscious mixing of two different types of sensory experience.
> A raw, red wind rushed from the north.
> "Leaves cast in casual potpourris / Whisper their scents from pits and
> cellar-holes." (Richard Wilbur)

Allegory and Symbol

Related to the figurative devices are the various types of symbolism that may occur
in poems. In many cases, a poem may seem so simple on the surface that we feel
impelled to read deeper meanings into it; Robert Frost's "Stopping by Woods on
a Snowy Evening" is a classic case in point. There is nothing wrong with search-
ing for larger significance in a poem, but the reader should perhaps be wary of
leaping to conclusions about symbolic meanings before fully exhausting the lit-
eral sense of a poem. Whatever the case, both **allegory** and **symbolism** demand
that the reader supply abstract or general meanings to the specific concrete details
of the poem.

The simplest form that this substitution takes occurs in allegory. An **alle-
gory** is a narrative that exists on at least two levels, a concrete literal level and a
second level of abstract meaning; throughout an allegory there is a consistent
sequence of parallels between the literal and the abstract. Sometimes allegories
may imply third or fourth levels of meaning as well, especially in long allegori-
cal works like Dante's *The Divine Comedy*, which has been interpreted in per-
sonal, political, ethical, and Christian terms. The characters and actions in an
allegory explicitly signify the abstract level of meaning, and generally this sec-
ond level of meaning is what the poet primarily intends to convey. For example,
Robert Southwell's "The Burning Babe" is filled with fantastic incidents and
paradoxical speech that are made clear in the poem's last line: "And straight I
callèd unto mind that it was Christmas day." The literal burning babe of the title
is the Christ child, who predicts his own future to the amazed watcher. Thus, in
interpreting the poem the reader must substitute theological terms like
"redemption" or "original sin" for the literal details it contains.

Two types of prose allegories, the fable and parable, have been universally
popular. A fable is a short, nonrealistic narrative that is told to illustrate a uni-
versal moral concept. A parable is similar, but generally contains realistic charac-
ters and events. Thus, Aesop's fable of the tortoise and the hare, instead of telling
us something about animal behavior, illustrates the virtue of persistence against
seemingly unbeatable competition. Jesus's parable of the good Samaritan tells the
story of a man who is robbed and beaten and eventually rescued by a stranger of
another race in order to define the concept of "neighbor" for a questioning
lawyer. Poetic allegories like George Herbert's "Redemption" or Christina

Rossetti's "Uphill" can be read in Christian terms as symbolic accounts of the process of salvation.

Many poems contain symbolic elements that are somewhat more elusive in meaning than the simple one-for-one equivalencies presented by allegory. A **symbol,** then, is any concrete thing or action in a poem that implies a meaning beyond its literal sense. Many of these things or actions are called **traditional symbols,** that is, symbols that hold roughly the same meanings for members of a given society. Certain flowers, colors, natural objects, and religious emblems possess meanings that we can generally agree upon. A white lily and a red rose, for instance, suggest opposite occasions, mourning and passion. Few would associate black with gaiety or red with innocence, and dawn and rainbows are traditional natural symbols of hope and new beginnings. It would be unlikely for a poet to mention a cross without expecting readers to think of its Christian associations.

Other types of symbols can be identified in poems that are otherwise not allegorical. A **private symbol** is one that has acquired certain meanings from a single poet's repeated use of it. William Butler Yeats's use of "gyres" is explained in some of his prose writings as a symbol for the turning of historical cycles, and his use of the word in his poems obviously goes beyond a literal level. Some visionary poets like William Blake have devised complicated private symbolic systems, a sort of alternative mythology, and understanding the full import of these symbols becomes the task of the specialist. Other poets may employ **incidental symbols,** things that are not usually considered symbolic but may be in a particular poem, or **symbolic acts,** a situation or response that seems of greater than literal import. As earlier noted, one of the most famous poems using these two devices is Robert Frost's "Stopping by Woods on a Snowy Evening." In this poem some readers see the "lovely, dark and deep" woods as inviting, even threatening, and want to view the persona's rejection of their allure ("For I have promises to keep / And miles to go before I sleep.") as some sort of life-affirming act. Frost himself was not particularly helpful in guiding his readers, often scoffing at those who had read too much metaphysical portent into such a simple lyric, though in other of his poems he presents objects—a rock wall between neighboring farms, an abandoned woodpile—that obviously possess some larger significance. There are many modern poems that remain so enigmatic that readers have consistently returned to them looking for new interpretations. Poems like these were to a degree influenced by the Symbolists, a group of French poets of the late nineteenth century who deliberately wrote poems filled with vague nuances subject to multiple interpretations. Such American examples of the Symbolist experiments as Wallace Stevens's "Anecdote of the Jar" or "The Emperor of Ice-Cream" continue to perplex and fascinate readers, particularly those who are versed in recent schools of interpretation which focus on the indeterminacy of a poetic text.

Tone of Voice

Even the simplest statement is subject to multiple interpretations if it is delivered in several different tones of voice. Consider the shift in emphasis between "I *gave* you the money" and "I gave *you* the money." Even a seemingly innocent compliment like "You look lovely this morning" takes on a different meaning if it is delivered by a woman to her obviously hungover husband. Still, these variations in **tone,** the speaker's implied attitude toward the words he or she says, depend primarily on vocal inflection. Since a poet does not always get the opportunity to elucidate the poem's tones in a public performance, it is possible that readers may have difficulties in grasping the tone of a poem printed on the cold page. Still, some poems present few problems. The opening of Milton's sonnet "On the Late Massacre in Piedmont"—"Avenge, O Lord, thy slaughtered saints . . . "—establishes a tone of righteous anger that is consistent throughout the poem. Keats's initial apostrophe in "Ode on a Grecian Urn"—"Thou still unravished bride of quietness, / Thou foster child of silence and slow time . . . —strikes the reader as both passionate and reverent, the poet's response to an undamaged artifact of the ancient past. Thus, in many cases we can relate the tone of voice in poems to the emotions we employ in our own speech, and we would have to violate quite a few rules of common sense to argue that Milton is being flippant or that Keats is speaking sarcastically.

Irony is the element of tone by which a poet may imply an attitude that is in fact contrary to what his words appear to say. Of course, the simplest form of irony is **sarcasm,** the wounding tone of voice we use to imply exactly the opposite of what we say: "That's really a *great* excuse!" "What a *wonderful* performance!" **Verbal irony** is the conscious manipulation of tone by which the poet's actual attitude is the opposite of what he or she says. In a poem like Thomas Hardy's "The Ruined Maid" it is obvious that one speaker considers the meaning of "ruined" to be somewhat less severe than the other, and the whole poem hinges on this ironic counterpoint of definitions and the different moral and social attitudes they imply. Consider the opening lines of Oliver Wendell Holmes's "Old Ironsides," a piece of propaganda verse which succeeded in raising enough money to save the USS *Constitution* from the scrap yard: "Ay, tear her tattered ensign down! / Long has it waved on high, / And many an eye has danced to see / That banner in the sky . . . ." Since Holmes's poetic mission is to *save* the ship, it is obvious that he is speaking ironically in the opening line; he emphatically *does not* want the ship's flag stripped from her, an attitude that is made clear in the third and fourth lines. Verbal irony is also a conspicuous feature of verse **satire,** poetry that exists to mock or ridicule, though often with serious intent. One famous example, in the form of a short satirical piece, or **epigram,** is Sarah N. Cleghorn's "The Golf Links," a poem written before the advent of child-labor laws:

> The golf links lie so near the mill
>   That almost every day
> The laboring children can look out
>   And see the men at play.

Here the weight of the verbal irony falls on two words, "laboring" and "play," and the way each is incongruously applied to the wrong group of people.

"The Golf Links," taken as a whole, also represents a second form of irony, **situational irony,** in which the setting of the poem (laboring children watching playing adults) contains a built-in incongruity. One master of ironic situation is Thomas Hardy, who used the title "Satires of Circumstance" in a series of short poems illustrating this sort of irony. Hardy's "Ah, Are You Digging on My Grave" and A.E. Housman's "Is My Team Ploughing?" demonstrate similar ironic situations, a ghostly persona asking questions of living speakers who end up offering little comfort to the dead. **Dramatic irony,** the third type of irony, occurs when the persona of a poem is less aware of the full import of his or her words than the reader. William Blake's "The Chimney Sweeper" is spoken by a child; he does not seem to realize how badly he is being exploited by his employer, who has been using the promises of religion as a way of keeping his workers in line. A similar statement could be made of the persona of Walter Savage Landor's "Mother, I Cannot," a young girl who apparently has not realized (or is deliberately unwilling to admit) that she has been sexually deceived. Dramatic irony, as the term implies, is most often found in dramatic monologues, where the gap between the speaker's perception of the situation and the reader's may be wide indeed.

Repetition: Sounds and Schemes

Because poetry uses language at its most intense level we are constantly aware of the weight of individual words and phrases to a degree that is usually lacking when we read prose. Poets have long known that the meanings they attempt to convey often depend as much on the sound of the words as on their meaning. We have already mentioned one sound device, onomatopoeia. Consider how much richer the experience of "the murmuring of innumerable bees" is than a synonymous phrase, "the low sound of a lot of bees." It has often been said that all art aspires to the condition of music in the way that it affects an audience on some unconscious, visceral level. By carefully exploiting the repetition of sound devices, a poet may use some of the same effects that the musical composer does.

Of course, much of this sonic level of poetry is subjective; what strikes one listener as pleasant may overwhelm the ear of another. Still, it is useful to distinguish between a poet's use of **euphony,** a series of pleasant sounds, and **cacophony,** sounds that are unpleasant. Note the following passages from Alexander Pope's "An Essay on Criticism," a didactic poem which attempts to illustrate many of the devices poets use:

> Soft is the strain when Zephyr gently blows,
> And the smooth stream in smoother numbers flows . . .

The repetition of the initial consonant sounds is called **alliteration,** and here Pope concentrates on the *s* sound. The vowel sounds are generally long: *strain, blows, smooth,* and so on. Here the description of the gentle west wind is assisted by the generally pleasing sense of euphony. But Pope, to illustrate the opposite quality, follows this couplet with a second:

> But when loud surges lash the sounding shore,
> The hoarse, rough verse should like the torrent roar.

Now the wind is anything but gentle, and the repetition of the *r* sounds in *surges, shore, hoarse, rough, verse, torrent,* and *roar* force the reader into the back of the throat, making sounds that are anything but euphonious.

Repetition of sounds have no inherent meaning values, though some linguists might argue that certain sounds do stimulate particular emotions, but this repetition does call attention to itself and can be particularly effective when a poet wishes to emphasize a certain passage. We have already mentioned alliteration.

Other sound patterns are **assonance,** the repetition of similar vowel sounds (*steep, even, receive, veal*), and **consonance,** the repetition of similar consonant sounds (*duck, torque, strike, trickle*). It should go without saying that spelling has little to do with any sound pattern; an initial *f* will alliterate with an initial *ph*.

Rhyme is the most important sound device, and our pleasures in deftly executed rhymes (consider the possibilities of rhyming "neighbor" with "sabre," as Richard Wilbur does in one of his translations) goes beyond mere sound to include the pleasure we take when an unexpected word is magically made to fit with another. There are several types of rhyme. **Masculine rhyme** occurs between single stressed syllables: *fleece, release, surcease, Nice,* and so on. **Feminine rhyme,** also called **double rhyme,** matches two syllables, one stressed and one usually unstressed: *stinging, upbringing, flinging.* **Triple rhyme** goes further: *slithering, withering.* **Slant rhyme** (also called **near rhyme** and **off rhyme**) contains hints of sound repetition (sometimes related to assonance and consonance): *chill, dull, sale* are possibilities, though poets often grant themselves considerable leeway in counting as rhyming words pairs that often have only the slightest similarity. When rhymes fall in a pattern in a poem as **end rhymes,** occurring at the end of lines, then it is convenient to assign letters to the sounds and speak of a **rhyme scheme.** Thus, a stanza of four lines ending with *heaven, hell, bell, eleven* would be said to have a rhyme scheme of *abba*. Rhyme may also occasionally be found in the interior of lines, what is called **internal rhyme.**

More complicated patterns of repetition involve more than mere sounds but whole phrases and grammatical units. Ancient rhetoricians, teaching the art of public speaking, identified several of these which are also found in poetry. **Parallel structure** is simply the repetition of grammatically similar phrases or clauses: Tennyson's "To strive, to seek, to find, and not to yield." **Anaphora** and **epistrophe** are repeated words or phrases at, respectively, the beginnings and ends of lines. Walt Whitman uses these schemes extensively, often in the same lines. This passage from "Song of Myself" illustrates both anaphora and epistrophe:

> If they are not yours as much as mine they are nothing, or next to nothing,
> If they are not the riddle and the untying of the riddle they are nothing,
> If they are not just as close as they are distant they are nothing.

Antithesis is the matching of parallel units which contain contrasting meanings, such as Whitman's "I am of old and young, of the foolish as much as the wise, / Regardless of others, ever regardful of others, / Maternal as well as paternal, a child as well as a man . . . " While the rhetorical schemes are perhaps more native to the orator, the poet can still make effective use of them, particularly in open form poetry like that of Whitman, where the formal devices of meter, rhyme, and stanza are lacking.

Meter and Rhythm

The subject of poetic meter and rhythm can be a difficult one, to say the least, and it is doubtless true that such phrases as *trochaic octameter* or *spondaic substitution* have an intimidating quality. Still, discussions of meter need not be limited to experts, and even beginning readers should be able to apply a few of the metrical principles commonly found in poetry written in English.

First, let's distinguish between two terms that are often used synonymously: **poetry** and **verse.** Poetry refers to an entire genre of literature and thus stands with fiction and drama as one of the three major types of writing. Verse, on the other hand, refers to a mode of writing in lines of a certain length; thus, many poets still retain the practice of capitalizing the first word of each line to indicate its integrity as a unit of composition. Virtually any piece of writing can be versified (and sometimes rhymed as well). Especially useful are bits of **mnemonic verse,** in which information like the number of days in the months or simple spelling rules ("*I* before *E* / Except after *C* . . .) is cast in a form that is easy to remember. Although it is not strictly accurate to do so, many writers use verse to denote metrical writing that somehow does not quite measure up to the level of true poetry; phrases like **light verse** or **occasional verse** (lines written for a specific event, like a birthday or anniversary) are often used in this way.

If, on the other hand, a writer is unconcerned about the length of individual lines and is governed only by the width of the paper being used, then he or she is not writing verse but **prose.** Verse is metrical writing; prose is not. Surprisingly enough, there is a body of writing called **prose poetry,** writing that uses language in a poetic manner but avoids any type of meter; see Carolyn Forché's "The Colonel" for one example. Perhaps the simplest way to think of **meter** in verse is to think of its synonym **measure** (think of the use of *meter* in words like *odometer* or *kilometer*). Thus, meter refers to the method by which a poet determines line length. Even if a poet writes lines of varying length, what we usually call **free verse,** he or she is still making a conscious decision about what each line may contain and may be measuring it on the basis of grammatical phrases or his or her own breath units.

However, when we talk about meter in poetry we ordinarily mean that the poet is employing some kind of consistent **prosody** or system of measurement. There are many possible prosodies, depending on what the poet decides to count as the unit of measurement in the line, but only three of these systems are common in English poetry. Perhaps the simplest is **syllabic verse.** In verse of this type the length of the line is determined by counting the total number of syllables the line contains (see Sylvia Plath's "Metaphors" for one example). Much French poetry of the past was written in 12-syllable lines, or **Alexandrines,** and in English a word like **octasyllabic** denotes a line of eight syllables. Because English is a language of strong stresses, most of our poets have favored other prosodic systems, but syllabic poetry has been attempted by many poets, among them Marianne Moore, Richard Wilbur, and Dylan Thomas. Moore, in particular, often writes in **quantitative syllabics,** stanzas with identical numbers of syllables in corresponding lines.

More natural to the English language is **accentual verse,** a prosodic system in which only accented or strongly-stressed syllables are counted in a line, which can also contain a varying number of unaccented syllables. Much folk poetry, intended perhaps to be recited to beat of a percussion instrument, retains this stress-based pattern, and the oldest English verse, Anglo-Saxon poetry like that of *Beowulf,* is composed in four-stress lines which were recited to musical accompaniment. Many of the verses we recall from nursery rhymes, children's chanting games ("Red rover, red rover, / Send [any name from one to up to four syllables can be substituted here—Bill, Susan, Latisha, Elizabeth] right over") and sports cheers ("Two bits, four bits, six bits, a dollar! / All for the [Owls, Cowboys, Cardinals] stand up and holler!") retain the strong sense of rhythmical pulse that characterizes much accentual verse, a fact we recognize when we clap our hands and move rhythmically to the sound of the words. Indeed, the lyrics to most current rap songs are actually composed to a four-stress accentual line, and the stresses or "beats" can be heard plainly when we listen or dance. More subtle, perhaps, is the method of many contemporary poets; indeed, what often passes for free verse is revealed, on closer inspection, to be a poem written in accentual meter. Richard Wilbur's "The Writer," for example, is written in a stanza containing lines of three, five, and three strong stresses, respectively, but the stresses do not overwhelm the reader.

Accentual-syllabic verse is perhaps the most important prosodic system in English, dominating our poetry for the five centuries from Chaucer's time down to the early years of our century. It has only been within the last fifty years that free verse has become the prevailing style, although accentual-syllabic verse still has many able practitioners. An accentual-syllabic prosody is somewhat more complicated than the two systems we have mentioned because it requires that the poet count both the strongly-stressed syllables *and* the total number of syllables in the line. Because stressed and unstressed syllables alternate fairly regularly in this system, four **metrical feet,** representing the most common patterns, represent the subdivisions of rhythm that make up each line (think of a yardstick divided into three feet). These feet are the **iamb** (or **iambic foot**), one unstressed and one stressed syllable; the **trochee** (or **trochaic foot**), one stressed and one unstressed syllable; the **anapest** (or **anapestic foot**), two unstressed syllables and one stressed syllable; and the **dactyl** (or **dactylic foot**), one stressed and two unstressed syllables. The first two of these, iambic and trochaic, are called **double meters;** the second two, **triple meters.** Iambic and anapestic meters are sometimes called **rising meters** because they "rise" toward the stressed syllable; trochaic and dactylic meters are called **falling meters** for the opposite reason. Simple repetition of words or phrases can give us the sense of how these lines sound in a purely schematic sense. The **breve** (˘) and **ictus** (´) are used to denote unstressed and stressed syllables, respectively.

Iambic:

> rĕléase | rĕléase | rĕléase
>
> tŏ fáll | ĭntó | dĕspáir
>
> Mărié | dĭscóv|ĕrs cándy̆

Trochaic:

> Méltĭng | méltĭng | méltĭng | méltĭng
>
> Pétĕr | dĭsă|greéd ĕn|tírely̆
>
> Úttĕr | nónsĕnse | fílled thĕ | páge

Anapestic:

> tŏ thĕ tóp | tŏ thĕ tóp
>
> á rĕtríevlĕr ăppéared
>
> ănd ắ tĕr|rĭbl ĕ thúndĕr

Dactylic:

> shívĕrĭng | shívĕrĭng | shívĕrĭng | shívĕrĭng | shívĕrĭng
>
> térrĭblў | ĭll frŏm ă | cáse ŏf thĕl vír ăl pnĕulmŏnĩ ã
>
> héar hŏw thĕ | mínĭstĕr | whíspĕred ăt | Émĭl ý's | gráve

Because each of these lines contains a certain number of feet, another specialized term is used to denote how many times a pattern is repeated in a line:

one foot	*monometer*
two feet	*dimeter*
three feet	*trimeter*
four feet	*tetrameter*
five feet	*pentameter*
six feet	*hexameter*
seven feet	*heptameter*
eight feet	*octameter*

Thus, in the examples above, the first set of lines is iambic trimeter; the second trochaic tetrameter; the third anapestic dimeter; and the fourth dactylic pentameter. The third lines in the iambic and trochaic examples are **hypermetrical;** that is, they contain an extra unstressed syllable or **feminine ending.** Conversely, the third lines in the trochaic and dactylic examples are missing one and two unstressed final syllables, respectively, a common practice called **catalexis.** Although over thirty combinations of foot type and number per line are theoretically possible, relatively few are regularly encountered in poetry. The iambic foot is most common in English, followed by the anapest and the trochee; the dactylic foot is rare. Line lengths tend to be from three to five feet, with anything shorter or longer used sparingly. Still, there are famous exceptions like Poe's "The Raven," which is composed in trochaic octameter or Southwell's "The Burning Babe," composed in iambic heptameter.

    Meter denotes regularity, the "blueprint" for a line from which the poet works. Since iambic pentameter is the most common meter used in English, our subsequent discussion will focus on poems written in it. Most poets quickly learn that a metronomic regularity, five iambic feet marching in lockstep line after line, is not a virtue and quickly becomes predictable. Thus, there are several ways by which poets can add variety to their lines. One is by varying the placement of the **caesura (||)** or pause within a line (usually indicated by a mark of punctuation). Another is by mixing **end-stopped lines,** which clearly pause at their conclusion, with **enjambed lines,** which run on into the next line with no pause. These lines from Tennyson's "Ulysses" illustrate these techniques:

> This is my son, mine own Telemachus,

> To whom I leave the scepter and the isle—
> Well-loved of me, discerning to fulfil
> This labor, by slow prudence to make mild
> A rugged people, and through soft degrees
> Subdue them to the useful and the good.

Lines two and six have no caesurae; the others do, after either the third, fourth, or fifth syllable. Lines one, two, and six are end-stopped; the others are enjambed.

Another technique of varying regularity is **metrical substitution,** where feet of a different type are substituted for what the meter calls for. In iambic meter, trochaic feet are often encountered at the beginnings of lines, or after a caesura. Two other feet, the **pyrrhic** (⌣⌣), consisting of two unstressed syllables, and the **spondee** (´´), consisting of two stressed syllables, are also commonly substituted. Here are Tennyson's lines with their **scansion** marked.

> Thís ĭs | mý sŏn, || mĭne ówn | Tĕl´ĕmlăchŭs,
>
> Tŏ whóm | Ĭ leáve | thĕ scéptlĕr ănd | thĕ ísle—
>
> Wéll-lóved | ŏf mé, || dĭscérnlĭng tŏ | fŭlfí l
>
> Thís lálbŏr, || bў | slŏw prúdlĕnce tŏ | máke mí ld
>
> Ă rúglgĕd péoplĭe, || ănd | thrŏ͞ugh sóft | dĕgreés
>
> Sŭbdúe | thĕm tŏ | thĕ úselfŭl ănd | thĕ góod.

Even though these are fairly regular iambic pentameter lines it should be observed that no single line is without some substitution. Still, the dominant pattern of five iambic feet per line should be apparent (out of thirty total feet, about twenty are iambs); there is even a strong tendency on the reader's part to "promote" the middle syllable of three unstressed syllables ("thĕ úselfŭl ănd | thĕ góod") to keep the sense of the iambic rhythm.

How far can a poet depart from the pattern without losing contact with the original meter? That is a question that is impossible to answer in general terms. This scansion will probably strike us at first as a far departure from regular iambic pentameter:

$$ ´ \; || \; ´ \; | \; ⌣ \; || \; ´ \; | \; ⌣ \; ⌣ \; || \; ´ \; ⌣ \; | \; ⌣ \; ´ $$

Yet it is actually the opening line of one of Shakespeare's most often quoted passages, Mark Antony's funeral oration from *Julius Caesar.*

> Fríends, || Rólmăns, || cóunltrўmĕn, || lénd mĕ | yŏur eárs

Poets who have learned to use the resources of meter do not consider it a restraint; instead, they are able to stretch the pattern to its limits without breaking it. A good analogy might be made between poetry and dance. Beginning dancers watch their feet and count the steps while making them; after considerable practice, the movements become second nature, and a skillful pair of partners can add dips and passes without losing the basic step of the music.

Poetic Form: Open Versus Closed

All poems have form, the arrangement of the poem on the page that differentiates it from prose. An analysis of poetic form might note how the lines are arranged on the page, how long the lines are, and how they are grouped into blocks or **stanzas.** Further analysis might reveal the existence of types of repetition, rhyme or the use of a **refrain,** a repeated line or groups of lines. A substantial number of poems written in this century have been written in **open form,** which simply means that there is no strict pattern of regularity in the elements mentioned previously; in other words, there is no consistent meter and no rhyme scheme. Still, even a famous open-form poem like William Carlos Williams's "The Red Wheelbarrow" can be described in formal terms:

> so much depends
> upon
>
> a red wheel
> barrow
>
> glazed with rain
> water
>
> beside the white
> chickens

Here we might observe that the eight-line poem is divided into **uniform stanzas** of two lines each (or couplets). Line length varies between four and two syllables per line. The odd numbered lines each contain three words; the even, one. There is no apparent use of rhyme or repetition.

   Closed form, on the other hand, denotes the existence of some kind of regular pattern of meter, stanza, rhyme, or repetition. **Stanza forms** are consistent patterns in the individual units of the poem (*stanza* means "room" in Italian); **fixed forms** are patterns that encompass a complete poem, for example, a sonnet. **Traditional forms** are patterns that have been used for long periods of time and thus may be associated with certain subjects, themes, or types of poems. **Nonce forms** are patterns that originate in an individual poem and have not been widely used by other poets. Of course, it goes without saying that every traditional form was at first a nonce form; the Italian poet (now lost to memory) who first wrote a lyric consisting of fourteen rhymed iambic pentameter lines could not have foreseen that poets the world over in subsequent centuries would produce literally millions of sonnets that are all variations on the original model. Some of the most common stanza and fixed forms are briefly discussed below.

Stanza Forms

Blank verse is not, strictly speaking, a stanza form since it consists of individual lines of iambic pentameter that do not rhyme. However, long poems in blank verse may be arranged into **verse paragraphs** or stanzas with varying numbers of lines. Blank verse originally appeared in English with the Earl of Surrey's translation of the *Aeneid* in the fifteenth century; it has been used extensively for narrative and dramatic purposes since, particularly in epics like Milton's *Paradise Lost* and in Shakespeare's plays.

Paired rhyming lines are called **couplets,** though they are rarely printed as separate stanzas. **Short couplets** have a meter of iambic tetrameter (and are sometimes called **octosyllabic couplets**). If their rhymes are predominantly feminine and seem chosen for comic effect, they may be called **Hudibrastic couplets** after Samuel Butler's satirical poem of the late 1600s. **Heroic couplets** have a meter of iambic pentameter and take their name from John Dryden's translation of the *Aeneid* (1697) and Alexander Pope's hugely successful translation of Homer's *Iliad* and *Odyssey* (1720-1726), all of these "heroic" or epic poems. Heroic couplets have also been used effectively in satirical poems like Pope's "mock epic" *The Dunciad* (1728-1743) and even in dramatic monologues such as Browning's "My Last Duchess," where the rhymes are so effectively buried by enjambment that the poem approximates speech. Other couplet forms include **poulter's measure,** rhyming pairs of alternating lines of iambic hexameter and iambic heptameter, and **fourteeners,** pairs of iambic heptameter (fourteen syllable) lines, which, since there is generally a caesura after the fourth foot, closely resemble common measure (see below).

A three-line stanza is called a **tercet.** If it rhymes in an *aaa bbb* pattern it is a **triplet;** sometimes triplets appear in poems written in heroic couplets, especially at the end of sections or where special emphasis is desired. Iambic pentameter tercets rhyming *aba bcb cdc* form **terza rima,** a pattern invented by Dante for *The Divine Comedy.*

A four-line stanza is known as a **quatrain.** Alternating lines of tetrameter and trimeter in any foot, rhyming *abcb* or *abab,* make up a **ballad stanza;** if the feet are strictly iambic, the quatrain is called **common measure,** the form of many popular hymns like "Amazing Grace." **Long measure,** also widely used in hymns, consists of iambic tetrameter lines rhyming *abcb* or *abab.* The *In Memoriam* **stanza,** named after Tennyson's long poetic sequence, is iambic tetrameter rhyming abba. The *Rubaiyat* **stanza,** an import from ancient Persia, consists of lines of either iambic tetrameter or pentameter, rhyming *aaba bbcb . . .* ; Edward Fitzgerald's translation *The Rubaiyat of Omar Khayyám* employs this form. Four lines of iambic pentameter rhyming *abab* are known as an **English quatrain,** also known as the **elegiac stanza** (after Thomas Gray's "Elegy Written in a Country Churchyard"). Lines of the same meter rhyming *abba* make up an **Italian quatrain.** One other unusual quatrain stanza is an import from ancient Greece, the **Sapphic stanza,** named after the poet Sappho. The Sapphic stanza consists of three **hendecasyllabic** (or eleven-syllable) lines of this pattern (´ ˘ | ´ ˘ | ´ ˘ ˘ | ´ ˘ | ´ ˘) and a fourth line called an **adonic,** which is five syllables long and consists of one dactylic foot and one trochaic foot. The Sapphic is usually unrhymed. The quatrain stanza is also used in another import, the **pantoum,** a poem in which the second and fourth lines of the first stanza become the first and third of the second, and the second and fourth of the second become the first and third of the fourth, and so on. Pantoums may be written in any meter and may or may not employ rhyme.

A five-line stanza is known as a **quintet** and is relatively rare in English poetry. The **sestet,** or six-line stanza, can be found with a number of different meters and rhyme schemes. A seven-line stanza is called a **septet;** one of Chaucer's favorite stanza patterns was **rime royal,** seven lines of iambic pentameter rhyming *ababbcc* (see "The Knight's Tale" for one example). An eight-line stanza is called an **octave;** one widely used stanza of this length is **ottava rima,** iambic pentameter lines rhyming *abababcc.* Another octave form is the **Monk's Tale stanza,** named after one of Chaucer's tales. It is iambic pentameter and rhymes *ababbcbc.* The addition of a ninth line, rhyming *c* and having a meter of iambic hexameter, makes a **Spenserian stanza,** named after the poet who invented it for *The Faery Queen.*

Fixed Forms

Fixed forms are combinations of meter, rhyme scheme, and repetition that make up complete poems. One familiar three-line fixed form is the **haiku,** a Japanese import consisting of lines of five, seven, and five syllables, respectively. Related to haiku is the **tanka,** which adds two additional seven-syllable lines.

Two five-line fixed forms are the **limerick** and the **cinquain.** The limerick consists of anapestic trimeter in lines one, two, and five, and anapestic dimeter in three and four. The rhymes, *aabba,* are usually feminine for a comic effect. A cinquain, the invention of American poet Adelaide Crapsey, consists of five unrhymed lines of two, four, six, eight, and two syllables, respectively.

The most important of the fixed forms is the **sonnet,** fourteen lines of rhymed iambic pentameter. The original form of the sonnet is called the **Italian sonnet** or the **Petrarchan sonnet** after the fourteenth century poet who popularized it. An Italian sonnet is usually cast in two stanzas, an octave rhyming *abbaabba* and a sestet with a variable rhyme scheme; *cdcdcd, cdecde, cddcee* are some of the possible patterns. A **volta** or "turn," usually a conjunction or conjunctive adverb like "but" or "then" may appear at the beginning of the sestet, signifying a slight change of direction in thought. Many Italian sonnets have a strong logical connection between octave and sestet (problem/solution, cause/effect, question/answer) and the volta helps to clarify the transition. The **English sonnet,** also known as the **Shakespearean sonnet** after one of its prime exemplars, was developed in the sixteenth century after the sonnet was imported to England and employs a different rhyme scheme that takes into consideration the relative scarcity of rhymes in English (as compared to Italian). The English sonnet has a rhyme scheme of *ababcdcdefefgg* and is usually printed as a single stanza. The pattern of three English quatrains plus a heroic couplet often forces a slightly different organization scheme on the poet, though many of Shakespeare's sonnets still employ a strong volta at the beginning of the ninth line. Other English sonnets may withhold the turn until the beginning of the closing couplet. A third sonnet type, relatively rare, is the **Spenserian sonnet,** named after Edmund Spenser, author of *Amoretti,* one of the earliest sonnet sequences in English. The Spenserian sonnet rhymes *ababbcbccdcdee.* There have been other sonnets written over the years which have other rhyme schemes, often hybrids of the Italian and English types. These are usually termed **nonce sonnets;** Shelley's "Ozymandias," with its unusual rhyme scheme of *ababacdcedefef,* is one notable example. In "Ode to the West Wind" Shelley also employs a fourteen-line stanza rhyming *aba bcb cdc ded ff,* which has been called a **terza rima sonnet.**

Three other fixed forms, all French imports, have appeared from time to time in English poetry. The **villanelle** is a nineteen-line poem, usually written in iambic pentameter, employing two refrain lines, A_1 and A_2, in a pattern of five tercets and a final quatrain: A_1bA_2 abA_1 abA_2 abA_1 abA_2 abA_1A_2. The **ballade** is thirty-six lines of iambic tetrameter employing a refrain C that appears at the end of its three octaves and final quatrain or **envoy:** *ababbcbC ababbcbC ababbcbC bcbC.* Obviously the rhyming demands of both the villanelle and the ballade pose serious challenges to English-language poets. A final fixed form is the thirty-nine line **sestina,** which may be either metered or in free verse and which uses a complicated sequence repeating, in different order, the six words that end the lines of the initial stanza. The sequence for the first six sestets is *123456 615243 364125 532614 451362 246531.* A final tercet uses three words in the interior of the lines and three at the ends, in the pattern *(2)5(4)3(6)1.* Many sestinas hinge on the poet's choice of six end words that have multiple meanings and can serve as more than one part of speech.

There are many other less familiar types of stanza forms and fixed forms; Lewis Turco's *The New Book of Forms* and Miller Williams's *Patterns of Poetry* are two reference sources useful in identifying them. An appendix of poetic forms discussed here can be found beginning on page 349.

Literary History and Poetic Conventions

What a poet attempts to do in any given poem is always governed by the tension that exists between originality and convention, in other words, between the poet's desire, in Ezra Pound's famous phrase, to "make it new" and the various stylistic devices that other poets and readers are familiar with through their understanding of the poetic tradition. If we look at some of the most obscure passages of Pound's *Cantos* we may think that the poet has departed about as far from conventional modes of expression as possible, leaving his audience far behind him. Yet it is important to keep two facts in mind. First, this style was not arrived at overnight; Pound's early poetry is relatively traditional and should present little difficulty to most readers. He arrived at the style of the *Cantos* after a twenty-year apprenticeship to the styles of writers as different as Li-Po, Robert Browning, and William Butler Yeats. Second, by the time Pound was writing his mature poetry the modernist movement was in full flower, forcing the public not only to read poems but also to look at paintings and sculpture and to listen to music in ways that would have been unimaginable only a decade or two earlier. When we talk about the stylistic conventions of any given literary period, we should keep in mind that poets are rarely willing to go much beyond what they have educated their audiences to understand. This mutual sense of agreement is the essence of poetic convention.

One should be wary of making sweeping generalizations about "schools" of poetry or the shared conventions of literary periods. In any era, there is always a significant amount of diversity among individual poets. Furthermore, an anthology of this limited scope, which by its very nature must exclude most long poems, is likely to contribute to a misleading view of literary history and the development of poetry in English. When we read Shakespeare's sonnets or Milton's shorter poems, we should not forget that their major reputations rest on poetry of a very different sort. The Neo-classical era in English poetry, stretching from the late seventeenth century until almost the end of the eighteenth century is poorly represented here because the satires of Dryden and Pope and long philosophical poems like *The Essay on Man* do not readily lend themselves to being excerpted. Edgar Allan Poe once claimed that a long poem is "simply a contradiction in terms," but the continued high reputation of *The Faery Queen, Paradise Lost, Don Juan,* and even a modern verse-novella like Robinson Jeffers's "The Roan Stallion" demonstrate that Poe's was far from the last word on the subject.

The earliest poems in this volume, all anonymous, represent poetry's links to the oral folk tradition. The American folk songs that children learn to sing in elementary school represent our own inheritance of this rich legacy. The poets of the Tudor (1485-1558) and Elizabethan (1558-1603) eras excelled at lyrical poetry; Wyatt and Surrey had imported the sonnet form from Italy, and the form was perfected during this period. Much of the love poetry of the age is characterized by conventional imagery, so-called Petrarchan conceits, which even a later poet like Campion employs in "There Is a Garden in Her Face" and which Shakespeare satirizes brilliantly in his sonnet 130 ("My mistress' eyes are nothing like the sun").

The poetry of the first half of the seventeenth century has several major schools: a smooth lyricism influenced by Ben Jonson that can be traced through the work of Herrick, Waller, and Lovelace; a serious body of devotional poetry by Donne, Herbert, and Milton; and the Metaphysical style, which uses complex extended metaphors or Metaphysical conceits; Donne and Herbert are its chief exemplars, followed by early American poets Bradstreet and Taylor. Shortly after the English Restoration in 1660, a profound period of conservatism began in the arts, and the Neo-classical era, lasting through most of the eighteenth century, drew heavily on Greek and Roman models. Poetry during this period— the age of Swift, Pope, and Gray—was dominated by one form, the heroic couplet; the genres of epic and satire; and an emphasis on human reason as the poet's chief guide. Never has the private voice been so subordinated to the public as in this period when, as Pope put it, a poet's highest aspiration should be to utter "What oft was thought, but ne'er so well expressed."

The first inklings of the Romantic era coincide with the American and French Revolutions, and poets of the latter half of the eighteenth century like Freneau and Blake exhibit some of its characteristics. But it was not until the publication of *Lyrical Ballads,* a 1798 book containing the best early work of Wordsworth and Coleridge, that the Romantic era can be said to have truly flowered. Wordsworth's famous formulation of a poem as "the spontaneous overflow of powerful feeling recollected in tranquillity" remains one of Romanticism's key definitions, with its emphasis on emotion and immediacy and reflection, and Wordsworth's own poetry, with its focus on the natural world, was tremendously influential. Most of the English and American poets of the first half of the nineteenth century have ties to Romanticism in its various guises, and even a poet as late as Whitman (1819-1892) inherits many of its liberal, democratic attitudes. Poets of the Victorian era (1837-1901) continued to explore many of the same themes and genres as their Romantic forebears, but certainly much of the optimism of the early years of the century had dissipated by the time poets like Hardy, Housman, and Yeats, with their omnipresent irony and pessimism, came on the scene in the century's last decades.

The present century has been ruled by the upheavals that modernism caused in every art form. If anything characterized the first half of the century it was its tireless experimentation with the forms of poetry. There is a continuum in English-language poetry from Chaucer through Frost and Robinson, but Pound, Williams, and cummings, to mention only three chief modernists, published poetry that would have totally mystified readers of their grandparents' day, just as Picasso and Dali produced paintings that represented radical breaks with the forms of the past. Though many of the experiments of movements like imagism and surrealism seem quaint today, they parallel the general direction that most of the other arts took during the same period.

For the sake of convenience more than anything else, it has been useful to refer to the era following the end of World War II as the post-modern era. Certainly many of the hard-won modernist gains—open form and greater candor in language and subject matter—have been taken for granted by poets writing in the contemporary period. The confessional poem, a frankly autobiographical narrative that reveals what poets in earlier ages might have tried desperately to conceal, surfaced in the late 1950s in the works of Lowell, Snodgrass, Plath, and Sexton, and remains one of the chief post-modern genres. Still, as the selections here will attest, there is considerable variety to be found in the contemporary scene, and it will perhaps be many years before critics have the necessary hindsight to assess the unique characteristics of the present period.

Writing About Poetry

Writing assignments vary widely, and your teacher's instructions may range from the general ("Discuss any two poems in your text which contain an effective use of imagery") to very specific ("Write an explication, in not less than one thousand words, of one of Edwin Arlington Robinson's sonnets, focusing on his use of form and his psychological insights into character"). Such processes as choosing, limiting, and developing a topic; brainstorming by taking notes on random ideas and refining those ideas further through group discussion or conferences with your instructor; and revising a first draft in light of critical remarks are undoubtedly techniques you have practiced in other composition classes. Basic types of organizational schemes learned in theme-writing courses can also be applied to writing about poetry.

Writing assignments on poetry usually fall into two categories: explication (or close reading) of single poems and analysis of poetic techniques in one or more poems. Because explication involves the careful "unfolding" of individual poems on a line-by-line basis, an assignment of this type will usually focus on a single short poem or a passage from a longer one. Some poems yield most of their meaning in a single reading; others, however, may contain complexities and nuances that deserve closer inspection. A typical explication might examine both form and content. Since assignments in analysis usually involve many of the same techniques as explication, we will look at explication more closely. Here is a checklist of questions that you might ask before explicating a poem; the answers apply to a poem from this book, Edwin Arlington Robinson's "Firelight."

Form

1. How many lines does the poem contain? How are they arranged into stanzas? Is either the whole poem or the stanza an example of a traditional poetic form?

   "Firelight" is an Italian sonnet. It is divided into
   two stanzas, an octave and sestet, and there is a
   tonal shift, or what is known in sonnets as a "turn"
   or *volta*, at the beginning of line nine, though here
   there is no single word that signals the shift.

2. Is there anything striking in the visual arrangement of the poem—indentation, spacing, etc.? Are capitalization and punctuation unusual?

   Capitalization and punctuation are standard in the
   poem, and Robinson follows the traditional practice
   of capitalizing the first word of each line.

3. What meter, if any, is the poem written in? Does the poet use any notable examples of substitution in the meter? Are the lines primarily end-stopped or enjambed?

   The meter is fairly regular iambic pentameter ("Her
   thoughts a moment since of one who shines") with
   occasional substitution of trochees ("Wĭsĕr | fŏr
   síllĕnce") and spondees ("thĕir jóy | rĕcálls / Nó
   snăke, || nó swórd"). Enjambment occurs at the ends of
   lines two, five, six, seven, nine, ten, twelve, and
   thirteen; this has the effect of masking the regular
   meter and rhymes and enforcing a conversational tone,
   an effect that is assisted by the caesurae in lines
   six, seven, nine, and (most importantly) fourteen.
   The caesura in this last line calls attention to
   "Apart," which ironically contrasts with the poem's
   opening phrase: "Ten years together."

4. What is the rhyme scheme, if any, of the poem? What types of rhyme are used?

   The rhyme scheme of this poem is *abbaabba cdecde*.
   Robinson uses exact masculine rime; the only possible
   exception is "intervals," where the meter forces a
   secondary stress on the third syllable.

5. Are significant sound patterns evident? Is there any repetition of whole lines, phrases, or words?

   Alliteration is present in "firelight" and "four" in
   line three and "wan" and "one" in line eleven, and
   there are several instances of assonance ("Wiser for
   silence"; "endowed / And bowered") and consonance
   ("Serenely and perennially endowed"; the wan face of
   one somewhere alone"). However, these sound patterns

do not call excessive attention to themselves and
detract from the poem's relaxed, conversational
sound.

"Firelight" contains no prominent use of repeti-
tion, with the possible exception of the pronoun
"they" and its variant forms "their" and "them" and
the related use of the third person singular pronouns
"he" and "she" in the last five lines of the poem.
This pronoun usage, confusing at first glance,
indirectly expresses the separateness of the lovers'
thoughts. The only notable instance of parallel
phrasing occurs in line seven with "No snake, no
sword."

Content

1. To what genre (lyric, narrative, dramatic) does the poem belong? Does it con-
   tain elements of more than one genre?

   "Firelight" is a narrative poem. Even though it has
   little plot in the conventional sense, it contains
   two characters in a specific setting who perform
   actions that give the reader insight into the true
   nature of their relationship. The sonnet form has
   traditionally been used for lyrical poetry.

2. Who is the persona of the poem? Is there an auditor? If so, who? What is the
   relationship between persona and auditor? Does the poem have a specific set-
   ting? If so, where and when is it taking place? Is there any action that has taken
   place before the poem opens? What actions take place during the poem?

   The persona here is a third-person omniscient
   narrator such as might be encountered in a short
   story; the narrator has the ability to read "Her
   thoughts a moment since" and comments that the couple
   is "Wiser for silence." The unnamed characters in the
   poem are a man and woman who have been married for
   ten years. The poem is set in their home, apparently
   in a comfortable room with a fireplace where they are
   spending a quiet evening together. Neither character
   speaks during the poem; the only action is their
   looking at "each other's eyes at intervals / Of
   gratefulness." Much of the poem's ironic meaning
   hinges on the couple's silence, "what neither says
   aloud."

3. Does the poem contain any difficulties with grammar or syntax? What indi-
   vidual words or phrases are striking because of their denotation or connota-
   tion?

The syntax of "Firelight" is straightforward and
contains no inversions or ellipses. The poem's
sentence structure is deceptively simple. The first
four lines make up a single sentence with one main
clause; the second four lines also make up a single
sentence, this time with two main clauses; the final
six lines also make up a single sentence, broken into
two equal parts by the semicolon, and consisting of
both main and dependent clauses. The poem's
vocabulary is not unusual, though "obliteration"
(literally an *erasure*) seems at first a curious
choice to describe the effects of love. One should
note the allusion implied by "bowered," "snake," and
"sword" in the octave and the rather complicated use
of the subjunctive "were" in lines nine, ten, and
twelve. Again, this slight alteration in grammar
bears indirectly on the theme of the poem. "Yet" in
the first line provides an interesting touch since it
injects a slight negative note into the picture of
marital bliss.

4. Does the poem use any figures of speech? If so, how do they add to the overall
   meaning? Is the action of the poem to be taken literally, symbolically, or both
   ways?

"Firelight" uses several figures of speech. "Cloud"
is a metaphor commonly employed for "foreboding."
"Firelight" and "four walls" are a metonymy and
synecdoche, respectively, for the couple's
comfortable home. The allusion to the "snake" and
"sword" direct the reader to the Garden of Eden
story. "Wiser for silence" is a slight paradox. "The
graven tale of lines / on the wan face" is an implied
metaphor which compares the lines on a person's face
to the written ("graven") story of her life. To say
that a person "shines" instead of "excels" is another
familiar metaphor. "Firelight" is to be understood
primarily on the literal level. The characters are
symbolic only in that the man and woman are perhaps
representative of many married couples, who outwardly
express happiness yet inwardly carry regrets and
fantasies from past relationships.

5. Is the title of the poem appropriate? What are its subject, tone of voice, and
   theme? Is the theme stated or implied?

"Firelight" is a good title since it carries both the
connotation of domestic tranquillity and a hint of
danger. "To bring to the light" means to reveal the
truth, and the narrator in the poem does this.

Robinson's attitude toward the couple is ironic. On
the surface they seem to be the picture of ideal
happiness, but he reveals that this happiness has
been purchased, in the man's case, at the expense of
an earlier lover and, in the woman's, by settling for
someone who has achieved less than another man for
whom she apparently had unrequited love. Robinson's
ironic view of marital stability is summed up in the
phrase "Wiser for silence." Several themes are
implied: the difference between surface appearance
and deeper insight; the cynical idea that in love
ignorance of what one's partner is thinking may be
the key to bliss; the sense that individual happiness
is not without its costs. All of these are possible
ways to state Robinson's bittersweet theme.

Your instructor may ask you to employ specific strategies in your explication and may require a certain type of organization for the paper. In writing the body of the explication you will probably proceed through the poem from beginning to end, summarizing and paraphrasing some lines and quoting others fully when you feel an explanation is required. It should be stressed that there are many ways, in theory, to approach a poem and that no two explications of the same poem will match in every detail. Some instructors may favor an explication that links the poem to events in the author's life, to the socio-historical context in which it was written, or to some other theoretical approach. You may also be required to use secondary sources from the library in writing your paper. A subject search through your library's books is a good starting place, especially for older poets who have attracted extensive critical attention. Reference books like *Contemporary Authors* and the *Dictionary of Literary Biography* provide compact overviews of poets' careers. *Contemporary Literary Criticism* contains excerpts from critical pieces on poets' works, and the *MLA Index* will direct you to articles on the poet in scholarly journals. There are several popular indexes of book reviews; one of these, the annual *Book Review Digest* reprints brief passages from the most representative reviews. Finally, a useful index to poetry explications published in periodicals and books is *Poetry Explication: A Checklist of Interpretations Since 1925 of British and American Poems Past and Present;* many of the articles listed here first appeared in the *Explicator,* a periodical also worth inspecting.

An assignment in analysis, which looks closely at the way a single element— such as theme, dramatic situation, meter, form, imagery, one or more figures of speech, and so forth—functions in poetry, would probably require that you write about two or more poems; in such cases a comparison/contrast or definition/illustration paper might be called for. An assignment of this type might examine two related poems by the same poet, or might inspect the way several poets have used a poetic device or theme. Comparison/contrast essays look for both similarities and differences in two poems. Definition/illustration papers usually begin with a general discussion of the topic, say, a popular theme (such as *carpe diem* , "seize the day") and then go on to illustrate how this motif may be found in several different poems. Assignments in analysis often lead to longer papers which may require the use of secondary sources. An appendix to this book lists some groups of two or more poems which have elements in common.

No matter what type of assignment you are given, it is always necessary to support the statements you make about a poem, either by quoting directly from the poem itself or, if you are required, by using secondary sources for additional critical opinion. The *MLA Handbook,* which you will find in the reference section of almost any library, contains the format for bibliographies and manuscripts which most instructors consider standard; indeed, most of the handbooks of grammar and usage commonly used in college courses follow MLA style. However, if you have doubts, ask your instructor what format he or she prefers. The type of parenthetical citation used today to indicate the source of quotations is simple to learn and dispenses with such time-consuming and repetitive chores as footnotes and endnotes. In using parenthetical citations remember that your goal is to direct your reader from the quoted passage in the paper to its source in your bibliography and from there, if necessary, to the book or periodical from which the quote is taken. A good parenthetical citation gives only the minimal information needed to accomplish this. Here are a few examples from student papers on Edwin Arlington Robinson's poetry.

```
Robinson's insights into character are never sharper
than in "Miniver Cheevy," a portrait of a town drunk
who loves "the days of old / When swords were bright
and steeds were prancing" and dreams incongruously
"of Thebes and Camelot, / And Priam's neighbors"
(347).
```

Here you should note a couple of conventions regarding writing about poetry. One is that the present tense is used in discussing the poem; in general, use the present tense throughout your critical writing except when you are giving biographical or historical information. Second, note how only parts of lines are quoted here to support the sentence and how the parts fit smoothly into the author's sentence structure. In general, ellipses (. . .) are not necessary at the beginning or end of these quotes since it is clear that they are quoted fragmentarily; they should, however, be used if something is omitted from the middle of a quote ("the days of old / When . . . steeds were prancing"). The virgule or slash (/) is used to indicate line breaks; a double slash (//) indicates stanza breaks. Quotes of up to three lines should be treated in this manner. If a quote is longer than three lines it should be indented ten spaces (with no quotation marks) and printed as it appears in the original poem:

```
Robinson opens one of his most effective and pitiless
character sketches with an unsparing portrait:
              Miniver Cheevy, child of scorn,
                Grew lean while he assailed the seasons;
              He wept that he was ever born,
                And he had reasons. (347)
```

The parenthetical citation here lists only a page number since only one work by Robinson appears in the bibliography. If several works by the poet had been listed among the works cited, the parenthetical citation would clarify which one was being referred to by adding a shortened form of the book's title: (Collected 347). The reader finds the following entry among the sources:

```
Robinson, Edwin Arlington.  Collected Poems.  New York:
     MacMillan, 1934.
```

Similarly, quotes and paraphrases from secondary critical sources should follow the same rules of common sense.

```
Louis O. Coxe observes that Robinson, even in using
the most demanding forms, manages to avoid the
artificial-sounding poetic diction of most
sonneteers: "The best of Robinson's sonnets take an
anti-rhetorical line though they often ride to
eloquence as they progress" (50-51).
```

In this case the author of the quote is identified, so only the page numbers are included in the parenthetical citation. The reader knows where to look among the sources:

```
Coxe, Louis O.  Edwin Arlington Robinson: The Life of
     Poetry.  New York: Pegasus, 1969.
```

To simplify the whole matter of parenthetical citation, it is recommended that quotes from secondary sources be introduced, wherever possible, in a manner that identifies the author so that only the page number of the quote is needed inside of the parentheses.

Of course, different types of sources—reference book entries, poems in anthologies, articles in periodicals, and book reviews—require different bibliographical information, so be sure to check the *MLA Handbook* if you have questions. Here are a few of the most commonly used bibliographical formats:

A book with author and editor:

```
Robinson, Edwin Arlington.  Edwin Arlington Robinson's
     Letters to Edith Brower.  Ed. Richard Cary.
     Cambridge:  Harvard UP, 1968.
```

A casebook or collection of critical essays:

```
Barnard, Ellsworth, ed.  Edwin Arlington Robinson:
     Centenary Essays.  Athens: U of Georgia P, 1969.
```

A poem reprinted in an anthology or textbook:

```
Robinson, Edwin Arlington.  "Richard Cory."  Literature:
     An Introduction to Poetry, Fiction, and Drama.  5th
     ed. Ed. X. J. Kennedy.  New York: HarperCollins,
     1991. 610.
```

An article in a reference book:

> Seymour-Smith, Martin.   "Robinson, Edwin Arlington."
>   <u>Who's Who in Twentieth Century Literature</u>.   New York:
>   McGraw, 1976.

An article in a scholarly journal:

> Read, Arthur M., II.   "Robinson's 'The Man Against the
>   Sky.'"   <u>Explicator</u> 26 (Feb. 1968): 49.

A book review in a periodical:

> Hutchison, Percy.   "Robinson's Satire and Symbolism."
>   Rev. of <u>King Jasper</u>, by Edwin Arlington Robinson.
>   <u>New York Times Book Review</u> 10 Nov. 1935: 5.

Anonymous

Some of the popular ballads and lyrics of England and Scotland, composed for the most part between 1300 and 1500, were first collected in their current forms by Thomas Percy, whose *Reliques of Ancient English Poetry* (1765) helped to revive interest in folk poetry. Francis James Child (1825-1896), an American, gathered over a thousand variant versions of the three hundred-odd core of poems. The Romantic poets of the early nineteenth century showed their debt to the folk tradition by writing imitative "art ballads" (see Keats's "La Belle Dame sans Merci" or Whittier's "Skipper Ireson's Ride") which incorporate many of their stylistic devices.

Western Wind

Western wind, when will thou blow,
    The small rain down can rain?
Christ, if my love were in my arms
4   And I in my bed again!

—1450?

Bonny Barbara Allan

It was in and about the Martinmas° time,
    When the green leaves were a falling,
That Sir John Græme, in the West Country,
    Fell in love with Barbara Allan.

5   He sent his men down through the town,
    To the place where she was dwelling.
"O haste and come to my master dear,
    Gin° ye be Barbara Allan."

O hooly,° hooly rose she up,
10   To the place where he was lying,
And when she drew the curtain by:
    "Young man, I think you're dying."
"O it's I'm sick, and very, very sick,

---

1 Martinmas November 11   **8 Gin** if   **9 hooly** slowly

And 'tis a'° for Barbara Allan."
15 "O the better for me ye s'° never be,
      Though your heart's blood were a-spilling.

"O dinna° ye mind, young man," said she,
  "When ye was in the tavern a drinking,
That ye made the healths gae° round and round,
20   And slighted Barbara Allan?"

He turned his face unto the wall,
  And death was with him dealing:
"Adieu, adieu, my dear friends all,
  And be kind to Barbara Allan."

25 And slowly, slowly raise she up,
      And slowly, slowly left him,
    And sighing said she could not stay,
      Since death of life had reft him.

She had not gane° a mile but twa,°
30   When she heard the dead-bell ringing,
    And every jow° that the dead-bell geid,°
      It cried, "Woe to Barbara Allan!"

"O mother, mother, make my bed!
  O make it saft° and narrow!
35 Since my love died for me to-day,
    I'll die for him to-morrow."

                                               —1500?

Sir Patrick Spens

The king sits in Dumferling town,
  Drinking the blude-reid° wine:
"O whar will I get guid sailor,
  To sail this ship of mine?"

5 Up and spak an eldern knicht,°
    Sat at the king's richt° knee:
  "Sir Patrick Spens is the best sailor

---

14 a' all   **15 s'** shall   **17 dinna** do not   **19 gae** go   **29 gane** gone   **twa** two   **31 jow** stroke   **geid** gave
34 saft soft
2 blude-reid blood-red   **5 eldern knicht** elderly knight   **6 richt** right

That sails upon the sea."

The king has written a braid° letter,
10   And signed it wi' his hand,
And sent it to Sir Patrick Spens,
      Was walking on the sand.

The first line that Sir Patrick read,
      A loud lauch° lauched he;
15   The next line that Sir Patrick read,
      The tear blinded his ee.°

"O wha is this has done this deed,
      This ill deed done to me,
To send me out this time o' the year,
20   To sail upon the sea?

"Mak haste, mak haste, my mirry men all,
      Our guid ship sails the morn."
"O say na sae,° my master dear,
      For I fear a deadly storm.

25   "Late, late yestre'en° I saw the new moon,
      Wi' the auld moon in hir arm,
And I fear, I fear, my dear master,
      That we will come to harm."

O our Scots nobles wer richt laith°
30   To weet° their cork-heeled shoon,°
But lang or a'° the play were played,
      Their hats they swam aboon.°

O lang, lang may their ladies sit,
      Wi' their fans into their hand,
35   Or ere they see Sir Patrick Spens
      Come sailing to the land.

O lang, lang may the ladies stand,
      Wi' their gold kems° in their hair,
Waiting for their ain dear lords,

---

9 braid long   **14 lauch** laugh   **16 ee** eye   **23 na sae** not so   **25 yestre'en** last evening   **29 laith** loath
30 weet wet   **shoon** shoes   **31 lang or a'** long before   **32 Their hats they swam aboon** their hats
swam above them   **38 kems** combs

40   For they'll se them na mair.

Half o'er, half o'er to Aberdour
   It's fifty fadom deep,
And there lies guid Sir Patrick Spens
   Wi' the Scots lords at his feet.

—1500?

Sir Thomas Wyatt
(1503?-1542)

While serving Henry VIII as a diplomat in Italy, Wyatt read the
love poetry of Petrarch (1304-1374), and is generally credited
with having imported both the fashions of these lyrics—
hyperbolic "conceits" or metaphorical descriptions of the
woman's beauty and the lover's suffering—and their form, the
sonnet, to England. "They Flee from Me," an example of one of
his original lyrics, displays Wyatt's unique grasp of the rhythms of
speech.

They Flee from Me

They flee from me, that sometime did me seek,
With naked foot stalking in my chamber.
I have seen them gentle, tame and meek,
That now are wild, and do not remember
5   That sometime they put themself in danger
To take bread at my hand; and now they range,
Busily seeking with a continual change.

Thanked be Fortune it hath been otherwise,
Twenty times better; but once in special,
10   In thin array, after a pleasant guise,°
When her loose gown from her shoulders did fall,
And she me caught in her arms long and small,
And therewith all sweetly did me kiss
And softly said, "Dear heart, how like you this?"

15   It was no dream, I lay broad waking.
But all is turned, thorough° my gentleness,

---

10 guise appearance

Into a strange fashion of forsaking;
And I have leave to go, of her goodness,
And she also to use newfangleness.
20 But since that I so kindely° am served,
I fain° would know what she hath deserved.

—1557

Henry Howard,
Earl of Surrey
(ca. 1517-1547)

Like Wyatt, Surrey was heavily influenced by Petrarchan love
poetry. His two major innovations are formal: his translation of
Virgil's *Aeneid* introduced blank verse to English poetry, and he
was first to use the English sonnet form, with its relaxed rhyme
scheme (see Index). This type of sonnet became, in the hands
of Shakespeare and later poets, the most enduring of all
traditional poetic forms in English. In "The Soote Season" he
experiments with a sonnet turning on only two rhymes.

The Soote Season

The soote° season, that bud and bloom forth brings,
With green hath clad the hill and eke° the vale;
The nightingale with feathers new she sings;
The turtle° to her make° hath told her tale.
5 Summer is come, for every spray now springs;
The hart hath hung his old head on the pale;
The buck in brake his winter coat he flings,
The fishes float with new repairèd scale;
The adder° all her slough away she slings,
10 The swift swallow pursueth the flies small;
The busy bee her honey now she mings.°
Winter is worn, that was the flowers' bale.°
And thus I see among these pleasant things,
Each care decays, and yet my sorrow springs.

—1557

---

16 thorough through   **20 kindely** in this manner   **21 fain** gladly
1 soote sweet   **2 eke** also   **4 turtle** turtledove   **make** mate   **9 adder** any snake   **11 mings** remembers
12 bale threat

Queen Elizabeth I
(1533-1603)

Elizabeth's skills as an amateur poet drew praise from the
members of her court, many of whom were also versifiers. A
handful of her lyrics survives, as do translations she made from
the Roman writers Seneca and Horace. Her reign (1558-1603)
established England as a world power and also nurtured the
talents of Edmund Spenser, William Shakespeare, Christopher
Marlowe, and Ben Jonson.

When I Was Fair and Young

When I was fair and young, and favor gracèd me,
Of many was I sought, their mistress for to be;
But I did scorn them all, and answered them therefore,
   "Go, go, go seek some otherwhere!
5   Importune me no more!"

How many weeping eyes I made to pine with woe,
How many sighing hearts, I have no skill to show;
Yet I the prouder grew, and answered them therefore,
   "Go, go, go seek some otherwhere!
10   Importune me no more!"

Then spake fair Venus' son,° that proud victorious boy,
And said, "Fine dame, since that you be so coy,
I will so pluck your plumes that you shall say no more,
   'Go, go, go seek some otherwhere!
15   Importune me no more!'"

When he had spake these words, such change grew in my breast
That neither night nor day since that, I could take any rest.
Then lo! I did repent that I had said before,
   "Go, go, go seek some otherwhere!
20   Importune me no more!"

---

11 **Venus' son** Eros or Cupid, god of love

Edmund Spenser
(1552-1599)

Born in London, Spenser spent most of his adult life in Ireland, where he held a variety of minor government posts. *The Faery Queen*, a long allegorical romance about Elizabethan England, was uncompleted at his death. The eighty-odd sonnets that make up the sequence called *Amoretti* are generally thought to detail his courtship of his second wife, Elizabeth Boyle, whom he married in 1594.

Amoretti: Sonnet 75

One day I wrote her name upon the strand,
But came the waves and washèd it away:
Agayne I wrote it with a second hand,°
But came the tyde, and made my paynes his pray.
5   "Vayne man," sayd she, "that doest in vaine assay,°
A mortall thing so to immortalize,
For I my selve shall lyke° to this decay
And eek° my name bee wypèd out lykewize."
"Not so," quod° I, "let baser things devize
10   To dy in dust, but you shall live by fame:
My verse your vertues rare shall eternize,
And in the hevens wryte your glorious name.
Where whenas death shall all the world subdew
Our love shall live, and later life renew."

—1595

Sir Philip Sidney
(1554-1584)

Sidney embodied many of the aspects of the ideal man of the Renaissance; he was a courtier, scholar, patron of the arts, and soldier who died of wounds received at the battle of Zutphen. His sonnet sequence *Astrophel and Stella* appeared in 1591, several years before Spenser's *Amoretti*, and helped to

---

3 second hand second time   **5 assay** attempt   **7 lyke** be similar to   **8 eek** also   **9 quod** said

precipitate the fashion for sonnets in England that lasted well into
the next century.

from Astrophel and Stella

1

Loving in truth, and fain° in verse my love to show,
That she dear she might take some pleasure of my pain,
Pleasure might cause her read, reading might make her know,
Knowledge might pity win, and pity grace obtain,
5   I sought fit words to paint the blackest face of woe:
Studying inventions fine, her wits to entertain,
Oft turning others' leaves,° to see if thence would flow
Some fresh and fruitful showers upon my sunburned brain.
But words came halting forth, wanting Invention's stay;
10 Invention, Nature's child, fled stepdame Study's blows;
And others' feet° still seemed but strangers in my way.
Thus, great with child to speak, and helpless in my throes,
Biting my truant pen, beating myself for spite:
"Fool," said my Muse to me, "look in thy heart, and write."

                                                        —1582

Robert Southwell
(ca. 1561-1595)

Southwell, a Roman Catholic priest in Elizabeth's Protestant
England, was executed for his religious beliefs. His devotional
poems, most of them on the subject of spiritual love, were
largely written during his three years in prison. Southwell was
declared a saint in 1970.

The Burning Babe

As I in hoary winter's night stood shivering in the snow,
Surprised I was with sudden heat which made my heart to glow;
And lifting up a fearful eye to view what fire was near,
A pretty babe all burning bright did in the air appear;
5   Who, scorchéd with excessive heat, such floods of tears did shed
As though his floods should quench his flames which with his tears were fed.

---

1 fain glad   **7 leaves** pages   **11 feet** metrical feet in poetry

"Alas," quoth he, "but newly born in fiery heats I fry,
Yet none approach to warm their hearts or feel my fire but I!
My faultless breast the furnace is, the fuel wounding thorns,
10 Love is the fire, and sighs the smoke, the ashes shame and scorns;
The fuel justice layeth on, and mercy blows the coals,
The metal in this furnace wrought are men's defiléd souls,
For which, as now on fire I am to work them to their good,
So will I melt into a bath to wash them in my blood."
15 With this he vanished out of sight and swiftly shrunk away,
And straight I callèd unto mind that it was Christmas day.

—1602

Michael Drayton
(1563-1631)

Like his contemporary Shakespeare, Drayton excelled in several literary genres. He collaborated on plays with Thomas Dekker and wrote long poems on English history, biography, and topography. Drayton labored almost three decades on the sixty-three sonnets in *Idea*, publishing them in their present form in 1619.

Idea: Sonnet 61

Since there's no help, come let us kiss and part;
Nay, I have done, you get no more of me,
And I am glad, yea glad with all my heart
That thus so cleanly I myself can free;
5 Shake hands forever, cancel all our vows,
And when we meet at any time again,
Be it not seen in either of our brows
That we one jot of former love retain.
Now at the last gasp of love's latest breath,
10 When, his pulse failing, passion speechless lies,
When faith is kneeling by his bed of death,
And innocence is closing up his eyes,
    Now if thou wouldst, when all have given him over,
    From death to life thou mightst him yet recover.

—1619

William Shakespeare
(1564-1616)

Shakespeare's sonnets were first printed in 1609, during the last years of his active career as a playwright, but they had circulated privately a dozen years before. Given the lack of concrete details about Shakespeare's life outside the theatre, critics have found the sonnets fertile ground for biographical speculation, and the sequence of 154 poems does contain distinct characters—a handsome youth to whom most of the first 126 sonnets are addressed, a "Dark Lady" who figures strongly in the remaining poems, and the poet himself, whose name is the source of many puns in the poems. There is probably no definitive "key" to the sonnets, but there is also little doubt that their place is secure among the monuments of English lyric verse. Shakespeare's other non-dramatic poems include narratives, allegories, and songs, of which "When Daisies Pied," two companion pieces from his early comedy *Love's Labour's Lost*, are perhaps the best examples.

Sonnet 18

Shall I compare thee to a summer's day?
Thou art more lovely and more temperate:
Rough winds do shake the darling buds of May,
And summer's lease hath all too short a date:
5   Sometimes too hot the eye of heaven shines,
And often is his gold complexion dimmed;
And every fair from fair° sometimes declines,
By chance or nature's changing course untrimmed;°
But thy eternal summer shall not fade,
10 Nor lose possession of that fair thou ow'st;°
Nor shall death brag thou wander'st in his shade,
When in eternal lines to time thou grow'st:
So long as men can breathe, or eyes can see,
So long lives this, and this gives life to thee.

—1609

---

7 **fair from fair** every fair thing from its fairness 8 **untrimmed** stripped 10 **ow'st** ownest

Sonnet 29

When, in disgrace with fortune and men's eyes,
I all alone beweep my outcast state,
And trouble deaf heaven with my bootless° cries,
And look upon myself, and curse my fate,
5   Wishing me like to one more rich in hope,
Featured like him, like him with friends possessed,
Desiring this man's art and that man's scope,
With what I most enjoy contented least;
Yet in these thoughts myself almost despising,
10   Haply° I think on thee—and then my state,
Like to the lark at break of day arising
From sullen earth, sings hymns at heaven's gate;
For thy sweet love remembered such wealth brings
That then I scorn to change my state with kings.

—1609

Sonnet 30

When to the sessions° of sweet silent thought
I summon up remembrance of things past,
I sigh the lack of many a thing I sought,
And with old woes new wail my dear time's waste:
5   Then can I drown an eye, unused to flow,
For precious friends hid in death's dateless° night,
And weep afresh love's long since canceled woe,
And moan the expense of many a vanished sight:
Then can I grieve at grievances foregone,
10   And heavily from woe to woe tell o'er
The sad account of fore-bemoanèd moan,
Which I new pay as if not paid before.
But if the while I think on thee, dear friend,
All losses are restored and sorrows end.

—1609

---

3 bootless useless   **10 Haply** fortunately
1 sessions as in sessions of a court of law   **6 dateless** endless

Sonnet 73

That time of year thou mayst in me behold
When yellow leaves, or none, or few, do hang
Upon those boughs which shake against the cold,
Bare ruined choirs, where late the sweet birds sang.
5 In me thou see'st the twilight of such day
As after sunset fadeth in the west;
Which by and by black night doth take away,
Death's second self, that seals up all in rest.
In me thou see'st the glowing of such fire,
10 That on the ashes of his youth doth lie,
As the deathbed whereon it must expire,
Consumed with that which it was nourished by.
This thou perceiv'st, which makes thy love more strong,
To love that well which thou must leave ere long.

—1609

Sonnet 116

Let me not to the marriage of true minds
Admit impediments. Love is not love
Which alters when it alteration finds,
Or bends with the remover to remove:
5 Oh, no! it is an ever-fixèd mark,
That looks on tempests and is never shaken:
It is the star to every wandering bark,
Whose worth's unknown, although his height be taken.°
Love's not Time's fool, though rosy lips and cheeks
10 Within his bending sickle's compass° come;
Love alters not with his brief hours and weeks,
But bears it out even to the edge of doom.
If this be error and upon me proved,
I never writ, nor no man ever loved.

—1609

Sonnet 130

My mistress' eyes are nothing like the sun;
Coral is far more red than her lips' red;

---

8 height be taken elevation be measured   **10 compass** range

If snow be white, why then her breasts are dun;
If hairs be wires, black wires grow on her head.
5   I have seen roses damasked,° red and white,
But no such roses see I in her cheeks;
And in some perfumes is there more delight
Than in the breath that from my mistress reeks.
I love to hear her speak, yet well I know
10 That music hath a far more pleasing sound;
I grant I never saw a goddess go;
My mistress, when she walks, treads on the ground.
And yet, by heaven, I think my love as rare
As any she belied° with false compare.°

—1609

When Daisies Pied

Spring

When daisies pied and violets blue
   And ladysmocks all silver-white
And cuckoobuds of yellow hue
   Do paint the meadows with delight,
5 The cuckoo then, on every tree,
Mocks married men;° for thus sings he,
          Cuckoo;
Cuckoo, cuckoo: Oh word of fear,
Unpleasing to a married ear!

10 When shepherds pipe on oaten straws,
   And merry larks are plowmen's clocks,
When turtles tread,° and rooks, and daws,
   And maidens bleach their summer smocks,
The cuckoo then, on every tree,
15 Mocks married men; for thus sings he,
          Cuckoo:
Cuckoo, cuckoo: Oh word of fear,
Unpleasing to a married ear!

Winter

When icicles hang by the wall

---

5 damasked multi-colored   **14 belied** lied about **compare** comparisons
6 Mocks married men The pun is on the similarity between "cuckoo" and "cuckold."   **12 turtles tread** turtledoves mate

20 And Dick the shepherd blows his nail°
And Tom bears logs into the hall,
    And milk comes frozen home in pail,
When blood is nipped and ways be foul,
Then nightly sings the staring owl,
25   Tu-who;
Tu-whit tu-who: a merry note,
While greasy Joan doth keel° the pot.

When all aloud the wind doth blow,
    And coughing drowns the parson's saw,°
30 And birds sit brooding in the snow,
    And Marian's nose looks red and raw,
When roasted crabs° hiss in the bowl,
Then nightly sings the staring owl,
                    Tu-who;
35 Tu-whit, tu-who: a merry note
While greasy Joan doth keel the pot.

                                                            —1598

Thomas Campion
(1567-1620)

A poet and physician, Campion wrote music and lyrics in a manner that was "chiefly aimed to couple my words and notes lovingly together." The imagery in "There Is a Garden in Her Face" represents a late flowering of the conceits of Petrarchan love poetry, so wittily mocked by Shakespeare in "Sonnet 130."

There Is a Garden in Her Face

There is a garden in her face,
Where roses and white lilies grow,
A heavenly paradise is that place,
Wherein all pleasant fruits do flow.
5 There cherries grow which none may buy
Till "Cherry-ripe!" themselves do cry.

Those cherries fairly do enclose
Of orient pearl a double row,

---

20 nail fingernails **27 keel** stir **29 saw** saying **32 crabs** crabapples

Which when her lovely laughter shows,
10   They look like rosebuds filled with snow.
Yet them nor peer nor prince can buy,
Till "Cherry-ripe!" themselves do cry.

Her eyes like angels watch them still;
Her brows like bended bows do stand,
15   Threatening with piercing frowns to kill
All that attempt with eye or hand
Those sacred cherries to come nigh,
Till "Cherry-ripe!" themselves do cry.

—1617

John Donne
(1572-1631)

Trained in the law for a career in government service, Donne
became the greatest preacher of his day, ending his life as
dean of St. Paul's Cathedral in London. Only two of Donne's
poems and a handful of his sermons were printed during his life,
but both circulated widely in manuscript and his literary reputation
among his contemporaries was considerable. His poetry falls
into two distinct periods: the witty love poetry of his youth and the
sober religious meditations of his maturity. In both, however,
Donne shows remarkable originality in rhythm, diction, and the
use of metaphor and conceit which mark him as the chief poet
of what has become commonly known as the Metaphysical
style.

The Canonization

For God's sake hold your tongue, and let me love,
   Or chide my palsy, or my gout,
My five gray hairs, or ruined fortune, flout,
   With wealth your state, your mind with arts improve,
5   Take you a course, get you a place,
     Observe His Honor, or His Grace,
Or the king's real,° or his stampèd face
   Contèmplate; what you will, approve,°
   So you will let me love.

---

7 real coinage   **8 approve** attempt

10   Alas, alas, who's injured by my love?
        What merchant's ships have my sighs drowned?
    Who says my tears have overflowed his ground?
        When did my colds a forward° spring remove?
          When did the heats which my veins fill
15   Add one more to the plaguy bill?°
Soldiers find wars, and lawyers find out still
      Litigious men, which quarrels move,
      Though she and I do love.

Call us what you will, we're made such by love;
20   Call her one, me another fly,
We're tapers too, and at our own cost die,°
    And we in us find th' eagle and the dove.
      The phoenix° riddle hath more wit
      By us: we two being one, are it.
25   So, to one neutral thing both sexes fit,
      We die and rise the same, and prove
      Mysterious by this love.

We can die by it, if not live by love,
    And if unfit for tomb and hearse
30   Our legend be, it will be fit for verse;
      And if no piece of chronicle° we prove,
      We'll build in sonnets pretty rooms;
      As well a well-wrought urn becomes
The greatest ashes, as half-acre tombs;
35   And by these hymns, all shall approve
      Us canonized for love:

And thus invoke us, "You whom reverend love
    Made one another's hermitage;
You, to whom love was peace, that now is rage;
40   Who did the whole world's soul contract, and drove
      Into the glasses of your eyes
      (So made such mirrors, and such spies,°
That they did all to you epitomize)
    Countries, towns, courts: Beg from above
45   A pattern of your love!"

                          —1633

---

13 forward early **15 plaguy bill** list of dead by plague **21 die** i.e., to have sexual intercourse **23 phoenix** legendary bird which is reborn from its own ashes **31 chronicle** history **42 spies** telescopes

The Flea

Mark but this flea, and mark in this,
How little that which thou deniest me is;
Me it sucked first, and now sucks thee,
And in this flea our two bloods mingled be;
5   Thou know'st that this cannot be said
A sin, or shame, or loss of maidenhead,
    Yet this enjoys before it woo,
    And pampered swells with one blood made of two,
    And this, alas, is more than we would do.

10   Oh stay, three lives in one flea spare,
Where we almost, nay more than married are.
This flea is you and I, and this
Our marriage bed and marriage temple is;
Though parents grudge, and you, we are met,
15   And cloistered in these living walls of jet.°
    Though use° make you apt to kill me
    Let not to that, self-murder added be,
    And sacrilege, three sins in killing three.

Cruel and sudden, hast thou since
20   Purpled thy nail° in blood of innocence?
Wherein could this flea guilty be,
Except in that drop which it sucked from thee?
Yet thou triumph'st, and say'st that thou
Find'st not thy self nor me the weaker now;
25   'Tis true; then learn how false fears be:
    Just so much honor, when thou yield'st to me,
    Will waste, as this flea's death took life from thee.

—1633

Holy Sonnet 10

Death, be not proud, though some have callèd thee
Mighty and dreadful, for thou art not so;
For those whom thou think'st thou dost overthrow
Die not, poor Death, nor yet canst thou kill me.

---

15 **jet** black   16 **use** familiarity, especially in the sexual sense   20 **Purpled thy nail** bloodied your fingernail

5   From rest and sleep, which but thy pictures be,
     Much pleasure; then from thee much more must flow,
     And soonest our best men with thee do go,
     Rest of their bones, and soul's delivery.
     Thou'art slave to fate, chance, kings, and desperate men,
10   And dost with poison, war, and sickness dwell,
     And poppy° or charms can make us sleep as well
     And better than thy stroke; why swell'st thou then?
     One short sleep past, we wake eternally,
     And death shall be no more; Death, thou shalt die.

                                                     —1633

Holy Sonnet 14

     Batter my heart, three-personed God; for You
     As yet but knock, breathe, shine, and seek to mend;
     That I may rise, and stand, o'erthrow me, and bend
     Your force to break, blow, burn, and make me new.
5   I, like an usurped town, to another due,
     Labor to admit You, but O, to no end;
     Reason, your Viceroy in me, me should defend,
     But is captived, and proves weak or untrue.
     Yet dearly I love You, and would be lovèd fain,°
10   But am bethrothed unto Your enemy.
     Divorce me, untie or break that knot again;
     Take me to You, imprison me, for I,
     Except You enthrall me, never shall be free,
     Nor ever chaste, except You ravish me.

                                                     —1633

A Valediction:° Forbidding Mourning

     As virtuous men pass mildly away,
         And whisper to their souls to go,
     Whilst some of their sad friends do say
         The breath goes now, and some say, No;

5   So let us melt, and make no noise,
         No tear-floods, nor sigh-tempests move,
     'Twere profanation of our joys

---

11 poppy opium **9 fain** gladly
Valediction farewell speech; Donne is addressing his wife before leaving on a diplomatic mission.

To tell the laity our love.

Moving of th'earth brings harms and fears,
10   Men reckon what it did and meant;
But trepidation of the spheres,°
        Though greater far, is innocent.

Dull sublunary° lovers' love,
        (Whose soul is sense) cannot admit
15 Absence, because it doth remove
        Those things which elemented it.

But we by a love so much refined
        That our selves know not what it is,
Inter-assurèd of the mind,
20   Care less, eyes, lips, and hands to miss.

Our two souls therefore, which are one,
        Though I must go, endure not yet
A breach, but an expansion,
        Like gold to airy thinness beat.

25 If they be two, they are two so
        As stiff twin compasses° are two;
Thy soul, the fixed foot, makes no show
        To move, but doth if th' other do.

And though it in the center sit,
30   Yet when the other far doth roam,
It leans and hearkens after it,
        And grows erect, as that comes home.

Such wilt thou be to me, who must
        Like th' other foot, obliquely run;
35 The firmness makes my circle just,°
        And makes me end where I begun.

                                —1633

---

11 trepidation of the spheres natural trembling of the heavenly spheres, a concept of Ptolemaic astronomy   **13 sublunary** under the moon, hence, changeable (a Ptolemaic concept)   **26 stiff twin compassess** drafting compasses   **35 just** complete

Ben Jonson
(1573-1637)

Jonson was Shakespeare's chief rival on the stage, and their
contentious friendship has been the subject of much speculation.
Jonson became England's first unofficial poet laureate, receiving
a royal stipend from James I, and was a great influence on a
group of younger poets who became known as the "Tribe of
Ben." His tragedies are little regarded today, and his comedies,
while still performed occasionally, have nevertheless failed to
hold stage as brilliantly as Shakespeare's. Still, he was a poet of
considerable talents, particularly in short forms. His elegy on
Shakespeare contains a famous assessment: "He was not of an
age, but for all time!"

On My First Son

Farewell, thou child of my right hand,° and joy;
My sin was too much hope of thee, loved boy:
Seven years thou'wert lent to me, and I thee pay,
Exacted by thy fate, on the just day.°
5 Oh, could I lose all father now! for why
Will man lament the state he should envy,
To have so soon 'scaped world's and flesh's rage,
And, if no other misery, yet age?
Rest in soft peace, and asked, say, "Here doth lie
10 Ben Jonson his best piece of poetry."
For whose sake henceforth all his vows be such
As what he loves may never like too much.

—1616

Slow, Slow, Fresh Fount°

from Cynthia's Revels

Slow, slow, fresh fount, keep time with my salt tears;
Yet slower, yet, O faintly, gentle springs!
List to the heavy part the music bears,

---

1 child of my right hand Benjamin, the child's name, means this in Hebrew **4 the just day** Jonson's
son died on his seventh birthday
Slow, Slow Fresh Fount from *Cynthia's Revels;* spoken by the nymph Echo to the dead Narcissus

Woe weeps out her division,° when she sings.
5   Droop herbs and flowers;
      Fall grief in showers;
Our beauties are not ours. O, I could still,
Like melting snow upon some craggy hill,
      Drop, drop, drop, drop,
10   Since nature's pride is now a withered daffodil.

                                        —1600

Robert Herrick
(1591-1674)

The most distinguished member of the "Tribe of Ben," Herrick is
grouped with the Cavalier poets, whose graceful lyrics are
marked by wit and gentle irony. Surprisingly, Herrick was a
minister; his Royalist sympathies during the English Civil War
caused him hardship during the Puritan era, but his position in the
church was returned to him by Charles II after the Restoration.

To the Virgins, to Make Much of Time

Gather ye rosebuds while ye may,
   Old time is still a-flying;
And this same flower that smiles today
   Tomorrow will be dying.

5 The glorious lamp of heaven, the sun,
      The higher he's a-getting,
   The sooner will his race be run,
      And nearer he's to setting.

   That age is best which is the first,
10   When youth and blood are warmer;
   But being spent, the worse, and worst
      Times still succeed the former.

   Then be not coy, but use your time,
      And, while ye may, go marry;
15 For, having lost but once your prime,
      You may forever tarry.

                                        —1648

---

4 division part of a song

George Herbert
(1593-1633)

The great master of the English devotional lyric, Herbert was born into a distinguished family which included his mother, the formidable literary patroness Lady Magdalen Herbert, and the poet and statesman Edward, Lord Herbert of Cherbury. Like John Donne, with whom he shares the Metaphysical label, Herbert early aimed at a political career but turned to the clergy, spending several happy years as rector of Bemerton before his death at age 40. *The Temple*, which contains most of his poems, was published posthumously in 1633.

Easter Wings

Lord, who createdst man in wealth and store,°
Though foolishly he lost the same,
Decaying more and more
Till he became
5   Most poor:
With Thee
O let me rise
As larks, harmoniously,
And sing this day Thy victories:
10   Then shall the fall further the flight in me.

My tender age in sorrow did begin;
And still with sicknesses and shame
Thou didst so punish sin,
That I became
15   Most thin.
With Thee
Let me combine,
And feel this day thy victory;
For, if I imp my wing° on thine,
20   Affliction shall advance the flight in me.

                    —1633

---

1 store abundance **19 imp my wing on thine** to graft feathers from a strong wing onto a weak one, a term from falconry

The Pulley

When God at first made man,
Having a glass of blessings standing by,
　"Let us," said he, "pour on him all we can.
Let the world's riches, which dispersèd lie,
5　　Contract into a span."°

　So strength first made a way;
Then beauty flowed, then wisdom, honor, pleasure
　When almost all was out, God made a stay,
Perceiving that, alone of all his treasure,
10　　Rest in the bottom lay.

　"For if I should," said he,
"Bestow this jewel also on my creature,
　He would adore my gifts instead of me,
And rest in Nature, not the God of Nature;
15　　So both should losers be.

　"Yet let him keep the rest,
But keep them with repining restlessness.
　Let him be rich and weary, that at least,
If goodness lead him not, yet weariness
20　　May toss him to my breast."

　　　　　　　　　　　　　　　　—1633

Redemption

Having been tenant long to a rich lord,
　Not thriving, I resolvèd to be bold,
　And make a suit° unto him, to afford°
A new small-rented lease, and cancel the old.

5　In heaven at his manor I him sought;
　They told me there that he was lately gone
　About some land, which he had dearly bought
Long since on earth, to take possession.

I straight returned, and knowing his great birth,

---

5 span the distance between thumb tip and the tip of the little finger
3 make a suit formally request　**afford** grant (me)

10   Sought him accordingly in great resorts;
       In cities, theaters, gardens, parks, and courts;
    At length I heard a ragged noise and mirth
       Of thieves and murderers; there I him espied,°
       Who straight, *Your suit is granted,* said, and died.

                                                    —1633

Edmund Waller
(1606-1687)

Another Royalist sympathizer who suffered during Oliver
Cromwell's protectorate, Waller is noted for having pioneered
the use of the heroic couplet as a popular verse form. He has
been often praised for the smoothness of his rhythms and sound
patterns.

Song

       Go, lovely rose!
    Tell her that wastes her time and me
       That now she knows,
    When I resemble° her to thee,
5   How sweet and fair she seems to be.

       Tell her that's young,
    And shuns to have her graces spied,
       That hadst thou sprung
    In deserts, where no men abide,
10   Thou must have uncommended died.

       Small is the worth
    Of beauty from the light retired;
       Bid her come forth,
    Suffer herself to be desired,
15   And not blush so to be admired.

       Then die! that she
    The common fate of all things rare
       May read in thee;

---

13 him espied saw him
4 resemble compare

How small a part of time they share
20 That are so wondrous sweet and fair!

—1645

John Milton
(1608-1674)

Milton's true genius was realized in *Paradise Lost,* the greatest
English epic poem. His life included service in the Puritan
government of Cromwell, pamphleteering for liberal political
causes, brief imprisonment after the Restoration, and blindness in
his later years. He excelled in the sonnet, a form to which he
returned throughout his long literary life.

How Soon Hath Time

How soon hath Time, the subtle thief of youth,
   Stoln on his wing my three and twentieth year!
   My hasting days fly on with full career,
   But my late spring no bud or blossom shew'th.°
5 Perhaps my semblance might deceive the truth,
   That I to manhood am arrived so near,
   And inward ripeness doth much less appear,
   That some more timely-happy spirits endu'th.°
Yet be it less or more, or soon or slow,
10   It shall be still in strictest measure even°
   To that same lot, however mean or high,
Toward which Time leads me, and the will of Heaven;
   All is, if I have grace to use it so,
   As ever in my great Taskmaster's eye.

—1645

On the Late Massacre in Piedmont°

Avenge, O Lord, thy slaughtered saints, whose bones
   Lie scattered on the Alpine mountains cold,
   Even them who kept thy truth so pure of old
   When all our fathers worshiped stocks and stones,°

---

4 shew'th shows **8 endu'th** endows **10 even** equal

Massacre in Piedmont 1700 Protestants from this North Italian state were massacred by Papal forces
on Easter Day, 1655. **4 stocks and stones** idols

5   Forget not: in thy book record their groans
         Who were thy sheep and in their ancient fold
         Slain by the bloody Piedmontese that rolled
         Mother with infant down the rocks. Their moans
     The vales redoubled to the hills, and they
10   To Heaven. Their martyred blood and ashes sow
         O'er all th'Italian fields where still doth sway
     The triple tyrant:° that from these may grow
         A hundredfold, who having learnt thy way
         Early may fly the Babylonian woe.°

                                                        —1655

When I Consider How My Light Is Spent

     When I consider how my light is spent
         Ere half my days, in this dark world and wide,
         And that one talent which is death to hide°
         Lodged with me useless, though my soul more bent
5   To serve therewith my Maker, and present
         My true account, lest he returning chide;
         "Doth God exact day-labor, light denied?"
         I fondly° ask; but Patience to prevent
     That murmur, soon replies, "God doth not need
10   Either man's work or his own gifts; who best
         Bear his mild yoke, they serve him best. His state
     Is kingly. Thousands at his bidding speed
         And post o'er land and ocean without rest:
         They also serve who only stand and wait."

                                                        —1673

Anne Bradstreet
(1612-1672)

Bradstreet was an American Puritan who was one of the first
settlers of the Massachusetts Bay Colony, along with her husband
Simon, later governor of the colony. *The Tenth Muse Lately
Sprung Up in America*, published abroad without her knowledge
by a relative, was the first American book of poetry published in

---

12 **triple tyrant** the Pope   14 **Babylonian woe** Early Protestants often linked ancient Babylon to
modern Rome as centers of vice.

3 **talent which is death to hide** See the Parable of the Talents, Matthew 25:14-30   8 **fondly** foolishly

England, and the circumstances of its appearance lie behind the witty tone of "The Author to Her Book."

The Author to Her Book°

Thou ill-formed offspring of my feeble brain,
Who after birth didst by my side remain,
Till snatched from thence by friends, less wise than true,
Who thee abroad, exposed to public view,
5 Made thee in rags, halting to th' press° to trudge,
Where errors were not lessened (all may judge).
At thy return my blushing was not small,
My rambling brat (in print) should mother call,
I cast thee by as one unfit for light,
10 Thy visage was so irksome in my sight;
Yet being mine own, at length affection would
Thy blemishes amend, if so I could:
I washed thy face, but more defects I saw,
And rubbing off a spot still made a flaw.
15 I stretched thy joints to make thee even feet,°
Yet still thou run'st more hobbling than is meet;
In better dress to trim thee was my mind,
But nought save homespun cloth i'th' house I find.
In this array 'mongst vulgars° may'st thou roam.
20 In critic's hands beware thou dost not come,
And take thy way where yet thou art not known;
If for thy father asked, say thou hadst none;
And for thy mother, she alas is poor,
Which caused her thus to send thee out of door.

—1678

To My Dear and Loving Husband

If ever two were one, then surely we;
If ever man were loved by wife, then thee;
If ever wife was happy in a man,
Compare with me, ye women, if you can.
5 I prize thy love more than whole mines of gold,
Or all the riches that the East° doth hold.
My love is such that rivers cannot quench,

Her Book Bradstreet's first book was published in England without her knowledge, the act of a well-meaning relative **5 press** printing press; also a clothes closet or chest **15 even feet** a pun on metrical feet **19 vulgars** common people, i.e., average readers
6 East the Orient

Nor aught but love from thee give recompense.
Thy love is such I can no way repay;
10   The heavens reward thee manifold, I pray.
Then while we live in love let's so persevere
That when we live no more we may live ever.

—1678

Richard Lovelace
(1618-1658)

Another Cavalier lyricist, Lovelace composed many of his
poems in prison following the English Civil War, during which he
was a staunch supporter of Charles I, serving as a soldier in
Scotland and France.

To Lucasta, Going to the Wars

Tell me not, sweet, I am unkind
That from the nunnery
Of thy chaste breast and quiet mind,
To war and arms I fly.

5   True, a new mistress now I chase,
The first foe in the field;
And with a stronger faith embrace
A sword, a horse, a shield.

Yet this inconstancy is such
10   As you too shall adore;
I could not love thee, dear, so much,
Loved I not honor more.

—1649

Andrew Marvell
(1621-1678)

Although widely known for the playful sexual wit of this most
famous example of the *carpe diem* poem in English, Marvell was
a learned Latin scholar who moved in high circles of government
under both the Puritans and Charles II, serving as a member of
parliament for two decades. Oddly, Marvell was almost
completely forgotten as a lyric poet for almost two hundred

years after his death, though today he is considered the last of the great exemplars of the Metaphysical style.

To His Coy Mistress

Had we but world enough, and time,
This coyness,° lady, were no crime.
We would sit down, and think which way
To walk, and pass our long love's day.
5 Thou by the Indian Ganges' side
Shouldst rubies find; I by the tide
Of Humber° would complain. I would
Love you ten years before the flood,
And you should, if you please, refuse
10 Till the conversion of the Jews.°
My vegetable° love should grow
Vaster than empires, and more slow;
An hundred years should go to praise
Thine eyes, and on thy forehead gaze;
15 Two hundred to adore each breast,
But thirty thousand to the rest;
An age at least to every part,
And the last age should show your heart.
For, lady, you deserve this state,°
20 Nor would I love at lower rate.
    But at my back I always hear
Time's wingèd chariot hurrying near;
And yonder all before us lie
Deserts of vast eternity.
25 Thy beauty shall no more be found;
Nor, in thy marble vault, shall sound
My echoing song; then worms shall try°
That long-preserved virginity,
And your quaint° honor turn to dust,
30 And into ashes all my lust:
The grave's a fine and private place,
But none, I think, do there embrace.
    Now therefore, while the youthful hue
Sits on thy skin like morning glow,
35 And while thy willing soul transpires

---

2 **coyness** here, artificial sexual reluctance 7 **Humber** an English river near Marvell's home
10 **conversion of the Jews** at the end of time 11 **vegetable** flourishing 19 **state** estate 27 **try** test
29 **quaint** too subtle

At every pore with instant fires,
Now let us sport us while we may,
And now, like amorous birds of prey,
Rather at once our time devour
40   Than languish in his slow-chapped° power.
Let us roll all our strength and all
Our sweetness up into one ball,
And tear our pleasures with rough strife
Thorough the iron gates of life:
45   Thus, though we cannot make our sun
Stand still, yet we will make him run.

—1681

John Dryden
(1631-1700)

Short poems do not do justice to Dryden's talents, for he excelled at long forms—verse dramas like *All for Love*, his version of Shakespeare's *Antony and Cleopatra*, his translation of Virgil's *Aeneid*, political allegories like *Absalom and Achitophel*, and *MacFlecknoe*, the first great English literary satire. Dryden's balance and formal conservatism introduced the neoclassical style to English poetry, a manner that prevailed for a century after his death. He became poet laureate of England in 1668.

Song from Marriage à la Mode

1

Why should a foolish marriage vow,
  Which long ago was made,
Oblige us to each other now,
  When passion is decayed?
5 We loved, and we loved, as long as we could,
  Till our love was loved out in us both;
But our marriage is dead when the pleasure is fled:
  'Twas pleasure first made it an oath.

2

If I have pleasures for a friend,
10   And farther love in store,

---

40 chapped jawed

What wrong has he whose joys did end,
  And who could give no more?
'Tis a madness that he should be jealous of me,
  Or that I should bar him of another:
15 For all we can gain is to give ourselves pain,
  When neither can hinder the other.

—1673

Epigram on Milton

Three poets, in three distant ages born,
Greece,° Italy,° and England did adorn.
The first in loftiness of thought surpassed,
The next in majesty, in both the last:
5 The force of Nature could no farther go;
To make a third, she joined the former two.

—1688

Edward Taylor
(1642-1729)

Taylor was a Calvinist minister in a village outside of Boston whose eccentric religious poems (obviously influenced by Donne and Herbert) remained in manuscript for over two centuries after his death, when they were discovered in the Yale University Library. Taylor was a true amateur, writing in isolation and apparently intending his poems as meditative exercises to assist him in his clerical duties.

Housewifery

Make me, O Lord, thy spinning wheel complete.
  Thy holy word my distaff° make for me.
Make mine affections thy swift flyers° neat,
  And make my soul thy holy spool° to be.
5   My conversation make to be thy reel,°
  And reel the yarn thereon spun of thy wheel.

Make me thy loom then, knit therein this twine;
  And make thy holy spirit, Lord, wind quills.°
Then weave the web thyself. The yarn is fine.

---

2 **Greece** i.e., Homer **Italy** i.e., Virgil

2 **distaff** part of a spinning wheel that holds raw material 3 **flyers** impart twist to yarn 4 **spool** collects spun yarn 5 **reel** receives finished thread 8 **quills** spools

10   Thine ordinances make my fulling mills.°
Then dye the same in heavenly colors choice,
All pinked° with varnished° flowers of paradise.

Then clothe therewith mine understanding, will,
   Affections, judgment, conscience, memory,
15 My words, and actions, that their shine may fill
   My ways with glory and thee glorify.
Then mine apparel shall display before ye
That I am clothed in holy robes for glory.

                                  —c. 1685

Jonathan Swift
(1667-1745)

As the author of *Gulliver's Travels,* Swift stands unchallenged as
the greatest English prose satirist, but his poetry too is remarkable
in the unsparing realism of its best passages. Like many poets of
the neo-classical era, Swift adds tension to his poetry by
ironically emphasizing parallels between the heroic past and the
familiar characters and scenes of contemporary London. A
native of Dublin, Swift returned to Ireland in his maturity as dean
of St. Patrick's cathedral.

A Description of a City Shower

   Careful observers may foretell the hour
(By sure prognostics)° when to dread a shower:
While rain depends,° the pensive cat gives o'er
Her frolics, and pursues her tail no more.
5 Returning home at night, you'll find the sink°
Strike your offended sense with double stink.
If you be wise, then go not far to dine;
You'll spend in coach hire more than save in wine.
A coming shower your shooting corns presage,
10 Old achès throb, your hollow tooth will rage.
Sauntering in coffeehouse is Dulman° seen;
He damns the climate and complains of spleen.°
   Meanwhile the South, rising with dabbled wings,

---

10 fulling mills where cloth is cleaned after weaving **12 pinked** decorated **varnished** shiny
2 prognostics forecasts **3 depends** is imminent **5 sink** sewer **11 Dulman** i.e., dull man
12 spleen mental depression

A sable cloud athwart the welkin° flings,
15 That swilled more liquor than it could contain,
And, like a drunkard, gives it up again.
Brisk Susan whips her linen from the rope,
While the first drizzling shower is borne aslope:
Such is that sprinkling which some careless quean°
20 Flirts on you from her mop, but not so clean:
You fly, invoke the gods; then turning, stop
To rail; she singing, still whirls on her mop.
Not yet the dust had shunned the unequal strife,
But, aided by the wind, fought still for life,
25 And wafted with its foe by violent gust,
'Twas doubtful which was rain and which was dust.
Ah! where must needy poet seek for aid,
When dust and rain at once his coat invade?
Sole coat, where dust cemented by the rain
30 Erects the nap, and leaves a mingled stain.
    Now in contiguous drops the flood comes down,
Threatening with deluge this devoted° town.
To shops in crowds the daggled° females fly,
Pretend to cheapen° goods, but nothing buy.
35 The Templar° spruce, while every spout's abroach,°
Stays till 'tis fair, yet seems to call a coach.
The tucked-up sempstress walks with hasty strides,
While streams run down her oiled umbrella's sides.
Here various kinds, by various fortunes led,
40 Commence acquaintance underneath a shed.
Triumphant Tories and desponding Whigs°
Forget their feuds, and join to save their wigs.
Boxed in a chair° the beau impatient sits,
While spouts run clattering o'er the roof by fits,
45 And ever and anon with frightful din
The leather sounds; he trembles from within.
So when Troy chairmen bore the wooden steed,
Pregnant with Greeks impatient to be freed
(Those bully Greeks, who, as the moderns do,
50 Instead of paying chairmen, run them through),
Laocoön° struck the outside with his spear,
And each imprisoned hero quaked for fear.
    Now from all parts the swelling kennels° flow,

---

14 **welkin** sky   19 **quean** ill-mannered woman   32 **devoted** doomed   33 **daggled** spattered
34 **cheapen** inspect prices of   35 **Templar** law student   **abroach** pouring   41 **Tories . . . Whigs** rival
political factions   43 **chair** sedan chair   51 **Laocoön** For his attempt to warn the Trojans, he was
crushed by sea serpents sent by Poseidon   53 **kennels** storm drains

And bear their trophies with them as they go:
55 Filth of all hues and odors seem to tell
What street they sailed from, by their sight and smell.
They, as each torrent drives with rapid force,
From Smithfield° or St. Pulchre's shape their course,
And in huge confluence joined at Snow Hill ridge,
60 Fall from the conduit prone to Holborn Bridge.
Sweepings from butchers' stalls, dung, guts, and blood,
Drowned puppies, stinking sprats,° all drenched in mud,
Dead cats, and turnip tops, come tumbling down the flood.

                                                    —1710

Alexander Pope
(1688-1744)

A tiny man who was afflicted in childhood by a crippling disease,
Pope was the dominant poet of eighteenth century England,
particularly excelling as a master of mock-epic satire in "The
Rape of the Lock" and "The Dunciad." His translations of the *Iliad*
and the *Odyssey* made him famous and financially independent
and remained the standard versions of Homer for almost two
hundred years. "An Essay on Criticism," a long didactic poem
modeled on Horace's *Ars poetica*, remains the most complete
statement of the Neo-classical aesthetic.

from An Essay on Criticism

But most by numbers judge a poet's song,
And smooth or rough with them is right or wrong.
In the bright Muse though thousand charms conspire,
Her voice is all these tuneful fools admire,
5 Who haunt Parnassus° but to please their ear,
Not mend their minds; as some to church repair,
Not for the doctrine, but the music there.
These equal syllables alone require,
Though oft the ear the open vowels tire,
10 While expletives° their feeble aid do join,
And ten low words oft creep in one dull line:
While they ring round the same unvaried chimes,
With sure returns of still expected rhymes;

---

58 Smithfield site of London cattle exchange   **62 sprats** small fish
5 Parnassus mountain of the Muses   **10 expletives** unnecessary filler words

Where'er you find "the cooling western breeze,"
15   In the next line, it "whispers through the trees";
If crystal streams "with pleasing murmurs creep,"
The reader's threatened (not in vain) with "sleep";
Then, at the last and only couplet fraught
With some unmeaning thing they call a thought,
20   A needless Alexandrine° ends the song
That, like a wounded snake, drags its slow length along.
Leave such to tune their own dull rhymes, and know
What's roundly smooth or languishingly slow;
And praise the easy vigor of a line
25   Where Denham's strength and Waller's° sweetness join.
True ease in writing comes from art, not chance,
As those move easiest who have learned to dance.
'Tis not enough no harshness gives offense,
The sound must seem an echo to the sense.
30   Soft is the strain when Zephyr° gently blows,
And the smooth stream in smoother numbers flows;
But when loud surges lash the sounding shore,
The hoarse, rough verse should like the torrent roar.
When Ajax° strives some rock's vast weight to throw,
35   The line too labors, and the words move slow;
Not so when swift Camilla° scours the plain,
Flies o'er the unbending corn, and skims along the main.
Hear how Timotheus'° varied lays surprise,
And bid alternate passions fall and rise!
40   While at each change the son of Libyan Jove°
Now burns with glory, and then melts with love;
Now his fierce eyes with sparkling fury glow,
Now sighs steal out, and tears begin to flow:
Persians and Greeks like turns of nature found
45   And the world's victor stood subdued by sound!
The power of music all our hearts allow,
And what Timotheus was is Dryden now.
    Avoid extremes; and shun the fault of such
Who still are pleased too little or too much.
50   At every trifle scorn to take offense:
That always shows great pride, or little sense.
Those heads, as stomachs, are not sure the best,
Which nauseate all, and nothing can digest.

---

20 **Alexandrine** line of six iambic feet (as in the next line)   25 **Denham's ... Waller's** earlier
English poets praised by Pope **30 Zephyr** the west wind **34 Ajax** legendary strong man of the *Iliad*
36 Camilla messenger of the goddess Diana **38 Timotheus** a legendary musician **40 son of Libyan
Jove** Alexander the Great

Yet let not each gay turn thy rapture move;
55 For fools admire, but men of sense approve:
As things seem large which we through mists descry,
Dullness is ever apt to magnify.

—1709

Ode on Solitude

Happy the man whose wish and care
 A few paternal acres bound,
Content to breathe his native air,
   In his own ground.

5 Whose herds with milk, whose fields with bread,
 Whose flocks supply him with attire,
Whose trees in summer yield him shade,
   In winter fire.

Blest, who can unconcernedly find
10 Hours, days, and years slide soft away,
In health of body, peace of mind,
   Quiet by day,

Sound sleep by night; study and ease,
 Together mixed; sweet recreation;
15 And innocence, which most does please
   With meditation.

Thus let me live, unseen, unknown;
 Thus unlamented let me die;
Steal from the world, and not a stone
20   Tell where I lie.

—1736

Thomas Gray
(1716-1771)

Gray's contemporary reputation rests primarily on a single poem, but it remains one of the most often quoted in the whole English canon, and the quatrain stanza is often called "elegiac" in its honor. Gray lived almost all of his adult life at Cambridge University, where he was a professor of history and languages.

He declined the poet laureateship of England in 1757.

Elegy Written in a Country Churchyard

The curfew tolls the knell of parting day,
  The lowing herd wind slowly o'er the lea,
The plowman homeward plods his weary way,
  And leaves the world to darkness and to me.

5   Now fades the glimmering landscape on the sight,
  And all the air a solemn stillness holds,
Save where the beetle wheels his droning flight,
  And drowsy tinklings lull the distant folds;

Save that from yonder ivy-mantled tower
10   The moping owl does to the moon complain
Of such, as wandering near her secret bower,
  Molest her ancient solitary reign.

Beneath those rugged elms, that yew tree's shade,
  Where heaves the turf in many a moldering heap,
15   Each in his narrow cell forever laid,
  The rude° forefathers of the hamlet sleep.

The breezy call of incense-breathing morn,
  The swallow twittering from the straw-built shed,
The cock's shrill clarion, or the echoing horn,
20   No more shall rouse them from their lowly bed.

For them no more the blazing hearth shall burn,
  Or busy housewife ply her evening care;
No children run to lisp their sire's return,
  Or climb his knees the envied kiss to share.

25   Oft did the harvest to their sickle yield,
  Their furrow oft the stubborn glebe° has broke;
How jocund did they drive their team afield!
  How bowed the woods beneath their sturdy stroke!

Let not Ambition mock their useful toil,
30   Their homely joys, and destiny obscure;

---

16 rude unlearned **26 glebe** plot of farmland

Nor Grandeur hear with a disdainful smile
   The short and simple annals of the poor.

The boast of heraldry, the pomp of power,
   And all that beauty, all that wealth e'er gave,
35 Awaits alike the inevitable hour.
   The paths of glory lead but to the grave.

Nor you, ye proud, impute to these the fault,
   If Memory o'er their tomb no trophies raise,
Where through the long-drawn aisle and fretted° vault
40   The pealing anthem swells the note of praise.

Can storied urn or animated bust
   Back to its mansion call the fleeting breath?
Can Honor's voice provoke the silent dust,
   Or Flattery soothe the dull cold ear of Death?

45 Perhaps in this neglected spot is laid
   Some heart once pregnant with celestial fire;
Hands that the rod of empire might have swayed,
   Or waked to ecstasy the living lyre.

But Knowledge to their eyes her ample page
50   Rich with the spoils of time did ne'er unroll;
Chill Penury repressed their noble rage,
   And froze the genial current of the soul.

Full many a gem of purest ray serene,
   The dark unfathomed caves of ocean bear:
55 Full many a flower is born to blush unseen,
   And waste its sweetness on the desert air.

Some village Hampden,° that with dauntless breast
   The little tyrant of his field withstood;
Some mute inglorious Milton here may rest,
60   Some Cromwell° guiltless of his country's blood.

The applause of listening senates to command,
   The threats of pain and ruin to despise,
To scatter plenty o'er a smiling land,

---

39 fretted carved   **57 Hampden** hero of the English Civil War   **60 Cromwell** Lord Protector of England from 1653-1658

And read their history in a nation's eyes,

65 Their lot forbade: nor circumscribed alone
    Their growing virtues, but their crimes confined;
Forbade to wade through slaughter to a throne,
    And shut the gates of mercy on mankind,

The struggling pangs of conscious truth to hide,
70   To quench the blushes of ingenuous shame,
Or heap the shrine of Luxury and Pride
    With incense kindled at the Muse's flame.

Far from the madding° crowd's ignoble strife,
    Their sober wishes never learned to stray;
75 Along the cool sequestered vale of life
    They kept the noiseless tenor of their way.

Yet even these bones from insult to protect
    Some frail memorial still erected nigh,
With uncouth rhymes and shapeless sculpture decked,
80   Implores the passing tribute of a sigh.

Their name, their years, spelt by the unlettered Muse,
    The place of fame and elegy supply:
And many a holy text around she strews,
    That teach the rustic moralist to die.

85 For who to dumb Forgetfulness a prey,
    This pleasing anxious being e'er resigned,
Left the warm precincts of the cheerful day,
    Nor cast one longing lingering look behind?

On some fond breast the parting soul relies,
90   Some pious drops the closing eye requires;
Even from the tomb the voice of Nature cries,
    Even in our ashes live their wonted fires.

For thee, who mindful of the unhonored dead
    Dost in these lines their artless tale relate;
95 If chance, by lonely contemplation led,
    Some kindred spirit shall inquire thy fate,

---

73 madding frenzied

Haply some hoary°-headed swain° may say,
  "Oft have we seen him at the peep of dawn
Brushing with hasty steps the dews away
100   To meet the sun upon the upland lawn.

"There at the foot of yonder nodding beech
  That wreathes its old fantastic roots so high,
His listless length at noontide would he stretch,
  And pore upon the brook that babbles by.

105 "Hard by yon wood, now smiling as in scorn,
  Muttering his wayward fancies he would rove,
Now drooping, woeful wan, like one forlorn,
  Or crazed with care, or crossed in hopeless love.

"One morn I missed him on the customed hill,
110   Along the heath and near his favorite tree;
Another came; nor yet beside the rill,
  Nor up the lawn, nor at the wood was he;

"The next with dirges due in sad array
  Slow through the churchway path we saw him borne.
115 Approach and read (for thou canst read) the lay,
  Graved on the stone beneath yon aged thorn."

    The Epitaph

Here rests his head upon the lap of Earth
  A youth to Fortune and to Fame unknown.
Fair Science frowned not on his humble birth,
120 *And Melancholy marked him for her own.*

Large was his bounty, and his soul sincere,
  Heaven did a recompense as largely send:
He gave to Misery all he had, a tear,
  He gained from Heaven ('twas all he wished) a friend.

125 *No farther seek his merits to disclose,*
  Or draw his frailties from their dread abode
(There they alike in trembling hope repose),
  The bosom of his Father and his God.

                           —1751

---

97 hoary frosty, white **swain** peasant

Christopher Smart
(1722-1771)

Educated, like Thomas Gray, at Cambridge, Smart fell victim to religious mania and insanity but continued to write throughout his life. *Jubilate Agno* ("Rejoice in the Lamb") is a long mediation on the immanence of God, even in such insignificant forms as his cat Jeoffry. The poem is one of the earliest examples of free verse in English.

from Jublilate Agno

For I will consider my Cat Jeoffry.
For he is the servant of the Living God, duly and daily serving him.
For at the first glance of the glory of God in the East he worships in his way.
For is this done by wreathing his body seven times round with elegant quickness.
For then he leaps up to catch the musk,° which is the blessing of God upon his
5   prayer.
For he rolls upon prank to work it in.
For having done duty and received blessing he begins to consider himself.
For this he performs in ten degrees.
For first he looks upon his forepaws to see if they are clean.
10 For secondly he kicks up behind to clear away there.
For thirdly he works it upon stretch with the forepaws extended.
For fourthly he sharpens his paws by wood.
For fifthly he washes himself.
For sixthly he rolls upon wash.
15 For seventhly he fleas himself, that he may not be interrupted upon the beat.°
For eighthly he rubs himself against a post.
For ninthly he looks up for his instructions.
For tenthly he goes in quest of food.
For having considered God and himself he will consider his neighbor.
20 For if he meets another cat he will kiss her in kindness.
For when he takes his prey he plays with it to give it a chance.
For one mouse in seven escapes by his dallying.
For when his day's work is done his business more properly begins.
For he keeps the Lord's watch in the night against the adversary.°
25 For he counteracts the powers of darkness by his electrical skin and glaring eyes.
For he counteracts the Devil, who is death, by brisking about the life.

---

5 musk scented object or toy **15 beat** accustomed path **24 adversary** i.e., Satan

For in his morning orisons he loves the sun and the sun loves him.

For he is of the tribe of Tiger.

For the Cherub Cat is a term° of the Angel Tiger.

30 For he has the subtlety and hissing of a serpent, which in goodness he suppresses.

For he will not do destruction if he is well-fed, neither will he spit without
     provocation.

For he purrs in thankfulness when God tells him he's a good Cat.

For he is an instrument for the children to learn benevolence upon.

For every house is incomplete without him, and a blessing is lacking in the spirit.

For the Lord commanded Moses concerning the cats at the departure of the
35   Children of Israel from Egypt.

For every family had one cat at least in the bag.

For the English Cats are the best in Europe.

For he is the cleanest in the use of his forepaws of any quadruped.

For the dexterity of his defense is an instance of the love of God to him
     exceedingly.

40 For he is the quickest to his mark of any creature.

For he is tenacious of his point.

For he is a mixture of gravity and waggery.

For he knows that God is his Saviour.

For there is nothing sweeter than his peace when at rest.

45 For there is nothing brisker than his life when in motion.

For he is of the Lord's poor, and so indeed is he called by benevolence
     perpetually—Poor Jeoffry! poor Jeoffry! the rat has bit thy throat.

For I bless the name of the Lord Jesus that Jeoffry is better.

For the divine spirit comes about his body to sustain it in complete cat.

For his tongue is exceeding pure so that it has in purity what it wants in music.

50 For he is docile and can learn certain things.

For he can sit up with gravity, which is patience upon approbation.

For he can fetch and carry, which is patience in employment.

For he can jump over a stick, which is patience upon proof positive.

For he can spraggle upon waggle at the word of command.

55 For he can jump from an eminence into his master's bosom.

For he can catch the cork and toss it again.

For he is hated by the hypocrite and miser.

For the former is afraid of detection.

For the latter refuses the charge.

60 For he camels his back to bear the first notion of business.

For he is good to think on, if a man would express himself neatly.

For he made a great figure in Egypt for his signal services.

For he killed the Icneumon° rat, very pernicious by land.

For his ears are so acute that they sting again.

---

29 term immature version   **63 Icneumon** resembling the mongoose *(Herpestes ichneumon)*

65 For from this proceeds the passing quickness of his attention.
For by stroking of him I have found out electricity.
For I perceived God's light about him both wax and fire.
For the electrical fire is the spiritual substance which God sends from heaven to
    sustain the bodies both of man and beast.
For God has blessed him in the variety of his movements.
70 For, though he cannot fly, he is an excellent clamberer.
For his motions upon the face of the earth are more than any other quadruped.
For he can tread to all the measures upon the music.
For he can swim for life.
For he can creep.

—ca. 1760

Philip Freneau
(1752-1832)

A friend and political ally of Thomas Jefferson, Freneau was a
popular journalist and writer whose patriotic verse earned him the
moniker "Poet of the Revolution." This reputation has unfortunately
overshadowed his considerable talents as a lyric poet whose
fine eye for nature prefigures next generation of American
Romantic poets.

The Wild Honey Suckle

Fair flower, that dost so comely grow,
Hid in this silent, dull retreat,
Untouched thy honied blossoms blow,
Unseen thy little branches greet:
5   No roving foot shall crush thee here,
    No busy hand provoke a tear.°

By Nature's self in white arrayed,
She bade thee shun the vulgar° eye,
And planted here the guardian shade,
10 And sent soft waters murmuring by;
    Thus quietly thy summer goes,
    Thy days declining to repose.

Smit with those charms, that must decay,

---

6 provoke a tear i.e., the nectar of the flower **8 vulgar** common

I grieve to see your future doom;
15 They died—nor were those flowers more gay,
The flowers that did in Eden bloom;
    Unpitying frosts, and Autumn's power
    Shall leave no vestige of this flower.

From morning suns and evening dews
20 At first thy little being came:
If nothing once, you nothing lose,
For when you die you are the same;
    The space between, is but an hour,
    The fail duration of a flower.

                              —1788

William Blake
(1757-1827)

Poet, painter, engraver, and visionary, Blake does not fit into any
easy categories, though his political sympathies link him to the
later Romantic poets. His first book, *Poetical Sketches*, attracted
little attention, but his mature works, starting with *Songs of
Innocence* and *Songs of Experience*, combine poetry with his
own remarkable illustrations and are unique in English literature.
Thought mad by many in his own day, Blake anticipated many
future directions of both literature and modern psychology.

The Chimney Sweeper

When my mother died I was very young,
And my father sold me while yet my tongue
Could scarcely cry " 'weep! 'weep! 'weep! 'weep!"
So your chimneys I sweep & in soot I sleep.

5   There's little Tom Dacre, who cried when his head
That curl'd like a lamb's back, was shav'd, so I said,
"Hush, Tom! never mind it, for when your head's bare,
You know that the soot cannot spoil your white hair."

And so he was quiet, & that very night,
10 As Tom was a-sleeping, he had such a sight!
That thousands of sweepers, Dick, Joe, Ned, & Jack,
Were all of them lock'd up in coffins of black;

And by came an Angel who had a bright key,
And he open'd the coffins & set them all free;
15 Then down a green plain, leaping, laughing they run,
And wash in a river and shine in the Sun.

Then naked & white, all their bags left behind,
They rise upon clouds, and sport in the wind.
And the Angel told Tom, if he'd be a good boy,
20 He'd have God for his father, & never want joy.

And so Tom awoke; and we rose in the dark,
And got with our bags & our brushes to work.
Tho' the morning was cold, Tom was happy & warm;
So if all do their duty, they need not fear harm.

—1789

The Little Black° Boy

My mother bore me in the southern wild,
And I am black, but O! my soul is white;
White as an angel is the English child:
But I am black as if bereav'd of light.

5 My mother taught me underneath a tree,
And sitting down before the heat of day,
She took me on her lap and kissèd me,
And pointing to the east, began to say:

"Look on the rising sun: there God does live,
10 And gives his light, and gives his heat away;
And flowers and trees and beasts and men receive
Comfort in morning, joy in the noon day.

"And we are put on earth a little space,
That we may learn to bear the beams of love,
15 And these black bodies and this sun-burnt face
Is but a cloud, and like a shady grove.

"For when our souls have learn'd the heat to bear,
The cloud will vanish; we shall hear his voice,
Saying: 'Come out from the grove, my love & care,

Black probably Indian rather than African

20   And round my golden tent like lambs rejoice.'"

Thus did my mother say, and kissèd me;
And thus I say to little English boy:
When I from black and he from white cloud free,
And round the tent of God like lambs we joy,

25   I'll shade him from the heat till he can bear
To lean in joy upon our father's knee:
And then I'll stand and stroke his silver hair,
And be like him, and he will then love me.

—1789

A Poison Tree

I was angry with my friend:
I told my wrath, my wrath did end.
I was angry with my foe:
I told it not, my wrath did grow.

5   And I water'd it in fears,
Night & morning with my tears;
And I sunnèd it with smiles,
And with soft deceitful wiles.

And it grew both day and night,
10   Till it bore an apple bright;
And my foe beheld it shine,
And he knew that it was mine,

And into my garden stole
When the night had veil'd the pole;
15   In the morning glad I see
My foe outstretch'd beneath the tree.

—1794

The Tyger

Tyger! Tyger! burning bright
In the forests of the night,
What immortal hand or eye
Could frame thy fearful symmetry?

5   In what distant deeps or skies
      Burnt the fire of thine eyes?
      On what wings dare he aspire?
      What the hand, dare seize the fire?

      And what shoulder, & what art,
10   Could twist the sinews of thy heart?
      And when thy heart began to beat,
      What dread hand? & what dread feet?

      What the hammer? what the chain?
      In what furnace was thy brain?
15   What the anvil? what dread grasp
      Dare its deadly terrors clasp?

      When the stars threw down their spears,
      And water'd heaven with their tears,
      Did he smile his work to see?
20   Did he who made the Lamb make thee?

      Tyger! Tyger! burning bright
      In the forests of the night,
      What immortal hand or eye,
      Dare frame thy fearful symmetry?

—1794

Robert Burns
(1759-1796)

Burns, a Scot known in his day as the "Ploughman Poet," was one
of the first English poets to put dialect to serious literary purpose.
Chiefly known for his realistic depictions of peasant life, he was
also an important lyric poet who prefigured many of the later
concerns of the Romantic era.

A Red, Red Rose

O my luve's like a red, red rose,
   That's newly sprung in June;
O my luve's like the melodie
   That's sweetly played in tune.

5   As fair art thou, my bonnie lass,
         So deep in luve am I;
     And I will luve thee still, my dear,
         Till a' the seas gang° dry.

     Till a' the seas gang dry, my dear,
10   And the rocks melt wi' the sun;
     O I will luve thee still, my dear,
         While the sands o' life shall run.

     And fare thee weel, my only luve,
         And fare thee weel awhile!
15   And I will come again, my luve
         Though it were ten thousand mile.

                                                —1796

William Wordsworth
(1770-1850)

Wordsworth is generally considered the first of the English
Romantics, and *Lyrical Ballads*, the 1798 volume that introduced
both his poetry and Samuel Taylor Coleridge's to a wide read-
ership remains one of the most influential collections of poetry
ever published. Wordsworth's preface to the revised edition of
1800 contains the famous Romantic formulation of poetry as the
"spontaneous overflow of powerful feelings," a theory exempli-
fied in short lyrics like "I Wandered Lonely as a Cloud" and in
longer meditative pieces like "Tintern Abbey." Wordsworth
served as poet laureate from 1843 to his death.

I Wandered Lonely as a Cloud

     I wandered lonely as a cloud
     That floats on high o'er vales and hills,
     When all at once I saw a crowd,
     A host, of golden daffodils;
5   Beside the lake, beneath the trees,
     Fluttering and dancing in the breeze.

     Continuous as the stars that shine
     And twinkle on the milky way,

─────────────────────

8 gang go

They stretched in never-ending line
10   Along the margin of a bay:
Ten thousand saw I at a glance,
Tossing their heads in sprightly dance.

The waves beside them danced; but they
Outdid the sparkling waves in glee;
15   A poet could not but be gay,
In such a jocund company;
I gazed—and gazed—but little thought
What wealth the show to me had brought:

For oft, when on my couch I lie
20   In vacant or in pensive mood,
They flash upon that inward eye
Which is the bliss of solitude;
And then my heart with pleasure fills,
And dances with the daffodils.

                                        —1807

It Is a Beauteous Evening

It is a beauteous evening, calm and free,
The holy time is quiet as a Nun
Breathless with adoration; the broad sun
Is sinking down in its tranquility;
5   The gentleness of heaven broods o'er the Sea:
Listen! the mighty Being is awake,
And doth with his eternal motion make
A sound like thunder—everlastingly.

Dear Child! dear Girl!° that walkest with me here,
10   If thou appear untouched by solemn thought,
Thy nature is not therefore less divine:
Thou liest in Abraham's bosom° all the year,
And worship'st at the Temple's inner shrine,
God being with thee when we know it not.

                                        —1807

---

9 Dear Child! dear Girl! the poet's daughter   **12 Abraham's bosom** where souls rest in Heaven

Lines

*Composed a Few Miles Above Tintern Abbey on Revisiting
the Banks of the Wye During a Tour. July 13, 1798*

Five years have passed; five summers, with the length
Of five long winters! and again I hear
These waters, rolling from their mountain-springs
With a sweet inland murmur. Once again
5   Do I behold these steep and lofty cliffs,
That on a wild secluded scene impress
Thoughts of more deep seclusion; and connect
The landscape with the quiet of the sky.
The day is come when I again repose
10   Here, under this dark sycamore, and view
These plots of cottage ground, these orchard tufts,
Which at this season, with their unripe fruits,
Are clad in one green hue, and lose themselves
'Mid groves and copses. Once again I see
15   These hedgerows, hardly hedgerows, little lines
Of sportive wood run wild; these pastoral farms,
Green to the very door; and wreathes of smoke
Sent up, in silence, from among the trees!
With some uncertain notice, as might seem
20   Of vagrant dwellers in the houseless woods,
Or of some Hermit's cave, where by his fire
The Hermit sits alone.

                  Those beauteous forms,
Through a long absence, have not been to me
As is a landscape to a blind man's eye;
25   But oft, in lonely rooms, and 'mid the din
Of towns and cities, I have owed to them,
In hours of weariness, sensations sweet,
Felt in the blood, and felt along the heart;
And passing even into my purer mind,
30   With tranquil restoration:—feelings too
Of unremembered pleasure; such, perhaps,
As have no slight or trivial influence
On that best portion of a good man's life,
His little, nameless, unremembered, acts
35   Of kindness and of love. Nor less, I trust,
To them I may have owed another gift,

Of aspect more sublime; that blessed mood,
In which the burthen° of the mystery,
In which the heavy and the weary weight

40   Of all this unintelligible world,
Is lightened—that serene and blessed mood,
In which the affections gently lead us on—
Until, the breath of this corporeal frame
And even the motion of our human blood

45   Almost suspended, we are laid asleep
In body, and become a living soul;
While with an eye made quiet by the power
Of harmony, and the deep power of joy,
We see into the life of things.

                              If this

50   Be but a vain belief, yet, oh! how oft—
In darkness and amid the many shapes
Of joyless daylight; when the fretful stir
Unprofitable, and the fever of the world,
Have hung upon the beatings of my heart—

55   How oft, in spirit, have I turned to thee,
O sylvan Wye! Thou wanderer through the woods,
How often has my spirit turned to thee!

   And now, with gleams of half-extinguished thought,
With many recognitions dim and faint,

60   And somewhat of a sad perplexity,
The picture of the mind revives again:
While here I stand, not only with the sense
Of present pleasure, but with pleasing thoughts
That in this moment there is life and food

65   For future years. And so I dare to hope,
Though changed, no doubt, from what I was when first
I came among these hills; when like a roe
I bounded o'er the mountains, by the sides
Of the deep rivers, and the lonely streams,

70   Wherever nature led—more like a man
Flying from something that he dreads than one
Who sought the thing he loved. For nature then
(The coarser pleasures of my boyish days.
And their glad animal movements all gone by)

75   To me was all in all.—I cannot paint

———————————

38 burthen burden

What then I was. The sounding cataract
Haunted me like a passion: the tall rock,
The mountain, and the deep and gloomy wood,
Their colours and their forms, were then to me

80   An appetite: a feeling and a love,
That had no need of a remoter charm,
By thought supplied, or any interest
Unborrowed from the eye.—That time is past,
And all its aching joys are now no more,

85   And all its dizzy raptures. Not for this
Faint I, nor mourn nor murmur: other gifts
Have followed; for such loss, I would believe,
Abundant recompence. For I have learned
To look on nature, not as in the hour

90   Of thoughtless youth, but hearing oftentimes
The still, sad music of humanity,
Not harsh nor grating, though of ample power
To chasten and subdue. And I have felt
A presence that disturbs me with the joy

95   Of elevated thoughts; a sense sublime
Of something far more deeply interfused,
Whose dwelling is the light of setting suns,
And the round ocean and the living air,
And the blue sky, and in the mind of man:

100   A motion and a spirit, that impels
All thinking things, all objects of all thought,
And rolls through all things. Therefore am I still
A lover of the meadows and the woods,
And mountains; and of all that we behold

105   From this green earth; of all the mighty world
Of eye, and ear—both what they half create,
And what perceive; well pleased to recognize
In nature and the language of the sense
The anchor of my purest thoughts, the nurse,

110   The guide, the guardian of my heart, and soul
Of all my moral being.

                          Nor, perchance,
If I were not thus taught, should I the more
Suffer my genial spirits° to decay:
For thou art with me, here, upon the banks

115   Of this fair river; thou, my dearest Friend,°

---

113 genial spirits natural abilities   **115 Friend** the poet's sister Dorothy (1771-1855)

My dear, dear Friend; and in thy voice I catch
The language of my former heart, and read
My former pleasures in the shooting lights
Of thy wild eyes. Oh! yet a little while
120 May I behold in thee what I was once,
My dear, dear Sister! And this prayer I make,
Knowing that Nature never did betray
The heart that loved her; 'tis her privilege,
Through all the years of this our life, to lead
125 From joy to joy: for she can so inform
The mind that is within us, so impress
With quietness and beauty, and so feed
With lofty thoughts, that neither evil tongues,
Rash judgments, nor the sneers of selfish men,
130 Nor greetings where no kindness is, nor all
The dreary intercourse of daily life,
Shall e'er prevail against us, or disturb
Our cheerful faith that all which we behold
Is full of blessings. Therefore let the moon
135 Shine on thee in thy solitary walk;
And let the misty mountain winds be free
To blow against thee: and in after years,
When these wild ecstasies shall be matured
Into a sober pleasure; when thy mind
140 Shall be a mansion for all lovely forms,
Thy memory be as a dwelling place
For all sweet sounds and harmonies; Oh! then,
If solitude, or fear, or pain, or grief,
Should be thy portion, with what healing thoughts
145 Of tender joy wilt thou remember me,
And these my exhortations! Nor, perchance—
If I should be, where I no more can hear
Thy voice, nor catch from thy wild eyes these gleams
Of past existence, wilt thou then forget
150 That on the banks of this delightful stream
We stood together; and that I, so long
A worshipper of Nature, hither came,
Unwearied in that service: rather say
With warmer love, oh! with far deeper zeal
155 Of holier love. Nor wilt thou then forget,
That after many wanderings, many years
Of absence, these steep woods and lofty cliffs,
And this green pastoral landscape, were to me

More dear, both for themselves, and for thy sake!

—1798

Ode

Intimations of Immortality
from Recollections of Early Childhood

> *The Child is Father of the Man;*
> *And I could wish my days to be*
> *Bound each to each by natural piety.*°

1

There was a time when meadow, grove and stream,
The earth, and every common sight,
   To me did seem
  Apparelled in celestial light,
5 The glory and the freshness of a dream.
It is not now as it hath been of yore;—
   Turn wheresoe'er I may,
    By night or day,
The things which I have seen I now can see no more.

2

10   The Rainbow comes and goes,
    And lovely is the Rose,
    The Moon doth with delight
Look round her when the heavens are bare,
    Waters on a starry night
15   Are beautiful and fair;
   The sunshine is a glorious birth;
   But yet I know, where'er I go,
That there hath past away a glory from the earth.

3

Now, while the birds thus sing a joyous song,
20 And while the young lambs bound
   As to the tabor's° sound,
To me alone there came a thought of grief:
A timely utterance gave that thought relief,
   And I again am strong:
25 The cataracts blow their trumpets from the steep;

The Child . . . natural piety last three lines of the poet's "My Heart Leaps Up" **21 tabor's** small
drum's

No more shall grief of mine the season wrong;
I hear the Echoes through the mountains throng,
The Winds come to me from the fields of sleep,
    And all the earth is gay;
30   Land and sea
    Give themselves up to jollity,
    And with the heart of May
    Doth every Beast keep holiday;—
       Thou child of Joy,
35 Shout round me, let me hear thy shouts, thou happy Shepherd-boy!

4

Ye blessed Creatures, I have heard the call
    Ye to each other make; I see
The heavens laugh with you in your jubilee;
    My heart is at your festival,
40   My head hath its coronal,°
The fulness of your bliss, I feel—I feel it all.
    Oh evil day! if I were sullen
    While Earth herself is adorning,
     This sweet May-morning,
45   And the Children are culling
      On every side,
    In a thousand valleys far and wide,
    Fresh flowers; while the sun shines warm,
And the Babe leaps up on his Mother's arm:—
50   I hear, I hear, with joy I hear!
    —But there's a Tree, of many, one,
A single Field which I have looked upon,
Both of them speak of something that is gone:
     The Pansy at my feet
55   Doth the same tale repeat:
Whither is fled the visionary gleam?
Where is it now, the glory and the dream?

5

Our birth is but a sleep and a forgetting:
The Soul that rises with us, our life's Star,
60   Hath had elsewhere its setting,
     And cometh from afar:
    Not in entire forgetfulness,
    And not in utter nakedness,

---

41 coronal floral crown

But trailing clouds of glory do we come
65   From God, who is our home:
Heaven lies about us in our infancy!
Shades of the prison-house begin to close
        Upon the growing Boy,
But He beholds the light, and whence it flows,
70   He sees it in his joy;
The Youth, who daily farther from the east
        Must travel, still is Nature's Priest,
        And by the vision splendid
        Is on his way attended;
75 At length the Man perceives it die away,
And fade into the light of common day.

                                        6

Earth fills her lap with pleasures of her own;
Yearnings she hath in her own natural kind,
And even with something of a Mother's mind,
80   And no unworthy aim,
        The homely Nurse doth all she can
To make her Foster-child, her Inmate Man,
        Forget the glories he hath known,
And that imperial palace whence he came.

                                        7

85 Behold the Child among his new-born blisses,
A six years' Darling of a pigmy size!
See where 'mid work of his own hand he lies,
Fretted° by sallies of his mother's kisses,
With light upon him from his father's eyes!
90 See, at his feet, some little plan or chart,
Some fragment from his dream of human life,
Shaped by himself with newly-learnèd art;
        A wedding or a festival,
        A mourning or a funeral;
95   And this hath now his heart,
        And unto this he frames his song:
            Then will he fit his tongue
To dialogues of business, love, or strife;
        But it will not be long
100   Ere this be thrown aside,
        And with new joy and pride

---

89 fretted annoyed or marked

The little Actor cons another part;
Filling from time to time his "humorous stage"°
With all the Persons, down to palsied Age,
105 That Life brings with her in her equipage;
   As if his whole vocation
   Were endless imitation.

     8

Thou whose exterior semblance doth belie
   Thy Soul's immensity;
110 Thou best Philosopher, who yet dost keep
Thy heritage, thou Eye among the blind,
That, deaf and silent, read'st the eternal deep,
Haunted for ever by the eternal mind,—
   Mighty Prophet! Seer blest!
115   On whom those truths do rest,
Which we are toiling all our lives to find,
In darkness lost, the darkness of the grave;
Thou, over whom thy Immortality
Broods like the Day, a Master o'er a Slave,
120 A Presence which is not to be put by;
Thou little Child, yet glorious in the might
Of heaven-born freedom on thy being's height,
Why with such earnest pains dost thou provoke
The years to bring the inevitable yoke,
125 Thus blindly with thy blessedness at strife?
Full soon thy Soul shall have her earthly freight,
And custom lie upon thee with a weight,
Heavy as frost, and deep almost as life!

     9

   O joy! that in our embers
130   Is something that doth live,
   That nature yet remembers
   What was so fugitive!
The thought of our past years in me doth breed
Perpetual benediction: not indeed
135 For that which is most worthy to be blest;
Delight and liberty, the simple creed
Of Childhood, whether busy or at rest,
With new-fledged hope still fluttering in his breast:—
   Not for these I raise

---

104 **"humorous stage"** phrase from poet Samuel Daniel (1563-1619)

140   The song of thanks and praise;
           But for those obstinate questionings
           Of sense and outward things,
           Fallings from us, vanishings;
           Blank misgivings of a Creature
145 Moving about in worlds not realized,
    High instincts before which our mortal Nature
    Did tremble like a guilty Thing surprised:
           But for those first affections,
           Those shadowy recollections,
150   Which, be they what they may,
    Are yet the fountain light of all our day,
    Are yet a master light of all our seeing;
           Uphold us, cherish, and have power to make
    Our noisy years seem moments in the being
155 Of the eternal Silence: truths that wake,
           To perish never;
    Which neither listlessness, nor mad endeavour,
           Nor Man nor Boy,
    Nor all that is at enmity with joy,
160 Can utterly abolish or destroy!
       Hence in a season of calm weather
         Though inland far we be,
    Our Souls have sight of that immortal sea
         Which brought us hither,
165   Can in a moment travel thither,
    And see the Children sport upon the shore,
    And hear the mighty waters rolling evermore.

10

    Then sing, ye Birds, sing, sing a joyous song!
         And let the young Lambs bound
170   As to the tabor's sound!
    We in thought will join your throng,
         Ye that pipe and ye that play,
         Ye that through your hearts to-day
         Feel the gladness of the May!
175 What though the radiance which was once so bright
    Be now for ever taken from my sight,
         Though nothing can bring back the hour
    Of splendour in the grass, of glory in the flower;
         We will grieve not, rather find
180   Strength in what remains behind;
           In the primal sympathy

Which having been must ever be;
In the soothing thoughts that spring
Out of human suffering;
185   In the faith that looks through death,
In years that bring the philosophic mind.

11

And O, ye Fountains, Meadows, Hills, and Groves,
Forbode not any severing of our loves!
Yet in my heart of hearts I feel your might;
190 I only have relinquished one delight
To live beneath your more habitual sway.
I love the Brooks which down their channels fret,
Even more than when I tripped lightly as they;
The innocent brightness of a new-born Day
195   Is lovely yet;
The Clouds that gather round the setting sun
Do take a sober colouring from an eye
That hath kept watch o'er man's mortality;
Another race hath been, and other palms are won.
200 Thanks to the human heart by which we live,
Thanks to its tenderness, its joys, and fears,
To me the meanest° flower that blows can give
Thoughts that do often lie too deep for tears.

—1807

Samuel Taylor Coleridge
(1772-1834)

The inspired but erratic Coleridge did his best work, like Wordsworth, during the great first decade of their friendship, the period that produced *Lyrical Ballads*. Coleridge's later life is a tragic tale of financial and marital problems, unfinished projects, and a ruinous addiction to opium. A brilliant critic, Coleridge lectured on Shakespeare and other writers and wrote the *Biographia Literaria*, perhaps the greatest literary autobiography ever written.

---

203 **meanest** least significant

Frost at Midnight

The Frost performs its secret ministry,
Unhelped by any wind. The owlet's cry
Came loud—and hark, again! loud as before.
The inmates of my cottage, all at rest,
5   Have left me to that solitude, which suits
Abstruser musings: save that at my side
My cradled infant° slumbers peacefully.
'Tis calm indeed! so calm, that it disturbs
And vexes meditation, with its strange
10   And extreme silentness. Sea, hill, and wood,
This populous village! Sea, and hill, and wood,
With all the numberless goings-on of life,
Inaudible as dreams! the thin blue flame
Lies on my low-burnt fire, and quivers not;
15   Only that film,° which fluttered on the grate,
Still flutters there, the sole unquiet thing.
Methinks its motion in this hush of nature
Gives it dim sympathies with me who live,
Making it a companionable form,
20   Whose puny flaps and freaks the idling Spirit
By its own moods interprets, everywhere
Echo or mirror seeking of itself,
And makes a toy of Thought.

                     But O! how oft,
25   How oft, at school, with most believing mind,
Presageful, have I gazed upon the bars,
To watch that fluttering *stranger!* and as oft
With unclosed lids, already had I dreamt
Of my sweet birthplace, and the old church tower,
30   Whose bells, the poor man's only music, rang
From morn to evening, all the hot fair-day,
So sweetly, that they stirred and haunted me
With a wild pleasure, falling on mine ear
Most like articulate sounds of things to come!
35   So gazed I, till the soothing things, I dreamt,
Lulled me to sleep, and sleep prolonged by dreams!
And so I brooded all the following morn,
Awed by the stern preceptor's face, mine eye
Fixed with mock study on my swimming book:

---

7 **My cradled infant** the poet's son Hartley (1796-1849)   15 **film** a piece of ash

40 Save if the door half opened, and I snatched
A hasty glance, and still my heart leaped up,
For still I hoped to see the *stranger's* face,
Townsman, or aunt, or sister more beloved,
My playmate when we both were clothed alike!

45   Dear Babe, that sleepest cradled by my side,
Whose gentle breathings, heard in this deep calm,
Fill up the interspersèd vacancies
And momentary pauses of the thought!
My babe so beautiful! it thrills my heart
50 With tender gladness, thus to look at thee,
And think that thou shalt learn far other lore,
And in far other scenes! For I was reared
In the great city, pent 'mid cloisters dim,
And saw nought lovely but the sky and stars.
55 But *thou*, my babe! shalt wander like a breeze
By lakes and sandy shores, beneath the crags
Of ancient mountain, and beneath the clouds,
Which image in their bulk both lakes and shores
And mountain crags: so shalt thou see and hear
60 The lovely shapes and sounds intelligible
Of that eternal language, which thy God
Utters, who from eternity doth teach
Himself in all, and all things in himself.
Great universal Teacher! he shall mold
65 Thy spirit, and by giving make it ask.

      Therefore all seasons shall be sweet to thee,
Whether the summer clothe the general earth
With greenness, or the redbreast sit and sing
Betwixt the tufts of snow on the bare branch
70 Of mossy apple tree, while the nigh thatch
Smokes in the sun-thaw whether the eave-drops fall
Heard only in the trances of the blast,
Or if the secret ministry of frost
Shall hang them up in silent icicles,
75 Quietly shining to the quiet Moon.

—February 1798

Kubla Khan°

Or a vision in a dream,° a fragment

In Xanadu did Kubla Khan
A stately pleasure-dome decree:
Where Alph, the sacred river, ran
Through caverns measureless to man
5   Down to a sunless sea.
So twice five miles of fertile ground
With walls and towers were girdled round:
And there were gardens bright with sinuous rills,
Where blossomed many an incense-bearing tree;
10   And here were forests ancient as the hills,
Enfolding sunny spots of greenery.

But oh! that deep romantic chasm which slanted
Down the green hill athwart a cedarn cover!
A savage place! as holy and enchanted
15   As e'er beneath a waning moon was haunted
By woman wailing for her demon lover!
And from this chasm, with ceaseless turmoil seething,
As if this earth in fast thick pants were breathing,
A mighty fountain momently was forced:
20   Amid whose swift half-intermitted burst
Huge fragments vaulted like rebounding hail,
Or chaffy grain beneath the thresher's flail:
And 'mid these dancing rocks at once and ever
It flung up momently the sacred river.
25   Five miles meandering with a mazy motion
Through wood and dale the sacred river ran,
Then reached the caverns measureless to man,
And sank in tumult to a lifeless ocean:
And 'mid this tumult Kubla heard from far
30   Ancestral voices prophesying war!

The shadow of the dome of pleasure
Floated midway on the waves;

Kubla Khan ruler of China (1216-1294)   **vision in a dream** Coleridge's own account tells how he took opium for an illness and slept for three hours, during which time he envisioned a complete poem of some 300 lines. When he awoke, he began to write down the details of his dream. "At this moment he was unfortunately called out by a person on business from Porlock, and detained by him above an hour, and on his return to the room found, to his no small surprise and mortification, that though he still retained some vague and dim recollection of the general purport of the vision, yet, with the exception of some eight or ten scattered lines and images on the surface of a stream into which a stone has been cast . . . [Coleridge's note]"

Where was heard the mingled measure
From the fountain and the caves.
35   It was a miracle of rare device,
A sunny pleasure dome of ice!

A damsel with a dulcimer
In a vision once I saw:
It was an Abyssinian maid,
40   And on her dulcimer she played,
Singing of Mount Abora.
Could I revive within me
Her symphony and song,
To such a deep delight 'twould win me,
45   That with music loud and long,
I would build that dome in air,
That sunny dome! those caves of ice!
And all who heard should see them there,
And all should cry, Beware! Beware!
50   His flashing eyes, his floating hair!
Weave a circle round him thrice,
And close your eyes with holy dread,
For he on honey-dew hath fed,
And drunk the milk of Paradise.

—1797-98

Work Without Hope

Lines Composed 21st February 1825

All nature seems at work. Slugs leave their lair—
The bees are stirring—birds are on the wing—
And Winter slumbering in the open air
Wears on his smiling face a dream of Spring!
5   And I the while, the sole unbusy thing,
Nor honey make, nor pair, nor build, nor sing.

Yet well I ken the banks where amaranths° blow,
Have traced the fount whence streams of nectar flow.
Bloom, O ye amaranths! bloom for whom ye may,
10   For me ye bloom not! Glide, rich streams, away!
With lips unbrightened, wreathless brow, I stroll:
And would you learn the spells that drowse my soul?

---

7 amaranths legendary flowers that never fade

Work without Hope draws° nectar in a sieve,
And Hope without an object cannot live.

—1828

Walter Savage Landor
(1775-1864)

Landor attained considerable celebrity in his final decades as
the last living Romantic poet. An author of epic poems and
verse dramas, he is best known today for his brilliant epigrams
and other short poems, which often employ dramatis personae.

Dying Speech of an Old Philosopher

I strove with none, for none was worth my strife:
   Nature I loved, and, next to Nature, Art:
I warmed both hands before the fire of Life;
4   It sinks; and I am ready to depart.

—1849

Mother, I Cannot

Mother, I cannot mind my wheel;°
   My fingers ache, my lips are dry:
Oh! if you felt the pain I feel!
   But oh, who ever felt as I?

5 No longer could I doubt him true;
   All ofther men may use deceit:
He always said my eyes were blue,
   And often swore my lips were sweet.

—1806

George Gordon, Lord Byron
(1788-1824)

The flamboyant Byron, whose celebrity status and unconven-

---

13 draws dips
1 wheel spinning wheel

tional lifestyle contributed to his notoriety, was the most widely read of all the English Romantic poets, but his verse romances and mock-epic poems like *Don Juan* have not proven as popular in this century. An English aristocrat who was committed to revolutionary ideals, Byron died while lending military assistance to the cause of Greek freedom.

Stanzas

When A Man Hath No Freedom To Fight For At Home

When a man hath no freedom to fight for at home,
    Let him combat for that of his neighbors;
Let him think of the glories of Greece and of Rome,
    And get knocked on his head for his labors.

5 To do good to mankind is the chivalrous plan,
    And is always as noble requited;
Then battle for freedom wherever you can,
    And, if not shot or hanged, you'll get knighted.

                —1824

Percy Bysshe Shelley
(1792-1822)

Like his friend Byron, Shelley has not found as much favor as the other English Romantics in this century, though his political liberalism anticipates many currents of our own day. Perhaps his unbridled emotionalism sometimes is too intense for modern readers. His wife, Mary Wollstonecraft Shelley, will be remembered as the author of the classic horror novel *Frankenstein*.

Ode to the West Wind

1

O wild West Wind, thou breath of Autumn's being,
Thou, from whose unseen presence the leaves dead
Are driven, like ghosts from an enchanter fleeing,

Yellow, and black, and pale, and hectic red,
5 Pestilence-stricken multitudes: O thou,
Who chariotest to their dark wintry bed

The wingèd seeds, where they lie cold and low,
Each like a corpse within its grave, until
Thine azure sister of the Spring° shall blow

10   Her clarion o'er the dreaming earth, and fill
(Driving sweet buds like flocks to feed in air)
With living hues and odors plain and hill:

Wild Spirit, which art moving everywhere;
Destroyer and preserver; hear, oh, hear!

2

15   Thou on whose stream, mid the steep sky's commotion,
Loose clouds like earth's decaying leaves are shed,
Shook from the tangled boughs of Heaven and Ocean,

Angels of rain and lightning: there are spread
On the blue surface of thine aëry surge,
20   Like the bright hair uplifted from the head

Of some fierce Mænad,° even from the dim verge
Of the horizon to the zenith's height,
The locks of the approaching storm. Thou dirge

Of the dying year, to which this closing night
25   Will be the dome of a vast sepulcher,
Vaulted with all thy congregated might

Of vapors, from whose solid atmosphere
Black rain, and fire, and hail will burst: oh, hear!

3

Thou who didst waken from his summer dreams
30   The blue Mediterranean, where he lay,
Lulled by the coil of his crystàlline streams,

Beside a pumice isle in Baiae's° bay,
And saw in sleep old palaces and towers
Quivering within the wave's intenser day,

35   All overgrown with azure moss and flowers

---

9 azure sister of the Spring i.e., the South Wind   **21 Mænad** female worshipper of the Bacchus, god
of wine   **32 Baiae's bay** near Naples

So sweet, the sense faints picturing them! Thou
For whose path the Atlantic's level powers

Cleave themselves into chasms, while far below
The sea-blooms and the oozy woods which wear
40   The sapless foliage of the ocean, know

Thy voice, and suddenly grow gray with fear,
And tremble and despoil themselves: oh, hear!

4

If I were a dead leaf thou mightest bear;
If I were a swift cloud to fly with thee;
45   A wave to pant beneath thy power, and share

The impulse of thy strength, only less free
Than thou, O uncontrollable! If even
I were as in my boyhood, and could be

The comrade of thy wanderings over Heaven,
50   As then, when to outstrip thy skyey speed
Scarce seemed a vision; I would ne'er have striven

As thus with thee in prayer in my sore need.
Oh, lift me as a wave, a leaf, a cloud!
I fall upon the thorns of life! I bleed!

55   A heavy weight of hours has chained and bowed
One too like thee: tameless, and swift, and proud.

5

Make me thy lyre, even as the forest is:
What if my leaves are falling like its own!
The tumult of thy mighty harmonies

60   Will take from both a deep, autumnal tone,
Sweet though in sadness. Be thou, Spirit fierce,
My spirit! Be thou me, impetuous one!

Drive my dead thoughts over the universe
Like withered leaves to quicken a new birth!
65   And, by the incantation of this verse,

Scatter, as from an unextinguished hearth

Ashes and sparks, my words among mankind!
Be through my lips to unawakened earth

The trumpet of a prophecy! O Wind,
70   If Winter comes, can Spring be far behind?

—1820

Ozymandias°

I met a traveler from an antique land
Who said: Two vast and trunkless legs of stone
Stand in the desert . . . Near them, on the sand,
Half sunk, a shattered visage lies, whose frown,
5   And wrinkled lip, and sneer of cold command,
Tell that its sculptor well those passions read
Which yet survive, stamped on these lifeless things,
The hand that mocked them, and the heart that fed:
And on the pedestal these words appear:
10 "My name is Ozymandias, king of kings:
Look on my works, ye Mighty, and despair!"
Nothing beside remains. Round the decay
Of that colossal wreck, boundless and bare
The lone and level sands stretch far away.

—1818

William Cullen Bryant
(1794-1878)

Bryant was often called "the American Wordsworth" for his
adaptation of the techniques of English Romanticism to the
American landscape. A precocious writer, Bryant wrote some of
his best poems when he was barely out of his teens, and "To a
Waterfowl" reflects the uncertainty of a young poet unsure of his
future vocation.

To a Waterfowl

Whither, 'midst falling dew,
While glow the heavens with the last steps of day,
Far, through their rosy depths, dost thou pursue

Ozymandias Ramses II of Egypt (c. 1250 B.C.)

Thy solitary way?

5 Vainly the fowler's eye
Might mark thy distant flight, to do thee wrong,
As, darkly seen against the crimson sky,
  Thy figure floats along.

Seek'st thou the plashy brink
10 Of weedy lake, or marge of river wide,
Or where the rocking billows rise and sink
  On the chaféd ocean side?

There is a Power, whose care
Teaches thy way along that pathless coast,—
15 The desert and illimitable air,
  Lone wandering, but not lost.

All day thy wings have fanned,
At that far height, the cold thin atmosphere;
Yet stoop not, weary, to the welcome land,
20 Though the dark night is near.

And soon that toil shall end;
Soon shalt thou find a summer home, and rest,
And scream among thy fellows; reeds shall bend,
  Soon, o'er thy sheltered nest.

25 Thou'rt gone, the abyss of heaven
Hath swallowed up thy form, yet, on my heart
Deeply hath sunk the lesson thou hast given,
  And shall not soon depart.

He, who, from zone to zone,
30 Guides through the boundless sky thy certain flight,
In the long way that I must tread alone,
  Will lead my steps aright.

        —1815

John Keats
(1795-1821)

Among his fellow poets, Keats is perhaps the most admired of all
the major Romantics. Certainly his tragic death from tuberculosis
in his twenties gives poignancy to thoughts of the doomed

young poet writing feverishly in a futile race against time; "Here
lies one whose name was writ in water" are the words he chose
for his own epitaph. Many of Keats's poems are concerned with
glimpses of the eternal, whether a translation of an ancient epic
poem or a pristine artifact of a vanished civilization.

La Belle Dame sans Merci°

O what can ail thee, Knight at arms,
   Alone and palely loitering?
The sedge has withered from the Lake
   And no birds sing!

5   O what can ail thee, Knight at arms,
   So haggard, and so woebegone?
The squirrel's granary is full
   And the harvest's done.

I see a lily on thy brow
10   With anguish moist and fever dew,
And on thy cheeks a fading rose
   Fast withereth too.

"I met a Lady in the Meads,
   Full beautiful, a faery's child,
15   Her hair was long, her foot was light,
   And her eyes were wild.

"I made a Garland for her head,
   And bracelets too, and fragrant Zone;°
She looked at me as she did love
20   And made sweet moan.

"I set her on my pacing steed
   And nothing else saw all day long,
For sidelong would she bend and sing
   A faery's song.

25   "She found me roots of relish sweet,
   And honey wild, and manna dew,
And sure in language strange she said
   'I love thee true.'

La Belle Dame sans Merci the beautiful lady without pity   **18 Zone** belt

"She took me to her elfin grot°
30   And there she wept and sighed full sore,
And there I shut her wild wild eyes
        With kisses four.

"And there she lullèd me asleep,
        And there I dreamed, Ah Woe betide!
35 The latest dream I ever dreamt
        On the cold hill side.

"I saw pale Kings, and Princes too,
        Pale warriors, death-pale were they all;
They cried, 'La belle Dame sans merci
40   Hath thee in thrall!'

"I saw their starved lips in the gloam
        With horrid warning gapèd wide,
And I awoke, and found me here
        On the cold hill's side.

45 "And this is why I sojourn here
        Alone and palely loitering;
Though the sedge is withered from the Lake,
        And no birds sing."

                                                        —1819

Ode on a Grecian Urn

1

Thou still unravished bride of quietness,
        Thou foster-child of silence and slow time,
Sylvan historian, who canst thus express
        A flowery tale more sweetly than our rhyme:
5 What leaf-fringed legend haunts about thy shape
        Of deities or mortals, or of both,
                In Tempe or the dales of Arcady?°
        What men or gods are these? What maidens loath?°
What mad pursuit? What struggle to escape?
10   What pipes and timbrels?° What wild ecstasy?

---

29 grot cave

7 Tempe or the dales of Arcady idealized Greek settings   **8 loath** reluctant   **10 timbrels**
tambourines

2

Heard melodies are sweet, but those unheard
  Are sweeter; therefore, ye soft pipes, play on;
Not to the sensual ear, but, more endeared,
  Pipe to the spirit ditties of no tone:
15 Fair youth, beneath the trees, thou canst not leave
    Thy song, nor ever can those trees be bare;
      Bold Lover, never, never canst thou kiss,
  Though winning near the goal—yet, do not grieve;
    She cannot fade, though thou hast not thy bliss,
20   Forever wilt thou love, and she be fair!

3

Ah, happy, happy boughs! that cannot shed
  Your leaves, nor ever bid the Spring adieu;
And, happy melodist, unwearièd,
  Forever piping songs forever new;
25 More happy love! more happy, happy love!
    Forever warm and still to be enjoyed,
      Forever panting, and forever young;
All breathing human passion far above,
  That leaves a heart high-sorrowful and cloyed,
30   A burning forehead, and a parching tongue.

4

Who are these coming to the sacrifice?
  To what green altar, O mysterious priest,
Lead'st thou that heifer lowing at the skies,
  And all her silken flanks with garlands dressed?
35 What little town by river or sea shore,
    Or mountain-built with peaceful citadel,
      Is emptied of this folk, this pious morn?
And, little town, thy streets forevermore
  Will silent be; and not a soul to tell
40   Why thou art desolate, can e'er return.

5

O Attic shape! Fair attitude! with brede°
  Of marble men and maidens overwrought,
With forest branches and the trodden weed;
  Thou, silent form, dost tease us out of thought
45 As doth eternity: Cold Pastoral!

---

41 Attic Greek **brede** ornamental pattern

When old age shall this generation waste,
   Thou shalt remain, in midst of other woe
Than ours, a friend to man, to whom thou say'st,
"Beauty is truth, truth beauty,"— that is all
50   Ye know on earth, and all ye need to know.

                       —1819

Ode to a Nightingale

1

My heart aches, and a drowsy numbness pains
   My sense, as though of hemlock° I had drunk,
Or emptied some dull opiate to the drains
   One minute past, and Lethe-wards° had sunk.
5 'Tis not through envy of thy happy lot,
   But being too happy in thine happiness—
      That thou, light-wingèd Dryad° of the trees,
        In some melodious plot
Of beechen green, and shadows numberless,
10   Singest of summer in full-throated ease.

2

O, for a draught of vintage! that hath been
   Cooled a long age in the deep-delvèd earth,
Tasting of Flora° and the country green,
   Dance, and Provençal° song, and sunburnt mirth!
15 O for a beaker full of the warm South,
   Full of the true, the blushful Hippocrene,°
      With beaded bubbles winking at the brim,
        And purple-stainèd mouth;
That I might drink, and leave the world unseen,
20   And with thee fade away into the forest dim:

3

Fade far away, dissolve, and quite forget
   What thou among the leaves hast never known,
The weariness, the fever, and the fret
   Here, where men sit and hear each other groan;
25 Where palsy shakes a few, sad, last gray hairs,
   Where youth grows pale, and specter-thin, and dies;

---

2 **hemlock** a deadly poison   4 **Lethe-wards** toward the waters of forgetfulness   7 **Dryad** tree nymph
13 **Flora** Roman goddess of spring   14 **Provencal** of Provence, in the South of France
16 **Hippocrene** fountain of the Muses

Where but to think is to be full of sorrow
    And leaden-eyed despairs,
Where Beauty cannot keep her lustrous eyes,
    Or new Love pine at them beyond tomorrow.

30

4

Away! away! for I will fly to thee,
    Not charioted by Bacchus° and his pards,°
But on the viewless wings of Poesy,
    Though the dull brain perplexes and retards:
35 Already with thee! tender is the night,
    And haply the Queen-Moon is on her throne,
        Clustered around by all her starry Fays;°
            But here there is no light,
    Save what from heaven is with the breezes blown
40   Through verdurous glooms and winding mossy ways.

5

I cannot see what flowers are at my feet,
    Nor what soft incense hangs upon the boughs,
But, in embalmèd darkness, guess each sweet
    Wherewith the seasonable month endows
45 The grass, the thicket, and the fruit-tree wild;
    White hawthorn, and the pastoral eglantine;
        Fast fading violets covered up in leaves;
            And mid-May's eldest child,
    The coming musk-rose, full of dewy wine,
50   The murmurous haunt of flies on summer eves.

6

Darkling° I listen; and for many a time
    I have been half in love with easeful Death,
Called him soft names in many a musèd rhyme,
    To take into the air my quiet breath;
55 Now more than ever seems it rich to die,
    To cease upon the midnight with no pain,
        While thou art pouring forth thy soul abroad
            In such an ecstasy!
    Still wouldst thou sing, and I have ears in vain—
60   To thy high requiem become a sod.

7

Thou wast not born for death, immortal Bird!

---

32 **Bacchus** Roman god of wine   **pards** leopards   37 **Fays** fairies   51 **Darkling** in the dark

No hungry generations tread thee down;
The voice I hear this passing night was heard
In ancient days by emperor and clown;
65 Perhaps the selfsame song that found a path
Through the sad heart of Ruth, when, sick for home,
She stood in tears amid the alien corn;°
The same that ofttimes hath
Charmed magic casements, opening on the foam
70 Of perilous seas, in faery lands forlorn.

8

Forlorn! the very word is like a bell
To toll me back from thee to my sole self!
Adieu! the fancy cannot cheat so well
As she is famed to do, deceiving elf.
75 Adieu! adieu! thy plaintive anthem fades
Past the near meadows, over the still stream,
Up the hill side; and now 'tis buried deep
In the next valley-glades:
Was it a vision, or a waking dream?
80 Fled is that music:—Do I wake or sleep?

—1819

On First Looking into Chapman's Homer°

Much have I traveled in the realms of gold,
And many goodly states and kingdoms seen;
Round many western islands have I been
Which bards in fealty to Apollo° hold.
5 Oft of one wide expanse had I been told
That deep-browed Homer ruled as his demesne;
Yet did I never breathe its pure serene
Till I heard Chapman speak out loud and bold:
Then felt I like some watcher of the skies
10 When a new planet swims into his ken;
Or like stout Cortez° when with eagle eyes
He stared at the Pacific—and all his men
Looked at each other with a wild surmise—
Silent, upon a peak in Darien.°

—1816

66-67 Ruth . . . alien corn in the Old Testament she is a stranger working in the grain fields of Judah
Chapman's Homer translation of the *Iliad* and *Odyssey* by George Chapman (1559-1634) **4 Apollo**
here, the god of poetry **11 Cortez** Balboa was actually the first European to see the Pacific **14 Darien**
in modern-day Panama

When I Have Fears

When I have fears that I may cease to be
   Before my pen has gleaned my teeming brain,
Before high-pilèd books, in charact'ry,°
   Hold like rich garners the full ripened grain;
5   When I behold, upon the night's starred face,
   Huge cloudy symbols of a high romance,
And think that I may never live to trace
   Their shadows, with the magic hand of chance;
And when I feel, fair creature of an hour,
10   That I shall never look upon thee more,
Never have relish in the faery power
   Of unreflecting love!—then on the shore
Of the wide world I stand alone, and think
Till Love and Fame to nothingness do sink.

                                                      —1818

Ralph Waldo Emerson
(1803-1882)

Emerson was more widely known in his own day as an essayist
and lecturer than as a poet, and in brilliant addresses like "The
American Scholar" or "The Poet" he called for a truly American
literature freed from its intellectual dependence on European
models. Many of his lyrics explore the mystical aspects of his
Transcendentalist philosophy.

Concord Hymn

Sung at the Completion of the Battle Monument, July 4, 1837

By the rude bridge that arched the flood,
   Their flag to April's breeze unfurled,
Here once the embattled farmers stood
   And fired the shot heard round the world.

5   The foe long since in silence slept;
   Alike the conqueror silent sleeps;
And Time the ruined bridge has swept

---

3 charact'ry writing

Down the dark stream which seaward creeps.

On this green bank, by this soft stream,
10   We set to-day a votive stone;
That memory may their deed redeem,
     When, like our sires, our sons are gone.

Spirit, that made those heroes dare
     To die, and leave their children free,
15   Bid Time and Nature gently spare
     The shaft we raise to them and thee.

—1876

Each and All

Little thinks, in the field, yon red-cloaked clown°
Of thee from the hill-top looking down;
The heifer that lows in the upland farm,
Far-heard, lows not thine ear to charm;
5   The sexton, tolling his bell at noon,
Deems not that great Napoleon
Stops his horse, and lists with delight,
Whilst his files sweep round yon Alpine height;
Nor knowest thou what argument
10   Thy life to thy neighbor's creed has lent.
All are needed by each one;
Nothing is fair or good alone.
I thought the sparrow's note from heaven,
Singing at dawn on the alder bough;
15   I brought him home, in his nest, at even;
He sings the song, but it cheers not now,
For I did not bring home the river and sky;—
He sang to my ear,—they sang to my eye.
The delicate shells lay on the shore;
20   The bubbles of the latest wave
Fresh pearls to their enamel gave,
And the bellowing of the savage sea
Greeted their safe escape to me.
I wiped away the weeds and foam,
25   I fetched my sea-born treasures home;
But the poor, unsightly, noisome things
Had left their beauty on the shore

---

1 **clown** peasant

With the sun and the sand and the wild uproar
The lover watched his graceful maid,
30   As 'mid the virgin train she strayed,
Nor knew her beauty's best attire
Was woven still by the snow-white choir.
At last she came to his hermitage,
Like the bird from the woodlands to the cage:—
35   The gay enchantment was undone,
A gentle wife, but fairy none.
Then I said, "I covet truth;
Beauty is unripe childhood's cheat;
I leave it behind with the games of youth:"—
40   As I spoke, beneath my feet
The ground-pine curled its pretty wreath,
Running over the club-moss burrs;
I inhaled the violet's breath;
Around me stood the oaks and firs;
45   Pine-cones and acorns lay on the ground;
Over me soared the eternal sky,
Full of light and of deity;
Again I saw, again I heard,
The rolling river, the morning bird;—
50   Beauty through my senses stole;
I yielded myself to the perfect whole.

—1847

Elizabeth Barrett Browning
(1806-1861)

Elizabeth Barrett was already a famous poet when she met her
husband-to-be, Robert Browning, who had been corresponding
with her on literary matters. She originally published her famous
sonnet sequence, written in the first years of her marriage, in the
guise of a translation of Portuguese poems, perhaps to mask
their personal revelations.

Sonnets from the Portuguese, 43

How do I love thee? Let me count the ways.
I love thee to the depth and breadth and height
My soul can reach, when feeling out of sight
For the ends of Being and ideal Grace.

5   I love thee to the level of everyday's
    Most quiet need, by sun and candle-light.
    I love thee freely, as men strive for Right;
    I love thee purely, as they turn from Praise.
    I love thee with the passion put to use
10 In my old griefs, and with my childhood's faith.
    I love thee with a love I seemed to lose
    With my lost saints—I love thee with the breath,
    Smiles, tears, of all my life!—and, if God choose,
    I shall but love thee better after death.

                                    —1845-46

Henry Wadsworth Longfellow
(1807-1882)

Longfellow was by far the most prominent nineteenth century American poet, and his international fame led to his bust's being placed in Westminster Abbey after his death. The long epic poems like *Evangeline* and *Hiawatha* that were immensely popular among contemporary readers are seldom read today, but his shorter poems reveal a level of craftsmanship that few poets have equaled.

The Arsenal at Springfield

This is the Arsenal. From floor to ceiling,
   Like a huge organ, rise the burnished arms;
But from their silent pipes no anthem pealing
   Startles the villages with strange alarms.

5   Ah! what a sound will rise, how wild and dreary,
   When the death-angel touches those swift keys!
What loud lament and dismal Miserere°
   Will mingle with their awful symphonies!

I hear even now the infinite fierce chorus,
10   The cries of agony, the endless groan,
Which, through the ages that have gone before us,
   In long reverberations reach our own.

---

7 Miserere Latin hymn from Psalm 1: "Have mercy on me, Lord."

On helm and harness rings the Saxon hammer,
  Through Cimbric° forest roars the Norseman's song,
15 And loud, amid the universal clamor,
  O'er distant deserts sounds the Tartar gong.

I hear the Florentine, who from his palace
  Wheels out his battle-bell with dreadful din,
And Aztec priests upon their teocallis°
20 Beat the wild war-drums made of serpent's skin;

The tumult of each sacked and burning village;
  The shout that every prayer for mercy drowns;
The soldiers' revels in the midst of pillage;
  The wail of famine in beleaguered towns;

25 The bursting shell, the gateway wrenched asunder,
  The rattling musketry, the clashing blade;
And ever and anon, in tones of thunder
  The diapason° of the cannonade.

Is it, O man, with such discordant noises,
30 With such accursed instruments as these,
Thou drownest Nature's sweet and kindly voices,
  And jarrest the celestial harmonies?

Were half the power, that fills the world with terror,
  Were half the wealth bestowed on camps and courts,
35 Given to redeem the human mind from error,
  There were no need of arsenals or forts:

The warrior's name would be a name abhorred!
  And every nation, that should lift again
Its hand against a brother, on its forehead
40 Would wear forevermore the curse of Cain!

Down the dark future, through long generations,
  The echoing sounds grow fainter and then cease;
And like a bell, with solemn, sweet vibrations,
  I hear once more the voice of Christ say, "Peace!"

45 Peace! and no longer from its brazen portals

---

14 **Cimbric** in Denmark   19 **teocallis** temples atop pyramids   28 **diapason** full range of pipe organ

The blast of War's great organ shakes the skies!
But beautiful as songs of the immortals,
   The holy melodies of love arise.

—1846

The Cross of Snow

In the long, sleepless watches of the night,
   A gentle face—the face of one long dead—
   Looks at me from the wall, where round its head
   The night-lamp casts a halo of pale light.
5 Here in this room she died; and soul more white
   Never through martyrdom of fire° was led
   To its repose; nor can in books be read
   The legend of a life more benedight.°
There is a mountain in the distant West
10 That, sun-defying, in its deep ravines
   Displays a cross of snow upon its side.
Such is the cross I wear upon my breast
   These eighteen years, through all the changing scenes
   And seasons, changeless since the day she died.

—1886

John Greenleaf Whittier
(1807-1892)

Whittier came from a Quaker background and remained close
to his rural origins in his vigorous poetry. An abolitionist and
political activist, he retained strong convictions about poetry's
moral content, and many of his once-popular poems seem stri-
dently propagandistic today. He is at his best in his vigorous
recreations of events from New England's history.

Skipper Ireson's Ride

Of all the rides since the birth of time,
Told in story or sung in rhyme,—
On Apuleius's Golden Ass,°

---

6 martyrdom of fire Longfellow's second wife, Frances, died as the result of a household fire in 1861
8 benedight blessed
3 Apuleius's Golden Ass story from the *Metamorphoses* (c. 150 B.C.)

Or one-eyed Calender's horse of brass,°
5   Witch astride of a human back,
Islam's prophet on Al-Borák;—°
The strangest ride that ever was sped
Was Ireson's, out from Marblehead!°
    Old Floyd Ireson, for his hard heart,
10   Tarred and feathered and carried in a cart
        By the women of Marblehead!

Body of turkey, head of owl,
Wings a-droop like a rained-on fowl,
Feathered and ruffled in every part,
15 Skipper Ireson stood in the cart.
Scores of women, old and young.
Strong of muscle, and glib of tongue,
Pushed and pulled up the rocky lane,
Shouting and singing the shrill refrain:
20   "Here's Flud Oirson, fur his horrd horrt,
        Torr'd an' futherr'd an' corr'd in a corrt
        By the women o' Morble'ead!"

Wrinkled scolds with hands on hips.
Girls in bloom of cheek and lips,
25 Wild-eyed, free-limbed, such as chase
Bacchus round some antique vase,
Brief of skirt, with ankles bare,
Loose of kerchief and loose of hair,
With conch-shells blowing and fish-horns' twang,
30 Over and over the Mænads° sang:
        "Here's Flud Oirson, fur his horrd horrt,
        Torr'd an' futherr'd an' corr'd in a corrt
        By the women o' Morble'ead!"

Small pity for him!—He sailed away
35 From a leaking ship in Chaleur Bay,—
Sailed away from a sinking wreck,
With his own town's-people on her deck!
"Lay by! lay by!" they called to him.
Back he answered, "Sink or swim!
40 Brag of your catch of fish again!"
And off he sailed through the fog and rain!

---

4 one-eyed Calendar's horse of brass story told in the *Arabian Nights* **6 Islam's prophet on Al-Boràk** Mohammed, in one legend, rode on the back of Al-Boràk, a winged creature **8 Marblehead** in Massachusetts **30 Mænads** female worshipers of Bacchus

Old Floyd Ireson, for his hard heart,
Tarred and feathered and carried in a cart
    By the women of Marblehead!

45 Fathoms deep in dark Chaleur
That wreck shall lie forevermore.
Mother and sister, wife and maid,
Looked from the rocks of Marblehead
Over the moaning and rainy sea,—
50 Looked for the coming that might not be!
What did the winds and the sea-birds say
Of the cruel captain who sailed away?—
    Old Floyd Ireson, for his hard heart,
    Tarred and feathered and carried in a cart
55   By the women of Marblehead!

Through the street, on either side,
Up flew windows, doors swung wide;
Sharp-tongued spinsters, old wives gray,
Treble lent the fish-horn's bray.
60 Sea-worn grandsires, cripple-bound,
Hulks of old sailors run aground,
Shook head, and fist, and hat, and cane,
And cracked with curses the hoarse refrain:
    "Here's Flud Oirson, fur his horrd horrt,
65 Torr'd an' futherr'd an' corr'd in a corrt
    By the women o' Morble'ead!"

Sweetly along the Salem road
Bloom of orchard and lilac showed.
Little the wicked skipper knew
70 Of the fields so green and the sky so blue.
Riding there in his sorry trim,
Like an Indian idol glum and grim,
Scarcely he seemed the sound to hear
Of voices shouting, far and near:
75 "Here's Flud Oirson, fur his horrd horrt,
    Torr'd an' futherr'd an' corr'd in a corrt
    By the women o' Morble'ead!"

"Hear me, neighbors!" at last he cried,—
80 "What to me is this noisy ride?
What is the shame that clothes the skin
To the nameless horror that lives within?

Waking or sleeping, I see a wreck,
And hear a cry from a reeling deck!
85   Hate me and curse me,—I only dread
The hand of God and the face of the dead!"
Said old Floyd Ireson, for his hard heart,
Tarred and feathered and carried in a cart
By the women of Marblehead!

90   Then the wife of the skipper lost at sea
Said, "God has touched him! why should we!"
Said an old wife mourning her only son,
"Cut the rogue's tether and let him run!"
So with soft relentings and rude excuse,
95   Half scorn, half pity, they cut him loose,
And gave him a cloak to hide him in,
And left him alone with his shame and sin.
Poor Floyd Ireson, for his hard heart,
Tarred and feathered and carried in a cart
100   By the women of Marblehead!

—1860

Edgar Allan Poe
(1809-1849)

The myth of Poe as a deranged, drug-crazed genius still lingers, despite the wealth of evidence to the contrary that can be gleaned from his brilliant, though erratic, career as a poet, short-story writer, critic, and editor. Poe's brand of Romanticism seems at odds with that of other American poets of his day and is perhaps more in keeping with the spirit of Coleridge than that of Wordsworth. "The Raven" has been parodied perhaps more than any other American poem, yet it still retains a powerful hold on its audience.

The Raven

Once upon a midnight dreary, while I pondered, weak and weary,
Over many a quaint and curious volume of forgotten lore—
While I nodded, nearly napping, suddenly there came a tapping,
As of some one gently rapping, rapping at my chamber door.
5   " 'T is some visitor," I muttered, "tapping at my chamber door—
Only this and nothing more."

Ah, distinctly I remember it was in the bleak December;
And each separate dying ember wrought its ghost upon the floor.
Eagerly I wished the morrow;—vainly I had sought to borrow
10 From my books surcease of sorrow—sorrow for the lost Lenore—
For the rare and radiant maiden whom the angels name Lenore—
                                        Nameless *here* for evermore.

And the silken, sad, uncertain rustling of each purple curtain
Thrilled me—filled me with fantastic terrors never felt before;
15 So that now, to still the beating of my heart, I stood repeating
" 'T is some visitor entreating entrance at my chamber door;—
Some late visitor entreating entrance at my chamber door;—
                                        This it is and nothing more."

Presently my soul grew stronger; hesitating then no longer,
20 "Sir," said I, "or Madam, truly your forgiveness I implore;
But the fact is I was napping, and so gently you came rapping,
And so faintly you come tapping, tapping at my chamber door,
That I scarce was sure I heard you"—here I opened wide the door;—
                                        Darkness there and nothing more.

25 Deep into that darkness peering, long I stood there wondering, fearing,
Doubting, dreaming dreams no mortal ever dared to dream before;
But the silence was unbroken, and the stillness gave no token,
And the only word there spoken was the whispered word, "Lenore?"
This I whispered, and an echo murmured back the word, "Lenore!"
30   Merely this and nothing more.

Back into the chamber turning, all my soul within me burning,
Soon I heard again a tapping somewhat louder than before.
"Surely," said I, "surely that is something at my window lattice;
Let me see, then, what thereat is, and this mystery explore—
35 Let my heart be still a moment and this mystery explore;—
                                        'T is the wind and nothing more!"

Open here I flung the shutter, when, with many a flirt and flutter,
In there stepped a stately Raven of the saintly days of yore;
Not the least obeisance made he; not a minute stopped or stayed he;
40 But, with mien of lord or lady, perched above my chamber door—
Perched upon a bust of Pallas° just above my chamber door—
                                        Perched, and sat, and nothing more.

---

41 Pallas Athena, goddess of wisdom

Then this ebony bird beguiling my sad fancy into smiling,
By the grave and stern decorum of the countenance it wore,
45   "Though thy crest be shorn and shaven, thou," I said, "art sure no craven,
Ghastly grim and ancient Raven wandering from the Nightly shore—
Tell me what thy lordly name is on the Night's Plutonian° shore!"
                            Quoth the Raven, "Nevermore."

Much I marvelled this ungainly fowl to hear discourse so plainly,
50   Though its answer little meaning—little relevancy bore;
For we cannot help agreeing that no living human being
Ever yet was blessed with seeing bird above his chamber door—
Bird or beast upon the sculptured bust above his chamber door,
                       With such name as "Nevermore."

55   But the Raven, sitting lonely on the placid bust, spoke only
That one word, as if his soul in that one word he did outpour.
Nothing farther then he uttered—not a feather then he fluttered—
Till I scarcely more than muttered, "Other friends have flown before—
On the morrow *he* will leave me, as my Hopes have flown before."
60   Then the bird said "Nevermore."

Startled at the stillness broken by reply so aptly spoken,
"Doubtless," said I, "what it utters is its only stock and store
Caught from some unhappy master whom unmerciful Disaster
Followed fast and followed faster till his songs one burden bore—
65   Till the dirges of his Hope that melancholy burden bore
                       Of 'Never—nevermore.'"

But the Raven still beguiling all my sad fancy into smiling,
Straight I wheeled a cushioned seat in front of bird and bust and door;
Then, upon the velvet sinking, I betook myself to linking
70   Fancy unto fancy, thinking what this ominous bird of yore—
What this grim, ungainly, ghastly, gaunt, and ominous bird of yore
                     Meant in croaking "Nevermore."

This I sat engaged in guessing, but no syllable expressing
To the fowl whose fiery eyes now burned into my bosom's core;
75   This and more I sat divining, with my head at ease reclining
On the cushion's velvet lining that the lamp-light gloated o'er,
But whose velvet-violet lining with the lamp-light gloating o'er,
                     She shall press, ah, nevermore!

---

47 Plutonian after Pluto, Roman god of the underworld

Then, methought, the air grew denser, perfumed from an unseen censer
80 Swung by seraphim whose foot-falls tinkled on the tufted floor.
"Wretch," I cried, "thy God hath lent thee—by these angels he hath sent thee.
Respite—respite and nepenthe° from thy memories of Lenore;
Quaff, oh quaff this kind nepenthe and forget this lost Lenore!"
                                          Quoth the Raven, "Nevermore."

85 "Prophet!" said I, "thing of evil!—prophet still, if bird or devil!—
Whether Tempter sent, or whether tempest tossed thee here ashore,
Desolate yet all undaunted, on this desert land enchanted—
On this home by Horror haunted—tell me truly, I implore—
Is there—*is* there balm in Gilead?—tell me—tell me, I implore!"
90   Quoth the Raven, "Nevermore."

"Prophet!" said I, "thing of evil!—prophet still, if bird or devil!
By that Heaven that bends above us—by that God we both adore—
Tell this soul with sorrow laden if, within the distant Aidenn,°
It shall clasp a sainted maiden whom the angels name Lenore—
95 Clasp a rare and radiant maiden whom the angels name Lenore."
                                          Quoth the Raven, "Nevermore."

"Be that word our sign of parting, bird or fiend!" I shrieked, upstarting—
"Get thee back into the tempest and the Night's Plutonian shore!
Leave no black plume as a token of that lie thy soul hath spoken!
100 Leave my loneliness unbroken!—quit the bust above my door!
Take thy beak from out my heart, and take thy form from off my door!"
                                          Quoth the Raven, "Nevermore."

And the Raven, never flitting, still is sitting, *still* is sitting
On the pallid bust of Pallas just above my chamber door;
105 And his eyes have all the seeming of a demon's that is dreaming,
And the lamp-light o'er him streaming throws his shadow on the floor;
And my soul from out that shadow that lies floating on the floor
                                  Shall be lifted—nevermore!
                                  —1845

Sonnet—To Science

Science! true daughter of Old Time thou art!
    Who alterest all things with thy peering eyes.
Why preyest thou thus upon the poet's heart,

---

82 **nepenthe** drug causing forgetfulness   93 **Aidenn** Eden

Vulture, whose wings are dull realities?
5 How should he love thee? or how deem thee wise?
Who wouldst not leave him in his wandering
To seek for treasure in the jeweled skies,
Albeit he soared with an undaunted wing?
Hast thou not dragged Diana° from her car?
10   And driven the Hamadryad° from the wood
To seek a shelter in some happier star?
Hast thou not torn the Naiad° from her flood,
The Elfin from the green grass, and from me
The summer dream beneath the tamarind° tree?

—1829

To Helen

Helen, thy beauty is to me
Like those Nicean° barks of yore,
That gently, o'er a perfumed sea
The weary, way-worn wanderer bore
5   To his own native shore.

On desperate seas long wont to roam,
Thy hyacinth° hair, thy classic face
Thy Naiad° airs have brought me home
To the glory that was Greece
10   And the grandeur that was Rome.

Lo! in yon brilliant window-niche
How statue-like I see thee stand!
The agate lamp within thy hand,
Ah! Psyche,° from the regions which
15   Are Holy Land!

—1823

Alfred, Lord Tennyson
(1809-1892)

Tennyson became the most famous English poet with the 1850
publication of *In Memoriam*, a sequence of poems on the death

---

9 **Diana** Roman goddess of the moon   10 **Hamadryad** wood nymph   12 **Naiad** water nymph
14 **tamarind** exotic Oriental tree

2 **Nicean** possibly of Nice (in the South of France); or Phoenician   7 **hyacinth** reddish, like the
flower of Greek myth   8 **Naiad** water nymph   14 **Psyche** the soul

of his friend A. H. Hallam The same year he became Poet Laureate. Modern critical opinion has focused more favorably on Tennyson's lyrical gifts than on his talents for narrative or drama. T. S. Eliot and W. H. Auden, among other critics, praised Tennyson's rhythms and sound patterns but had reservations about his depth of intellect, especially when he took on the role of official apologist for Victorian England.

The Eagle

Fragment

He clasps the crag with crooked hands;
Close to the sun in lonely lands,
Ringed with the azure world, he stands.

5 The wrinkled sea beneath him crawls;
He watches from his mountain walls,
And like a thunderbolt he falls.

—1851

In Memoriam A. H. H.,° 54

O, yet we trust that somehow good
   Will be the final goal of ill,
   To pangs of nature, sins of will,
Defects of doubt, and taints of blood;

5 That nothing walks with aimless feet;
   That not one life shall be destroyed,
   Or cast as rubbish to the void,
When God hath made the pile complete;

That not a worm is cloven in vain;
10   That not a moth with vain desire
   Is shriveled in a fruitless fire,
Or but subserves another's gain.

Behold, we know not anything;
   I can but trust that good shall fall
15   At last—far off—at last, to all,
And every winter change to spring.

A. H. H. the poet's college friend Arthur Henry Hallam (1811-1833)

So runs my dreams; but what am I?
  An infant crying in the night;
  An infant crying for the light,
20 And with no language but a cry.

—1833

Tears, Idle Tears

from The Princess

Tears, idle tears, I know not what they mean,
Tears from the depth of some divine despair
Rise in the heart, and gather to the eyes,
In looking on the happy autumn-fields,
5 And thinking of the days that are no more.

Fresh as the first beam glittering on a sail,
That brings our friends up from the underworld,
Sad as the last which reddens over one
That sinks with all we love below the verge;
10 So sad, so fresh, the days that are no more.

Ah, sad and strange as in dark summer dawns
The earliest pipe of half-awakened birds
To dying ears, when unto dying eyes
The casement slowly grows a glimmering square;
15 So sad, so strange, the days that are no more.

Dear as remembered kisses after death,
And sweet as those by hopeless fancy feigned
On lips that are for others; deep as love,
Deep as first love, and wild with all regret;
20 O Death in Life, the days that are no more!

—1847

Ulysses°

It little profits that an idle king,
By this still hearth, among these barren crags,
Matched with an aged wife, I mete and dole
Unequal laws unto a savage race,

Ulysses Homer's *Odyssey* ends with the return of Odysseus (Ulysses) to his island kingdom, Ithaca.
Tennyson's poem takes place some years later

5   That hoard, and sleep, and feed, and know not me.
       I cannot rest from travel; I will drink
       Life to the lees. All times I have enjoyed
       Greatly, have suffered greatly, both with those
       That loved me, and alone; on shore, and when
10   Through scudding drifts the rainy Hyades°
       Vexed the dim sea. I am become a name;
       For always roaming with a hungry heart
       Much have I seen and known—cities of men
       And manners, climates, councils, governments,
15   Myself not least, but honored of them all—
       And drunk delight of battle with my peers,
       Far on the ringing plains of windy Troy.
       I am a part of all that I have met;
       Yet all experience is an arch wherethrough
20   Gleams that untraveled world whose margin fades
       For ever and for ever when I move.
       How dull it is to pause, to make and end,
       To rust unburnished, not to shine in use!
       As though to breathe were life! Life piled on life
25   Were all too little, and of one to me
       Little remains; but every hour is saved
       From that eternal silence, something more,
       A bringer of new things; and vile it were
       For some three suns to store and hoard myself,
30   And this gray spirit yearning in desire
       To follow knowledge like a sinking star,
       Beyond the utmost bound of human thought.
            This is my son, mine own Telemachus,
       To whom I leave the scepter and the isle,
35   Well-loved of me, discerning to fulfill
       This labor, by slow prudence to make mild
       A rugged people, and through soft degrees
       Subdue them to the useful and the good.
       Most blameless is he, centered in the sphere
40   Of common duties, decent not to fail
       In offices of tenderness, and pay
       Meet adoration to my household gods,
       When I am gone. He works his work, I mine.
            There lies the port; the vessel puffs her sail;
45   There gloom the dark, broad seas. My mariners,
       Souls that have toiled, and wrought, and thought with me,

---

10 Hyades a constellation thought to predict rain

That ever with a frolic welcome took
The thunder and the sunshine, and opposed
Free hearts, free foreheads—you and I are old;
50 Old age hath yet his honor and his toil.
Death closes all; but something ere the end,
Some work of noble note, may yet be done,
Not unbecoming men that strove with gods.
The lights begin to twinkle from the rocks;
55 The long day wanes; the low moon climbs; the deep
Moans round with many voices. Come, my friends,
'Tis not too late to seek a newer world.
Push off, and sitting well in order smite
The sounding furrows; for my purpose holds
60 To sail beyond the sunset, and the baths
Of all the western stars, until I die.
It may be that the gulfs will wash us down;
It may be we shall touch the Happy Isles,°
And see the great Achilles, whom we knew.
65 Though much is taken, much abides; and though
We are not now that strength which in old days
Moved earth and heaven, that which we are, we are,
One equal temper of heroic hearts,
Made weak by time and fate, but strong in will
70 To strive, to seek, to find, and not to yield.

—1833

Robert Browning
(1812-1889)

Browning's many successful dramatic monologues are his lasting
legacy, for he brings the genre to a level of achievement rarely
equaled. Less regarded during his lifetime than his contemporary
Tennyson, he has consistently risen in the esteem of modern
readers. Often overlooked in his gallery of often grotesque
characters are his considerable metrical skills and ability to
simulate speech while working in demanding poetic forms.

---

63 Happy Isles Elysium, the resting place of dead heroes

My Last Duchess

Ferrara°

That's my last duchess painted on the wall,
Looking as if she were alive. I call
That piece a wonder, now: Frà Pandolf's° hands
Worked busily a day, and there she stands.
5 Will't please you sit and look at her? I said
"Frà Pandolf" by design, for never read
Strangers like you that pictured countenance,
The depth and passion of its earnest glance,
But to myself they turned (since none puts by
10 The curtain I have drawn for you, but I)
And seemed as they would ask me, if they durst,
How such a glance came there; so, not the first
Are you to turn and ask thus. Sir, 'twas not
Her husband's presence only, called that spot
15 Of joy into the Duchess' cheek: perhaps
Frà Pandolf chanced to say "Her mantle laps
Over my lady's wrist too much," or "Paint
Must never hope to reproduce the faint
Half-flush that dies along her throat": such stuff
20 Was courtesy, she thought, and cause enough
For calling up that spot of joy. She had
A heart—how shall I say?—too soon made glad,
Too easily impressed; she liked whate'er
She looked on, and her looks went everywhere.
25 Sir, 'twas all one! My favor at her breast,
The dropping of the daylight in the West,
The bough of cherries some officious fool
Broke in the orchard for her, the white mule
She rode with round the terrace—all and each
30 Would draw from her alike the approving speech,
Or blush, at least. She thanked men—good! but thanked
Somehow—I know not how—as if she ranked
My gift of a nine-hundred-years-old name
With anybody's gift. Who'd stoop to blame
35 This sort of trifling? Even had you skill
In speech—which I have not—to make your will
Quite clear to such an one, and say, "Just this
Or that in you disgusts me; here you miss,

Ferrara The speaker is probably Alfonso II d'Este, Duke of Ferrara (1533-158?)   **3 Frà Pandolf** an imaginary painter

Or there exceed the mark"—and if she let
40 Herself be lessoned so, nor plainly set
Her wits to yours, forsooth, and made excuse,
—E'en then would be some stooping; and I choose
Never to stoop. Oh sir, she smiled, no doubt,
Whene'er I passed her; but who passed without
45 Much the same smile? This grew; I gave commands;
Then all smiles stopped together. There she stands
As if alive. Will't please you rise? We'll meet
The company below, then. I repeat,
The Count your master's° known munificence
50 Is ample warrant that no just pretense
Of mine for dowry will be disallowed;
Though his fair daughter's self, as I avowed
At starting, is my object. Nay, we'll go
Together down, sir. Notice Neptune, though,
55 Taming a sea horse, thought a rarity,
Which Claus of Innsbruck cast in bronze for me!

                                                    —1842

Porphyria's° Lover

The rain set early in tonight,
        The sullen wind was soon awake,
It tore the elm-tops down for spite,
        And did its worst to vex the lake:
5   I listened with heart fit to break.
When glided in Porphyria; straight
        She shut the cold out and the storm,
And kneeled and made the cheerless grate
        Blaze up, and all the cottage warm;
10   Which done, she rose, and from her form
Withdrew the dripping cloak and shawl,
        And laid her soiled gloves by, untied
Her hat and let the damp hair fall,
        And, last, she sat down by my side
15   And called me. When no voice replied,
She put my arm about her waist,
        And made her smooth white shoulder bare,
And all her yellow hair displaced,

---

49 Count your master's The auditor is apparently an envoy sent to arrange a marriage between the
Duke of Ferrara and a count's daughter

Porphyria name suggesting purple, the color of nobility and royalty

And, stooping, made my cheek lie there,
20   And spread, o'er all, her yellow hair,
Murmuring how she loved me—she
    Too weak, for all her heart's endeavor,
To set its struggling passion free
    From pride, and vainer ties dissever,
25   And give herself to me forever.
But passion sometimes would prevail,
    Nor could tonight's gay feast restrain
A sudden thought of one so pale
    For love of her, and all in vain:
30   So, she was come through wind and rain.
Be sure I looked up at her eyes
    Happy and proud; at last I knew
Porphyria worshipped me; surprise
    Made my heart swell, and still it grew
35   While I debated what to do.
That moment she was mine, mine, fair,
    Perfectly pure and good: I found
A thing to do, and all her hair
    In one long yellow string I wound
40   Three times her little throat around,
And strangled her. No pain felt she;
    I am quite sure she felt no pain.
As a shut bud that holds a bee,
    I warily oped her lids: again
45   Laughed the blue eyes without a stain.
And I untightened next the tress
    About her neck; her cheek once more
Blushed bright beneath my burning kiss:
    I propped her head up as before,
50   Only, this time my shoulder bore
Her head, which droops upon it still:
    The smiling rosy little head
So glad it has its utmost will,
    That all it scorned at once is fled,
55   And I, its love, am gained instead!
Porphyria's love: she guessed not how
    Her darling one wish would be heard.
And thus we sit together now,
    And all night long we have not stirred,
60   And yet God has not said a word!

                        —1842

Walt Whitman
(1819-1892)

Whitman's pioneering use of free verse has established him as one of the forebears of modern poetry, but his subject matter, often dealing with sexual topics, and his unsparing realism were equally controversial in his day. An admirer of Emerson, he adapted many of the ideas of Transcendentalism in "Song of Myself," his first major sequence, and also incorporated many of Emerson's calls for poets to use American subjects and patterns of speech. *Leaves of Grass*, which he revised from 1855 until his death, expanded to include virtually all of his poems, including the graphic poems he wrote while serving as a volunteer in Civil War army hospitals.

A Sight in Camp in the Daybreak Gray and Dim

A sight in camp in the daybreak gray and dim,
As from my tent I emerge so early sleepless,
As slow I walk in the cool fresh air the path near by the hospital tent,
Three forms I see on stretchers lying, brought out there untended lying,
5   Over each the blanket spread, ample brownish woolen blanket,
Gray and heavy blanket, folding, covering all.

Curious I halt and silent stand,
Then with light fingers I from the face of the nearest the first just lift the
    blanket;
Who are you elderly man so gaunt and grim, with well-gray'd hair, and flesh all
    sunken about the eyes?
10   Who are you my dear comrade?
Then to the second I step—and who are you my child and darling?
Who are you sweet boy with cheeks yet blooming?

Then to the third—a face nor child nor old, very calm, as of beautiful yellow-
    white ivory;
Young man I think I know you—I think this face is the face of the Christ himself,
15   Dead and divine and brother of all, and here again he lies.
                         —1867

Crossing Brooklyn Ferry

1

Flood-tide below me! I see you face to face!

Clouds of the west—sun there half an hour high—I see you also face to face.

Crowds of men and women attired in the usual costumes, how curious you are to me!

On the ferry-boats the hundreds and hundreds that cross, returning home, are more curious to me than you suppose,

And you that shall cross from shore to shore years hence are more to me, and more in my meditations, than you might suppose.

2

The impalpable sustenance of me from all things at all hours of the day,

The simple, compact, well-join'd scheme, myself disintegrated, every one disintegrated yet part of the scheme,

The similitudes of the past and those of the future,

The glories strung like beads on my smallest sights and hearings, on the walk in the street and the passage over the river,

The current rushing so swiftly and swimming with me far away,

The others that are to follow me, the ties between me and them,

The certainty of others, the life, love, sight, hearing of others.

Others will enter the gates of the ferry and cross from shore to shore,

Others will watch the run of the flood-tide,

Others will see the shipping of Manhattan north and west, and the heights of Brooklyn to the south and east,

Others will see the islands large and small;

Fifty years hence, others will see them as they cross, the sun half an hour high,

A hundred years hence, or ever so many hundred years hence, others will see them,

Will enjoy the sunset, the pouring-in of the flood-tide, the falling-back to the sea of the ebb-tide.

3

It avails not, time nor place—distance avails not,

I am with you, you men and women of a generation, or ever so many generations hence,

Just as you feel when you look on the river and sky, so I felt,

Just as any of you is one of a living crowd, I was one of a crowd,

Just as you are refresh'd by the gladness of the river and the bright flow, I was refresh'd,

Just as you stand and lean on the rail, yet hurry with the swift current, I stood yet was hurried,

Just as you look on the numberless masts of ships and the thick-stemm'd pipes of steamboats, I look'd.

I too many and many a time cross'd the river of old,

Watched the Twelfth-month° sea-gulls, saw them high in the air floating with
    motionless wings, oscillating their bodies,
Saw how the glistening yellow lit up parts of their bodies and left the rest in
    strong shadow,
30 Saw the slow-wheeling circles and the gradual edging toward the south,
Saw the reflection of the summer sky in the water,
Had my eyes dazzled by the shimmering track of beams,
Look'd at the fine centrifugal spokes of light round the shape of my head in the
    sunlit water,
Look'd on the haze on the hills southward and south-westward,
35 Look'd on the vapor as it flew in fleeces tinged with violet,
Look'd toward the lower bay to notice the vessels arriving,
Saw their approach, saw aboard those that were near me,
Saw the white sails of schooners and sloops, saw the ships at anchor,
The sailors at work in the rigging or out astride the spars,
The round masts, the swinging motion of the hulls, the slender serpentine
40   pennants,
The large and small steamers in motion, the pilots in their pilothouses,
The white wake left by the passage, the quick tremulous whirl of the wheels,
The flags of all nations, the falling of them at sunset
The scallop-edged waves in the twilight, the ladled cups, the frolicsome crests
    and glistening,
The stretch afar growing dimmer and dimmer, the gray walls of the granite
45   storehouses by the docks,
On the river the shadowy group, the big steam-tug closely flank'd on each side by
    the barges, the hay boat, the belated lighter,
On the neighboring shore the fires from the foundry chimneys burning high and
    glaringly into the night,
Casting their flicker of black contrasted with wild red and yellow light over the
    tops of houses, and down into the clefts of streets.

4

These and all else were to me the same as they are to you,
50 I loved well those cities, loved well the stately and rapid river,
The men and women I saw were all near to me,
Others the same—others who look back on me because I look'd forward to them,
(The time will come, though I stop here to-day and to-night.)

5

What is it then between us?
55 What is the count of the scores or hundreds of years between us?

---

28 Twelfth-month Whitman's mother was a Quaker, hence this phrase for December

Whatever it is, it avails not—distance avails not, and place avails not,
I too lived, Brooklyn of ample hills was mine,
I too walk'd the streets of Manhattan island, and bathed in the waters around it,
I too felt the curious abrupt questionings stir within me,
In the day among crowds of people sometimes they came upon me,
In my walks home late at night or as I lay in my bed they came upon me,
I too had been struck from the float forever held in solution,
I too had receiv'd identity by my body,
That I was I knew was of my body, and what I should be I knew I should be of my body.

6

It is not upon you alone the dark patches fall,
The dark threw its patches down upon me also,
The best I had done seem'd to me blank and suspicious,
My great thoughts as I supposed them, were they not in reality meagre?
Nor is it you alone who know what it is to be evil,
I am he who knew what it was to be evil,
I too knitted the old knot of contrariety,
Blabb'd, blush'd, resented, lied, stole, grudg'd,
Had guile, anger, lust, hot wishes I dared not speak,
Was wayward, vain, greedy, shallow, sly, cowardly, malignant,
The wolf, the snake, the hog, not wanting in me,
The cheating look, the frivolous word, the adulterous wish, not wanting,
Refusals, hates, postponements, meanness, laziness, none of these wanting,
Was one with the rest, the days and haps of the rest,
Was call'd by my nighest name by clear loud voices of young men as they saw me approaching or passing,
Felt their arms on my neck as I stood, or the negligent leaning of their flesh against me as I sat,
Saw many I loved in the street or ferry-boat or public assembly, yet never told them a word,
Lived the same life with the rest, the same old laughing, gnawing, sleeping,
Play'd the part that still looks back on the actor or actress,
The same old role, the role that is what we make it, as great as we like,
Or as small as we like, or both great and small.

7

Closer yet I approach you,
What thought you have of me now, I had as much of you—I laid in my stores in advance,
I consider'd long and seriously of you before you were born.

Who was to know what should come home to me?

90   Who knows but I am enjoying this?
      Who knows, for all the distance, but I am as good as looking at you now, for all
          you cannot see me?

8

      Ah, what can ever be more stately and admirable to me than mast hemm'd
          Manhattan?
      River and sunset and scallop-edg'd waves of flood-tide?
      The sea-gulls oscillating their bodies, the hay-boat in the twilight, and the
          belated lighter?
      What gods can exceed these that clasp me by the hand, and with voices I love call
95   me promptly and loudly by my nighest name as I approach?
      What is more subtle than this which ties me to the woman or man that looks in my
          face?
      Which fuses me into you now, and pours my meaning into you?

      We understand then do we not?
      What I promis'd without mentioning it, have you not accepted?
      What the study could not teach—what the preaching could not accomplish is
100   accomplish'd, is it not?

9

      Flow on, river! flow with the flood-tide, and ebb with the ebb-tide!
      Frolic on, crested and scallop-edg'd waves!
      Gorgeous clouds of the sunset! drench with your splendor me, or the men and
          women generations after me!
      Cross from shore to shore, countless crowds of passengers!
105   Stand up, tall masts of Mannahatta! stand up, beautiful hills of Brooklyn!
      Throb, baffled and curious brain! throw out questions and answers!
      Suspend here and everywhere, eternal float of solution!
      Gaze, loving and thirsting eyes, in the house or street or public assembly!
      Sound out, voices of young men! loudly and musically call me by my nighest
          name!
110   Live, old life! play the part that looks back on the actor or actress!
      Play the old role, the role that is great or small according as one makes it!
      Consider, you who peruse me, whether I may not in unknown ways be looking
          upon you;
      Be firm, rail over the river, to support those who lean idly, yet haste with the
          hasting current;
      Fly on, sea-birds! fly sideways, or wheel in large circles high in the air;
      Receive the summer sky, you water, and faithfully hold it till all downcast eyes
115   have time to take it from you!
      Diverge, fine spokes of light, from the shape of my head, or any one's head, in the
          sunlit water!

Come on, ships from the lower bay! pass up or down, white-sail'd schooners,
    sloops, lighters!
Flaunt away, flags of all nations! be duly lower'd at sunset!
Burn high your fires, foundry chimneys! cast black shadows at nightfall! cast red
    and yellow light over the tops of the houses!
120 Appearances, now or henceforth, indicate what you are,
You necessary film, continue to envelop the soul
About my body for me, and your body for you, be hung our divinest aromas,
Thrive, cities—bring your freight, bring your shows, ample and sufficient
    rivers,
Expand, being than which none else is perhaps more spiritual,
125 Keep your places, objects than which none else is more lasting.

You have waited, you always wait, you dumb, beautiful ministers,
We receive you with free sense at last, and are insatiate henceforward,
Not you any more shall be able to foil us, or withhold yourselves from us,
We use you, and do not cast you aside—we plant you permanently within us,
130 We fathom you not—we love you—there is perfection in you also,
You furnish your parts toward eternity,
Great or small, you furnish your parts toward the soul.
                                            —1881-1882

A Noiseless Patient Spider

A noiseless patient spider,
I mark'd where on a little promontory it stood isolated,
Mark'd how to explore the vacant vast surrounding,
It launch'd forth filament, filament, filament, out of itself,
5   Ever unreeling them, ever tirelessly speeding them.

And you O my soul where you stand,
Surrounded, detached, in measureless oceans of space,
Ceaselessly musing, venturing, throwing, seeking the spheres to connect them,
Till the bridge you will need be form'd, till the ductile anchor hold,
10 Till the gossamer thread you fling catch somewhere, O my soul.
                                            —1871

Out of the Cradle Endlessly Rocking

Out of the cradle endlessly rocking,
Out of the mocking-bird's throat, the musical shuttle,

Out of the Ninth-month° midnight,
Over the sterile sands and the fields beyond, where the child leaving his bed
    wander'd alone, bareheaded, barefoot,
5   Down from the shower'd halo,
Up from the mystic play of shadows twining and twisting as if they were alive,
Out from the patches of briers and blackberries,
From the memories of the bird that chanted to me,
From your memories sad brother, from the fitful risings and fallings I heard,
10   From under that yellow half-moon late-risen and swollen as if with tears,
From those beginning notes of yearning and love there in the mist,
From the thousand responses of my heart never to cease,
From the myriad thence-arous'd words,
From the word stronger and more delicious than any,
15   From such as now they start the scene revisiting,
As a flock, twittering, rising, or overhead passing,
Borne hither, ere all eludes me, hurriedly,
A man, yet by these tears a little boy again,
Throwing myself on the sand, confronting the waves,
20   I, chanter of pains and joys, uniter of here and hereafter,
Taking all hints to use them, but swiftly leaping beyond them,
A reminiscence sing.

Once Paumanok,°
When the lilac-scent was in the air and Fifth-month° grass was growing,
25   Up this seashore in some briers,
Two feather'd guests from Alabama, two together,
And their nest, and four light-green eggs spotted with brown,
And every day the he-bird to and fro near at hand,
And every day the she-bird crouch'd on her nest, silent, with bright eyes,
30   And every day I, a curious boy, never too close, never disturbing them,
Cautiously peering, absorbing, translating.

Shine! shine! shine!
Pour down your warmth, great sun!
While we bask, we two together.

35   *Two together!*
Winds blow south, or winds blow north,
Day come white, or night come black,
Home, or rivers and mountains from home,
Singing all time, minding no time,

---

3 Ninth-month Quaker term for September   **23 Paumanok** Indian name for Long Island   **24 Fifth-month** May (Quaker)

40   *While we two keep together.*

Till of a sudden,
May-be kill'd, unknown to her mate,
One forenoon the she-bird crouch'd not on the nest,
Nor return'd that afternoon, nor the next,
45   Nor ever appear'd again.

And thenceforward all summer in the sound of the sea,
And at night under the full of the moon in calmer weather,
Over the hoarse surging of the sea,
Or flitting from brier to brier by day,
50   I saw, I heard at intervals the remaining one, the he-bird,
The solitary guest from Alabama.

Blow! blow! blow!
Blow up sea-winds along Paumanok's shore;
I wait and I wait till you blow my mate to me.

55   Yes, when the stars glisten'd,
All night long on the prong of a moss-scallop'd stake,
Down almost amid the slapping waves,
Sat the lone singer wonderful causing tears.

He call'd on his mate,
60   He pour'd forth the meaning which I of all men know.

Yes my brother I know,
The rest might not, but I have treasur'd every note,
For more than once dimly down to the beach gliding,
Silent, avoiding the moonbeams, blending myself with the shadows,
Recalling now the obscure shapes, the echoes, the sounds and sights after their
65   sorts,
The white arms out in the breakers tirelessly tossing,
I, with bare feet, a child, the wind wafting my hair,
Listen'd long and long.

Listen'd to keep, to sing, now translating the notes,
70   Following you my brother.

Soothe! soothe! soothe!
Close on its wave soothes the wave behind,
And again another behind embracing and lapping, every one close,
But my love soothes not me, not me.

75   *Low hangs the moon, it rose late,*
      It is lagging—O I think it is heavy with love, with love.

      O madly the sea pushes upon the land,
      With love, with love.

      O night! do I not see my love fluttering out among the breakers?
80   *What is that little black thing I see there in the white?*

      Loud! loud! loud!
      Loud I call to you, my love!

      High and clear I shoot my voice over the waves,
      Surely you must know who is here, is here,
85   *You must know who I am, my love.*

      Low-hanging moon!
      What is that dusky spot in your brown yellow?
      O it is the shape, the shape of my mate!
      O moon do not keep her from me any longer.

90   *Land! land! O land!*
      Whichever way I turn, O I think you could give me my mate back again if you
        only would,
      For I am almost sure I see her dimly whichever way I look.

      O rising stars!
      Perhaps the one I want so much will rise, will rise with some of you.

95   *O throat! O trembling throat!*
      Sound clearer through the atmosphere!
      Pierce the woods, the earth,
      Somewhere listening to catch you must be the one I want.

      Shake out carols!
100   *Solitary here, the night's carols!*
      Carols of lonesome love! death's carols!
      Carols under that lagging, yellow, waning moon!
      O under that moon where she droops almost down into the sea!
      O reckless despairing carols.

105   *But soft! sink low!*
      Soft! let me just murmur,

And do you wait a moment you husky-nois'd sea,
For somewhere I believe I heard my mate responding to me,
So faint, I must be still, be still to listen,
110   *But not altogether still, for then she might not come immediately to me.*

Hither my love!
Here I am! here!
With this just-sustain'd note I announce myself to you,
This gentle call is for you my love, for you.

115   *Do not be decoy'd elsewhere,*
That is the whistle of the wind, it is not my voice,
That is the fluttering, the fluttering of the spray,
Those are the shadows of leaves.

O darkness! O in vain!
120   *O I am very sick and sorrowful.*

O brown halo in the sky near the moon, drooping upon the sea!
O troubled reflection in the sea!
O throat! O throbbing heart!
And I singing uselessly, uselessly all the night.

125   *O past! O happy life! O songs of joy!*
In the air, in the woods, over fields,
Loved! loved! loved! loved! loved!
But my mate no more, no more with me!
We two together no more.

130   The aria sinking,
All else continuing, the stars shining,
The winds blowing, the notes of the bird continuous echoing,
With angry moans the fierce old mother incessantly moaning,
On the sands of Paumanok's shore gray and rustling,
The yellow half-moon enlarged, sagging down, drooping, the face of the sea
135   almost touching,
The boy ecstatic, with his bare feet the waves, with his hair the atmosphere
       dallying,
The love in the heart long pent, now loose, now at last tumultuously bursting,
The aria's meaning, the ears, the soul, swiftly depositing,
The strange tears down the cheeks coursing,
140   The colloquy there, the trio, each uttering,
The undertone, the savage old mother incessantly crying,
To the boy's soul's questions sullenly timing, some drown'd secret hissing,

To the outsetting bard.

Demon or bird! (said the boy's soul,)
145   Is it indeed toward your mate you sing? or is it really to me?
For I, that was a child, my tongue's use sleeping, now I have heard you,
Now in a moment I know what I am for, I awake,
And already a thousand singers, a thousand songs, clearer, louder and more
      sorrowful than yours,
A thousand warbling echoes have started to life within me, never to die.

150   O you singer solitary, singing by yourself, projecting me,
O solitary me listening, never more shall I cease perpetuating you,
Never more shall I escape, never more the reverberations,
Never more the cries of unsatisfied love be absent from me
Never again leave me to be the peaceful child I was before what there in the night,
155   By the sea under the yellow and sagging moon,
The messenger there arous'd, the fire, the sweet hell within,
The unknown want, the destiny of me.

O give me the clew!° (it lurks in the night here somewhere,)
O if I am to have so much, let me have more!

160   A word then, (for I will conquer it,)
The word final, superior to all,
Subtle, sent up—what is it?—I listen;
Are you whispering it, and have been all the time, you sea waves?
Is that it from your liquid rims and wet sands?

165   Whereto answering, the sea,
Delaying not, hurrying not,
Whisper'd me through the night, and very plainly before daybreak,
Lisp'd to me the low and delicious word death,
And again death, death, death, death,
170   Hissing melodious, neither like the bird nor like my arous'd child's heart,
But edging near as privately for me rustling at my feet,
Creeping thence steadily up to my ears and laving me softly all over,
Death, death, death, death, death.

Which I do not forget,
175   But fuse the song of my dusky demon and brother,
That he sang to me in the moonlight on Paumanok's gray beach,
With the thousand responsive songs at random,

---

158 **clew** clue

My own songs awaked from that hour,
And with them the key, the word up from the waves,
180 The word of the sweetest song and all songs,
That strong and delicious word which, creeping to my feet,
(Or like some old crone rocking the cradle, swathed in sweet garments, bending
   aside,)
The sea whisper'd me.

—1881-1882

Song of Myself, 6

A child said *What is the grass?* fetching it to me with full hands;
How could I answer the child? I do not know what it is anymore than he.

I guess it must be the flag of my disposition, out of hopeful green stuff woven.

Or I guess it is the handkerchief of the Lord,
5 A scented gift and remembrancer designedly dropped,
Bearing the owner's name someway in the corners, that we may see and remark, and
   say *Whose?*

Or I guess the grass is itself a child, the produced babe of the vegetation.

Or I guess it is a uniform hieroglyphic,
And it means, Sprouting alike in broad zones and narrow zones,
10 Growing among black folks as among white,
Kanuck,° Tuckahoe, Congressman, Cuff, I give them the same, I receive them the
   same.
And now it seems to me the beautiful uncut hair of graves.

Tenderly will I use you curling grass,
It may be you transpire from the breasts of young men,
15 It may be if I had known them I would have loved them,
It may be you are from old people, or from offspring taken soon out of their
   mothers' laps,
And here you are the mothers' laps.

This grass is very dark to be from the white heads of old mothers.
Darker than the colorless beards of old men.
20 Dark to come from under the faint red roofs of mouths.

O I perceive after all so many uttering tongues,
And I perceive they do not come from the roofs of mouths for nothing.

---

11 **Kanuck** French-Canadian   **Tuckahoe** coastal Virginian   **Cuff** a black slave

I wish I could translate the hints about the dead young men and women.
And the hints about old men and mothers. and the offspring taken soon out of
   their laps.

25 What do you think has become of the young and old men? .
And what do you think has become of the women and children?

They are alive and well somewhere,
The smallest sprout shows there is really no death,
And if ever there was it led forward life, and does not wait at the end to arrest it.
30 And ceased the moment life appeared.

All goes onward and outward, nothing collapses.
And to die is different from what anyone supposed, and luckier.

                                 —1865

When I Heard the Learn'd Astronomer

When I heard the learn'd astronomer,
When the proofs, the figures, were ranged in columns before me,
When I was shown the charts and diagrams, to add, divide, and measure them,
When I sitting heard the astronomer where he lectured with much applause in the
   lecture-room,
5 How soon unaccountable I became tired and sick,
Till rising and gliding out I wander'd off by myself,
In the mystical moist night-air, and from time to time,
Look'd up in perfect silence at the stars.

                                   —1865

Matthew Arnold
(1822-1888)

Arnold, son of the headmaster of Rugby School, served as an
inspector of schools during much of his adult life. An influential
essayist as well as a poet, Arnold was unsparing in his criticism of
middle-class "Philistinism." At least part of "Dover Beach" is
thought to date from his honeymoon in 1851.

Dover Beach°

The sea is calm tonight.
The tide is full, the moon lies fair
Upon the straits; on the French coast the light
Gleams and is gone; the cliffs of England stand,
5   Glimmering and vast, out in the tranquil bay.
Come to the window, sweet is the night-air!
Only, from the long line of spray
Where the sea meets the moon-blanched land,
Listen! you hear the grating roar
10   Of pebbles which the waves draw back, and fling,
At their return, up the high strand,
Begin, and cease, and then again begin,
With tremulous cadence slow, and bring
The eternal note of sadness in.

15   Sophocles° long ago
Heard it on the Aegaean, and it brought
Into his mind the turbid ebb and flow
Of human misery; we
Find also in the sound a thought,
20   Hearing it by this distant northern sea.

The Sea of Faith
Was once, too, at the full, and round earth's shore
Lay like the folds of a bright girdle° furled.
But now I only hear
25   Its melancholy, long, withdrawing roar,
Retreating, to the breath
Of the night-wind, down the vast edges drear
And naked shingles° of the world.

Ah, love, let us be true
30   To one another! for the world, which seems
To lie before us like a land of dreams,
So various, so beautiful, so new,
Hath really neither joy, nor love, nor light,
Nor certitude, nor peace, nor help for pain;
35   And we are here as on a darkling plain
Swept with confused alarms of struggle and flight,
Where ignorant armies clash by night.

—1867

Dover Beach The poem was first composed on the poet's honeymoon in 1851   **15 Sophocles**
Athenian tragic poet (496-406 B.C.)   **23 girdle** sash   **28 shingles** beach-pebbles

Emily Dickinson
(1830-1886)

Each generation tries to reinvent Dickinson, and readers' views of
her have ranged between two extremes—one perceiving her
as the abnormally shy "Belle of Amherst" making poetry out of
her own neuroses and another seeing her as a proto-feminist
carving out a world of her own in self-willed isolation. What
remains is her brilliant poetry—unique, original, and marked with
the stamp of individual talent. Dickinson published only seven
poems during her lifetime, but left behind hundreds of poems in
manuscript at her death. Published by her relatives, they were
immediately popular, but it was not until the edition of Thomas
Johnson in 1955 that they were read with Dickinson's eccentric
punctuation and capitalization intact.

Because I Could Not Stop for Death

Because I could not stop for Death—
He kindly stopped for me—
The Carriage held but just Ourselves—
And Immortality.

5   We slowly drove—He knew no haste
And I had put away
My labor and my leisure too,
For His Civility—

We passed the School, where Children strove
10 At Recess—in the Ring—
We passed the Fields of Gazing Grain—
We passed the Setting Sun—

Or rather—He passed Us—
The Dews drew quivering and chill—
15 For only Gossamer, my Gown—
My Tippet°—only Tulle°—

We paused before a House that seemed
A Swelling of the Ground—

---

16 **Tippet** shawl **Tulle** net-like fabric

The Roof was scarcely visible—
20 The Cornice—in the Ground—

Since then—'tis Centuries—and yet
Feels shorter than the Day
I first surmised the Horses' Heads
Were toward Eternity—

—1890

I Died for Beauty—But Was Scarce

I died for Beauty—but was scarce
Adjusted in the Tomb
When One who died for Truth, was lain
In an adjoining Room—

5 He questioned softly "Why I failed?"
"For Beauty," I replied—
"And I—for Truth—Themself are One—
We Brethren, are," He said—

And so, as Kinsmen, met a Night—
10 We talked between the Rooms—
Until the Moss had reached our lips—
And covered up—our names—

—1890

I Heard a Fly Buzz—When I Died—

I heard a Fly buzz—when I died—
The Stillness in the Room
Was like the Stillness in the Air—
Between the Heaves of Storm—

5 The Eyes around—had wrung them dry—
And Breaths were gathering firm
For that last Onset—when the King
Be witnessed—in the Room—

I willed my Keepsakes—Signed away
10 What portion of me be
Assignable—and then it was
There interposed a Fly—

With Blue—uncertain stumbling Buzz—
Between the light—and me—
15   And then the Windows failed—and then
I could not see to see—

                                                    —1896

My Life Closed Twice Before Its Close

My life closed twice before its close;
It yet remains to see
If Immortality unveil
A third event to me,

5   So huge, so hopeless to conceive
As these that twice befell.
Parting is all we know of heaven,
And all we need of hell.

                                                    —1896

A Narrow Fellow in the Grass

A narrow Fellow in the Grass
Occasionally rides—
You may have met Him—did you not
His notice sudden is—

5   The Grass divides as with a Comb—
A spotted shaft is seen—
And then it closes at your feet
And opens further on—

He likes a Boggy Acre
10   A Floor to cool for Corn—
Yet when a Boy, and Barefoot—
I more than once at Noon
Have passed, I thought, a Whip lash
Unbraiding in the Sun
15   When stooping to secure it
It wrinkled, and was gone—

Several of Nature's People
I know, and they know me—

20   I feel for them a transport
Of cordiality—

But never met this Fellow
Attended, or alone
Without a tighter breathing
And Zero at the Bone—

—1866

The Soul Selects Her Own Society—

The Soul selects her own Society—
Then—shuts the Door—
To her divine Majority—
Present no more—

5   Unmoved—she notes the Chariots pausing—
At her low Gate—
Unmoved—an Emperor be kneeling
Upon her Mat—

I've known her—from an ample nation—
10   Choose One—
Then—close the Valves of her attention—
Like Stone—

—1890

Christina Rossetti
(1830-1894)

The younger sister of Dante Gabriel and William, also distin-
guished writers, Rossetti was the author of numerous devotional
poems and prose works. Her collected poems, edited by her
brother William, appeared posthumously in 1904.

Up-Hill

Does the road wind uphill all the way?
    Yes, to the very end.
Will the day's journey take the whole long day?
    From morn to night, my friend.

5   But is there for the night a resting-place?
        A roof for when the slow, dark hours begin.
    May not the darkness hide it from my face?
        You cannot miss that inn.

    Shall I meet other wayfarers at night?
10   Those who have gone before.
    Then must I knock, or call when just in sight?
        They will not keep you waiting at that door.

    Shall I find comfort, travel-sore and weak?
        Of labor you shall find the sum.
15 Will there be beds for me and all who seek?
        Yea, beds for all who come.

                                                   —1858

Thomas Hardy
(1840-1928)

After the disappointing response to his novel *Jude the Obscure* in 1895, Hardy returned to his first love, writing poetry for the last thirty years of his long life. The language and life of Hardy's native Wessex inform both his novels and poems. His subject matter is very much of the 19th century, but his ironic, disillusioned point of view mark him as one of the chief predecessors of modernism.

Ah, Are You Digging on My Grave?

    "Ah, are you digging on my grave
        My loved one?—planting rue?"°
    —"No: yesterday he went to wed
    One of the brightest wealth has bred.
5   'It cannot hurt her now,' he said,
        'That I should not be true.'"

    "Then who is digging on my grave?
        My nearest dearest kin?"
    —"Ah, no; they sit and think, 'What use!

---

2 rue yellow flower traditionally associated with sadness

10   What good will planting flowers produce?
No tendance of her mound can loose
      Her spirit from Death's gin.'"

"But some one digs upon my grave?
      My enemy?—prodding sly?"
15   —"Nay: when she heard you had passed the Gate
That shuts on all flesh soon or late.
She thought you no more worth her hate,
      And cares not where you lie."

"Then who is digging on my grave?
20   Say—since I have not guessed!"
—"O it is I, my mistress dear,
Your little dog, who still lives near,
And much I hope my movements here
      Have not disturbed your rest?"

25   "Ah, yes! *You* dig upon my grave . . .
      Why flashed it not on me
That one true heart was left behind!
What felling do we ever find
To equal among human kind
30   A dog's fidelity!"

"Mistress, I dug upon your grave
      To bury a bone, in case
I should be hungry near this spot
When passing on my daily trot.
35   I am sorry, but I quite forgot
      It was your resting-place."

                       —1914

Neutral Tones

We stood by a pond that winter day,
And the sun was white, as though chidden of God,
And a few leaves lay on the starving sod;
      —They had fallen from an ash, and were gray.

5   Your eyes on me were as eyes that rove
Over tedious riddles of years ago;
And some words played between us to and fro
      On which lost the more by our love.

The smile on your mouth was the deadest thing
10   Alive enough to have strength to die;
And a grin of bitterness swept thereby
          Like an ominous bird a-wing . . .

Since then, keen lessons that love deceives,
And wrings with wrong, have shaped to me
15   Your face, and the God-curst sun, and a tree,
          And a pond edged with grayish leaves.

                                        —1898

The Oxen

Christmas Eve, and twelve of the clock.
  "Now they are all on their knees,"°
An elder said as we sat in a flock
  By the embers in hearthside ease.

5   We pictured the meek and mild creatures where
  They dwelt in their strawy pen,
Nor did it occur to one of us there
  To doubt they were kneeling then.

So fair a fancy few would weave
10   In these years! Yet, I feel,
If someone said on Christmas Eve,
  "Come; see the oxen kneel,

"In the lonely barton° by yonder coomb°
  Our childhood used to know,"
15   I should go with him in the gloom,
  Hoping it might be so.

                                        —1917

The Ruined Maid

"O 'Melia, my dear, this does everything crown!
Who could have supposed I should meet you in Town?
And whence such fair garments, such prosperi-ty?"
"O didn't you know I'd been ruined?" said she.

---

2 **Now they are on their knees** folk belief that the oxen pray at the moment of Christ's birth
13 **barton** barnyard   **coomb** valley

5   "You left us in tatters, without shoes or socks,
    Tired of digging potatoes, and spudding up docks;°
    And now you've gay bracelets and bright feathers three!"
    "Yes: that's how we dress when we we're ruined," said she.

    "At home in the barton° you said 'thee' and 'thou,'
10   And 'thik oon,' and 'theäs oon,'° and 't'other'; but now
    Your talking quite fits 'ee for high compa-ny!"
    "Some polish is gained with one's ruin," said she.

    "Your hands were like paws then, your face blue and bleak
    But now I'm bewitched by your delicate cheek,
15   And your little gloves fit as on any la-dy!"
    "We never do work when we're ruined," said she.

    "You used to call home-life a hag-ridden dream,
    And you'd sigh, and you'd sock; but at present you seem
    To know not of megrims° or melancho-ly!"
20   "True. One's pretty lively when ruined," said she.

    "I wish I had feathers, a fine sweeping gown,
    And a delicate face, and could strut about Town!"
    "My dear—a raw country girl, such as you be,
    Cannot quite expect that. You ain't ruined," said she.

                            —1866

Gerard Manley Hopkins
(1844-1889)

Hopkins was an English Jesuit priest who developed elaborate theories of poetic meter (what he called "sprung rhythm") and language to express his own spiritual ardor. Most of his work was posthumously printed through the efforts of his Oxford friend and lifelong correspondent Robert Bridges, who was Poet Laureate.

God's Grandeur

The world is charged with the grandeur of God.

---

6 docks weeds   **9 barton** barnyard   **10 thik oon and theäs oon** dialect: "that one and this one"
19 megrims migraines

It will flame out, like shining from shook foil;°
It gathers to a greatness, like the ooze of oil
Crushed.° Why do men then now not reck his rod?
5   Generations have trod, have trod, have trod;
    And all is seared with trade; bleared, smeared with toil;
    And wears man's smudge and shares man's smell: the soil
Is bare now, nor can foot feel, being shod.

And for all this, nature is never spent;
10   There lives the dearest freshness deep down things;
And though the last lights off the black West went
    Oh, morning, at the brown brink eastward, springs—
Because the Holy Ghost over the bent
    World broods with warm breast and with ah! bright wings.

                             —1918

Pied Beauty

Glory be to God for dappled things—
    For skies of couple-color as a brinded° cow;
        For rose-moles all in stipple upon trout that swim;
Fresh-firecoal chestnut-falls;° finches' wings;
5   Landscape plotted and pieced—fold, fallow, and plough;
        And all trades, their gear and tackle and trim.
All things counter, original, spare, strange;
    Whatever is fickle, freckled (who knows how?)
        With swift, slow; sweet, sour; adazzle, dim;
10   He fathers-forth whose beauty is past change:
                 Praise him.

                             —1877

A. E. Housman
(1859-1936)

Educated in the classics at Oxford, Housman was almost forty
before he began to write verse seriously. His ballad-like poems
of Shropshire (an area in which he never actually lived) have
proven some of the most popular lyrics in English, despite their
pervasive mood of bittersweet pessimism.

---

2 **foil** gold leaf   4 **Crushed** Hopkins is referring to olive oil
2 **brinded** streaked   4 **Fresh-firecoal chestnut-falls** according to the poet, chestnuts have a red color

"Terence, This Is Stupid Stuff..."

"Terence, this is stupid stuff:
You eat your victuals fast enough;
There can't be much amiss, 'tis clear,
To see the rate you drink your beer.
5 But oh, good Lord, the verse you make,
It gives a chap the belly-ache.
The cow, the old cow, she is dead;
It sleeps well, the hornèd head:
We poor lads, 'tis our turn now
10 To hear such tunes as killed the cow.
Pretty friendship 'tis to rhyme
Your friends to death before their time
Moping melancholy mad:
Come, pipe a tune to dance to, lad."

15   Why, if 'tis dancing you would be,
There's brisker pipes than poetry.
Say, for what were hop-yards meant,
Or why was Burton built on Trent?°
Oh many a peer of England brews
20 Livelier liquor than the Muse,
And malt does more than Milton can
To justify God's ways to man.
Ale, man, ale's the stuff to drink
For fellows whom it hurts to think:
25 Look into the pewter pot
To see the world as the world's not.
And faith, 'tis pleasant till 'tis past:
The mischief is that 'twill not last.
Oh I have been to Ludlow fair
30 And left my necktie God knows where,
And carried halfway home, or near,
Pints and quarts of Ludlow beer:
Then the world seemed none so bad,
And I myself a sterling lad;
35 And down in lovely muck I've lain,
Happy till I woke again.
Then I saw the morning sky:
Heigho, the tale was all a lie;
The world, it was the old world yet,

---

18 **Burton built on Trent** site of breweries

40 I was I, my things were wet,
    And nothing now remained to do
    But begin the game anew.

    Therefore, since the world has still
    Much good, but much less good than ill,
45 And while the sun and moon endure
    Luck's a chance, but trouble's sure,
    I'd face it as a wise man would,
    And train for ill and not for good.
    'Tis true, the stuff I bring for sale
50 Is not so brisk a brew as ale:
    Out of a stem that scored the hand
    I wrung it in a weary land.
    But take it: if the smack is sour,
    The better for the embittered hour;
55 It should do good to heart and head
    When your soul is in my soul's stead;
    And I will friend you, if I may,
    In the dark and cloudy day.

    There was a king reigned in the East:
60 There, when kings will sit to feast,
    They get their fill before they think
    With poisoned meat and poisoned drink.
    He gathered all that springs to birth
    From the many-venomed earth;
65 First a little, thence to more,
    He sampled all her killing store;
    An easy, smiling, seasoned sound,
    Sate the king when healths went round.
    They put arsenic in his meat
70 And stared aghast to watch him eat;
    They poured strychnine in his cup
    And shook to see him drink it up:
    They shook, they stared as white's their shirt:
    Them it was their poison hurt.
75 —I tell the tale that I heard told.
    Mithridates,° he died old.

                                        —1896

---

76 Mithradates legendary King of Pontus, he protected himself from poisons by taking small doses
regularly

Eight O'Clock

He stood, and heard the steeple
   Sprinkle the quarters° on the morning town.
One, two, three, four, to market-place and people
   It tossed them down.

5 Strapped, noosed, nighing his hour,
   He stood and counted them and cursed his luck;
And then the clock collected in the tower
   Its strength, and struck.

—1922

Is My Team Plowing

"Is my team plowing,
   That I was used to drive
And hear the harness jingle
   When I was man alive?"

5 Ay the horses trample,
   The harness jingles now;
No change though you lie under
   The land you used to plow.

"Is football playing
10   Along the river shore,
With lads to chase the leather,
   Now I stand up no more?"

Ay, the ball is flying,
   The lads play heart and soul;
15 The goal stands up, the keeper
   Stands up to keep the goal.

"Is my girl happy,
   That I thought hard to leave,
And has she tired of weeping
20   As she lies down at eve?"

---

2 quarters quarter hours

Ay, she lies down lightly,
   She lies not down to weep
Your girl is well contented
   Be still, my lad, and sleep.

25   "Is my friend hearty,
   Now I am thin and pine,
And has he found to sleep in
   A better bed than mine?"

Yes, lad, I lie easy,
30   I lie as lads would choose;
I cheer a dead man's sweetheart,
   Never ask me whose.

—1896

Loveliest of Trees, the Cherry Now

Loveliest of trees, the cherry now
Is hung with bloom along the bough,
And stands about the woodland ride
Wearing white for Eastertide.

5 Now, of my threescore years and ten,
Twenty will not come again,
And take from seventy springs a score,
It only leaves me fifty more.

And since to look at things in bloom
10 Fifty springs are little room,
About the woodlands I will go
To see the cherry hung with snow.

—1896

Rudyard Kipling
(1865-1936)

To pigeonhole Kipling as a simple-minded advocate of British imperialism is to disregard the considerable talents as poet and fiction writer that won him one of the first Nobel Prizes for literature. Best known for his dialect ballads of English military life in far-flung colonial posts, he was also an excellent writer of lyrics.

When Earth's Last Picture Is Painted

L'Envoi° to "The Seven Seas"

When Earth's last picture is painted and the tubes are twisted and dried,
When the oldest colors have faded, and the youngest critic has died,
We shall rest, and, faith, we shall need it—lie down for an æon or two,
Till the Master of All Good Workmen shall put us to work anew.

5 And those that were good shall be happy: they shall sit in a golden chair;
They shall splash at a ten-league canvas with brushes of comets' hair.
They shall find real saints to draw from—Magdalene, Peter, and Paul;
They shall work for an age at a sitting and never be tired at all!

And only The Master shall praise us, and only The Master shall blame;
And no one shall work for money, and no one shall work for fame,
But each for the joy of the working, and each, in his separate star,
10 Shall draw the Thing as he sees It for the God of Things as They are!
                                                        —1892

William Butler Yeats
(1865-1939)

Yeats is the greatest Irish poet and provides an important link
between the late Romantic era and early modernism. His early
poetry, focusing on Irish legend and landscape, is regional in the
best sense of the term, but his later work, with its prophetic tone
and symbolist texture, moves on a larger stage. Yeats lived in
London for many years and was at the center of British literary
life. He was awarded the Nobel prize in 1923.

The Lake Isle of Innisfree

I will arise and go now, and go to Innisfree,
And a small cabin build there, of clay and wattles° made:
Nine bean-rows will I have there, a hive for the honey-bee,
And live alone in the bee-loud glade.

5 And I shall have some peace there, for peace comes dropping slow,
Dropping from the veils of the morning to where the cricket sings;

L'Envoi closing summary
2 wattles woven poles and reeds

There midnight's all a glimmer, and noon a purple glow,
And evening full of the linnet's wings.

And I will arise and go now, for always night and day
10   I hear the lake water lapping with low sounds by the shore;
While I stand on the roadway, or on the pavements gray,
I hear it in the deep heart's core.

—1892

Leda° and the Swan

A sudden blow: the great wings beating still
Above the staggering girl, her thighs caressed
By the dark webs, her nape caught in his bill,
He holds her helpless breast upon his breast.

5   How can those terrified vague fingers push
The feathered glory from her loosening thighs?
And how can body, laid in that white rush,
But feel the strange heart beating where it lies?

A shudder in the loins engenders there
10   The broken wall, the burning roof and tower
And Agamemnon dead.°
                        Being so caught up,
So mastered by the brute blood of the air,
Did she put on his knowledge with his power
Before the indifferent beak could let her drop?

—1923

Sailing to Byzantium°

1

That is no country for old men. The young
In one another's arms, birds in the trees
—Those dying generations—at their song,
The salmon-falls, the mackerel-crowded seas,
5   Fish, flesh, or fowl, commend all summer long
Whatever is begotten, born, and dies.
Caught in that sensual music all neglect

Leda mortal mother of Helen of Troy and Clytemnestra, wife and assassin of Agamemnon   **10-11 The broken wall . . . Agamemnon dead** events during and after the Trojan War
Byzantium Constantinople or Istanbul, capital of the Eastern Roman Empire

Monuments of unaging intellect.

2

An aged man is but a paltry thing,
10 A tattered coat upon a stick, unless
Soul clap its hands and sing, and louder sing
For every tatter in its mortal dress,
Nor is there singing school but studying
Monuments of its own magnificence;
15 And therefore I have sailed the seas and come
To the holy city of Byzantium.

3

O sages standing in God's holy fire
As in the gold mosaic of a wall,
Come from the holy fire, perne in a gyre,°
20 And be the singing-masters of my soul.
Consume my heart away; sick with desire
And fastened to a dying animal
It knows not what it is; and gather me
Into the artifice of eternity.

4

25 Once out of nature I shall never take
My bodily form from any natural thing,
But such a form as Grecian goldsmiths make
Of hammered gold and gold enameling
To keep a drowsy Emperor awake;
30 Or set upon a golden bough to sing
To lords and ladies of Byzantium
Of what is past, or passing, or to come.

—1927

The Second Coming

Turning and turning in the widening gyre°
The falcon cannot hear the falconer;
Things fall apart; the center cannot hold;
Mere anarchy is loosed upon the world,
5 The blood-dimmed tide is loosed, and everywhere
The ceremony of innocence is drowned;

---

19 perne in a gyre descend in a spiral; the gyre for Yeats was a private symbol of historical cycles
1 gyre see note to "Sailing to Byzantium"

The best lack all conviction, while the worst
Are full of passionate intensity.

Surely some revelation is at hand;
10   Surely the Second Coming is at hand.
The Second Coming! Hardly are those words out
When a vast image out of *Spiritus Mundi*°
Troubles my sight: somewhere in the sands of the desert
A shape with lion body and the head of a man,
15   A gaze blank and pitiless as the sun,
Is moving its slow thighs, while all about it
Reel shadows of the indignant desert birds.
The darkness drops again; but now I know
That twenty centuries of stony sleep
20   Were vexed to nightmare by a rocking cradle,
And what rough beast, its hour come round at last,
Slouches towards Bethlehem to be born?

—1921

✧ ✧ ✧

Edwin Arlington Robinson
(1869-1935)

Robinson's poems set in "Tilbury," a recreation of his hometown
of Gardiner, Maine, continue to present readers with a memo-
rable cast of eccentric characters who somehow manifest uni-
versal human desires. Robinson languished in poverty and ob-
scurity for many years before his reputation began to flourish as
a result of the interest taken in his work by President Theodore
Roosevelt, who obtained a government job for Robinson and
wrote a favorable review of one of his books.

Firelight

Ten years together without yet a cloud,
They seek each other's eyes at intervals
Of gratefulness to firelight and four walls
For love's obliteration of the crowd.
5   Serenely and perennially endowed
And bowered as few may be, their joy recalls
No snake, no sword, and over them there falls

---

12 *Spiritus Mundi* World-Spirit

The blessing of what neither says aloud.

Wiser for silence, they were not so glad
10 Were she to read the graven° tale of lines
On the wan face of one somewhere alone;
Nor were they more content could he have had
Her thoughts a moment since of one who shines
Apart, and would be hers if he had known.

—1920

The Mill

The miller's wife had waited long,
    The tea was cold, the fire was dead;
And there might yet be nothing wrong
    In how he went and what he said:
5 "There are no millers any more,"
    Was all that she had heard him say;
And he had lingered at the door
    So long that it seemed yesterday.

Sick with a fear that had no form
10 She knew that she was there at last;
And in the mill there was a warm
    And mealy fragrance of the past.
What else there was would only seem
    To say again what he had meant;
15 And what was hanging from a beam
    Would not have heeded where she went.

And if she thought it followed her,
    She may have reasoned in the dark
That one way of the few there were
20 Would hide her and would leave no mark:
Black water, smooth above the weir
    Like starry velvet in the night,
Though ruffled once, would soon appear
    The same as ever to the sight.

—1920

Richard Cory

Whenever Richard Cory went down town,

---

10 graven engraved

We people on the pavement looked at him:
He was a gentleman from sole to crown,
Clean favored, and imperially slim.

5   And he was always quietly arrayed,
And he was always human when he talked;
But still he fluttered pulses when he said,
"Good-morning," and he glittered when he walked.

And he was rich—yes, richer than a king—
10 And admirably schooled in every grace:
In fine, we thought that he was everything
To make us wish that we were in his place.

So on we worked, and waited for the light,
And went without the meat, and cursed the bread;
15 And Richard Cory, one calm summer night,
Went home and put a bullet through his head.

—1896

Stephen Crane
(1871-1900)

The brilliant young journalist who wrote *The Red Badge of
Courage* was also an unconventional poet whose skeptical
epigrams and fables today seem far ahead of their time. In
many ways he mirrors the cosmic pessimism of contemporaries
like Hardy, Housman, and Robinson, all of whom were influenced
by the currents of Determinism that ran so strongly at the end of
the nineteenth century.

from The Black Riders

VI

God fashioned the ship of the world carefully.
With the infinite skill of an All-Master
Made He the hull and the sails,
Held He the rudder
5   Ready for adjustment.
Erect stood He, scanning His work proudly.
Then—at fateful time—a wrong called,
And God turned, heeding.

      Lo, the ship, at this opportunity, slipped slyly,
10   Making cunning noiseless travel down the ways.
      So that, for ever rudderless, it went upon the seas
      Going ridiculous voyages,
      Making quaint progress,
      Turning as with serious purpose
15   Before stupid winds.
      And there were many in the sky
      Who laughed at this thing.

—1895

from War Is Kind

XXI

A man said to the universe:
"Sir, I exist!"
"However," replied the universe,
"The fact has not created in me
5   A sense of obligation."

—1899

Paul Laurence Dunbar
(1872-1906)

A native of Dayton, Ohio, Dunbar was one of the first black
poets to make a mark in American literature. Many of his dialect
poems reflect a sentimentalized view of life in the South, which
he did not know directly. However, he was also capable of
powerful expressions of racial protest.

We Wear the Mask

We wear the mask that grins and lies,
It hides our cheeks and shades our eyes—
This debt we pay to human guile;
With torn and bleeding hearts we smile,
5   And mouth with myriad subtleties.

Why should the world be over-wise,
In counting all our tears and sighs?
Nay, let them only see us, while

We wear the mask.

10 We smile, but, O great Christ, our cries
To thee from tortured souls arise.
We sing, but oh the clay is vile
Beneath our feet, and long the mile;
But let the world dream otherwise,
15   We wear the mask!

—1896

Robert Frost
(1874-1963)

During the second half of his long life, Frost was a public figure
who attained a popularity unmatched by any American poet of
this century. His reading at the inauguration of John F. Kennedy in
1961 capped an impressive career that included four Pulitzer
prizes. Unattracted by the more exotic aspects of modernism,
Frost nevertheless remains a poet who speaks eloquently to
contemporary uncertainties about humanity's place in a universe
that does not seem to care much for its existence. While Frost is
rarely directly an autobiographical poet ("The Road Not Taken"
was intended to be about a friend, English poet Edward Thomas)
his work always bears the stamp of his powerful personality and
identification with the New England landscape.

Acquainted with the Night

I have been one acquainted with the night.
I have walked out in rain—and back in rain.
I have outwalked the furthest city light.

I have looked down the saddest city lane.
5 I have passed by the watchman on his beat
And dropped my eyes, unwilling to explain.

I have stood still and stopped the sound of feet
When far away an interrupted cry
Came over houses from another street,

10 But not to call me back or say good-by;
And further still at an unearthly height
One luminary clock against the sky

Proclaimed the time was neither wrong nor right.
I have been one acquainted with the night.

—1928

Design

I found a dimpled spider, fat and white,
On a white heal-all,° holding up a moth
Like a white piece of rigid satin cloth—
Assorted characters of death and blight
5   Mixed ready to begin the morning right,
Like the ingredients of a witches' broth—
A snow-drop spider, a flower like a froth,
And dead wings carried like a paper kite.

What had that flower to do with being white,
10 The wayside blue and innocent heal-all?
What brought the kindred spider to that height,
Then steered the white moth thither in the night?
What but design of darkness to appall?—
If design govern in a thing so small.

—1936

Home Burial

He saw her from the bottom of the stairs
Before she saw him. She was starting down,
Looking back over her shoulder at some fear.
She took a doubtful step and then undid it
5   To raise herself and look again. He spoke
Advancing toward her: "What is it you see
From up there always?—for I want to know."
She turned and sank upon her skirts at that,
And her face changed from terrified to dull.
10 He said to gain time: "What is it you see?"
Mounting until she cowered under him.
"I will find out now—you must tell me, dear."
She, in her place, refused him any help,
With the least stiffening of her neck and silence.
15 She let him look, sure that he wouldn't see,

---

2 **heal-all** a wildflower, usually blue

Blind creature; and awhile he didn't see.
But at last he murmured, "Oh," and again, "Oh."

"What is it—what?" she said.

            "Just that I see."

"You don't," she challenged. "Tell me what it is."

20   "The wonder is I didn't see at once.
I never noticed it from here before.
I must be wonted to it—that's the reason.
The little graveyard where my people are!
So small the window frames the whole of it.
25   Not so much larger than a bedroom, is it?
There are three stones of slate and one of marble,
Broad-shouldered little slabs there in the sunlight
On the sidehill. We haven't to mind *those*.

But I understand: it is not the stones,
But the child's mound—"

30   "Don't, don't, don't, don't," she cried.

She withdrew, shrinking from beneath his arm
That rested on the banister, and slid downstairs;
And turned on him with such a daunting look,
He said twice over before he knew himself:
35   "Can't a man speak of his own child he's lost?"

"Not you!—Oh, where's my hat? Oh, I don't need it!
I must get out of here. I must get air.—
I don't know rightly whether any man can."

"Amy! Don't go to someone else this time.
40   Listen to me. I won't come down the stairs."
He sat and fixed his chin between his fists.
"There's something I should like to ask you, dear."

"You don't know how to ask it."

            "Help me, then."

Her fingers moved the latch for all reply.

45 "My words are nearly always an offense.
I don't know how to speak of anything
So as to please you. But I might be taught,
I should suppose. I can't say I see how.
A man must partly give up being a man
50 With womenfolk. We could have some arrangement
By which I'd bind myself to keep hands off
Anything special you're a-mind to name.
Though I don't like such things 'twixt those that love.
Two that don't love can't live together without them.
55 But two that do can't live together with them."
She moved the latch a little. "Don't—don't go.
Don't carry it to someone else this time.
Tell me about it if it's something human.
Let me into your grief. I'm not so much
60 Unlike other folks as your standing there
Apart would make me out. Give me my chance.
I do think, though, you overdo it a little.
What was it brought you up to think it the thing
To take your mother-loss of a first child
65 So inconsolably—in the face of love.
You'd think his memory might be satisfied—"

"There you go sneering now!"

              "I'm not, I'm not!
You make me angry. I'll come down to you.
God, what a woman! And it's come to this,
70 A man can't speak of his own child that's dead."

"You can't because you don't know how to speak.
If you had any feelings, you that dug
With your own hand—how could you?—his little grave;
I saw you from that very window there,
75 Making the gravel leap and leap in air,
Leap up, like that, like that, and land so lightly
And roll back down the mound beside the hole.
I thought, Who is that man? I didn't know you.
And I crept down the stairs and up the stairs
80 To look again, and still your spade kept lifting.
Then you came in. I heard your rumbling voice
Out in the kitchen, and I don't know why,
But I went near to see with my own eyes.

You could sit there with the stains on your shoes
85   Of the fresh earth from your own baby's grave
And talk about your everyday concerns.
You had stood the spade up against the wall
Outside there in the entry, for I saw it."

"I shall laugh the worst laugh I ever laughed.
90   I'm cursed. God, if I don't believe I'm cursed."

"I can repeat the very words you were saying:
'Three foggy mornings and one rainy day
Will rot the best birch fence a man can build.'
Think of it, talk like that at such a time!
95   What had how long it takes a birch to rot
To do with what was in the darkened parlor?
You *couldn't* care! The nearest friends can go
With anyone to death, comes so far short
They might as well not try to go at all.
100 No, from the time when one is sick to death,
One is alone, and he dies more alone.
Friends make pretense of following to the grave,
But before one is in it, their minds are turned
And making the best of their way back to life
105 And living people, and things they understand.
But the world's evil. I won't have grief so
If I can change it. Oh, I won't, I won't!"

"There, you have said it all and you feel better.
You won't go now. You're crying. Close the door.
110 The heart's gone out of it: why keep it up?
Amy! There's someone coming down the road!"

"*You*—oh, you think the talk is all. I must go—
Somewhere out of this house. How can I make you—"

"If—you—do!" She was opening the door wider.
115 "Where do you mean to go? First tell me that.
I'll follow and bring you back by force. I *will!*—"

                                                          —1914

The Road Not Taken

Two roads diverged in a yellow wood,
And sorry I could not travel both

And be one traveler, long I stood
And looked down one as far as I could
5   To where it bent in the undergrowth;

Then took the other, as just as fair,
And having perhaps the better claim,
Because it was grassy and wanted wear;
Though as for that the passing there
10   Had worn them really about the same,

And both that morning equally lay
In leaves no step had trodden black.
Oh, I kept the first for another day!
Yet knowing how way leads on to way,
15   I doubted if I should ever come back.

I shall be telling this with a sigh
Somewhere ages and ages hence:
Two roads diverged in a wood, and I—
I took the one less traveled by,
20   And that has made all the difference.

—1916

Stopping by Woods on a Snowy Evening

Whose woods these are I think I know.
His house is in the village though;
He will not see me stopping here
To watch his woods fill up with snow.

5   My little horse must think it queer
To stop without a farmhouse near
Between the woods and frozen lake
The darkest evening of the year.

He gives his harness bells a shake
10   To ask if there is some mistake.
The only other sound's the sweep
Of easy wind and downy flake.

The woods are lovely, dark and deep,
But I have promises to keep,
15   And miles to go before I sleep,
And miles to go before I sleep.

—1923

Carl Sandburg
(1878-1967)

Like Frost, Sandburg was a visible presence in American life for
many years, not only as a poet but as the popular biographer of
Lincoln and as a collector and performer of folk songs. A mid-
westerner, many of his early poems seem a continuation of the
poetic tradition begun by Whitman.

Grass

Pile the bodies high at Austerlitz and Waterloo.°
Shovel them under and let me work—
      I am the grass; I cover all.

And pile them high at Gettysburg°
5 And pile them high at Ypres and Verdun.°
Shovel them under and let me work.
Two years, ten years, and passengers ask the conductor:
      What place is this?
      Where are we now?

10   I am the grass.
      Let me work.

                        —1918

Wallace Stevens
(1879-1955)

A lawyer specializing in surety bonds, Stevens rose to be a vice-
president of the Hartford Accident and Indemnity Company. His
poetry was collected for the first time in *Harmonium* when he was
forty-five, and, while he published widely during his lifetime, his
poetry was only slowly recognized as the work of a major
modernist whose originality has not been surpassed. Stevens's
idea of poetry as a force taking the place of religion has had a
profound influence on poets and critics of this century.

---

1 Austerlitz and Waterloo sites of battles in Napoleonic Wars **4 Gettysburg** battle in U.S. Civil
War **5 Ypres and Verdun** World War I battlefields

Anecdote of the Jar

I placed a jar in Tennessee,
And round it was, upon a hill.
It made the slovenly wilderness
Surround that hill.

5   The wilderness rose up to it,
And sprawled around, no longer wild.
The jar was round upon the ground
And tall and of a port in air.

10   It took dominion everywhere.
The jar was gray and bare.
It did not give of bird or bush,
Like nothing else in Tennessee.

                                                      —1923

Disillusionment of Ten O'Clock

The houses are haunted
By white night-gowns.
None are green,
Or purple with green rings,
5   Or green with yellow rings,
Or yellow with blue rings.
None of them are strange,
With socks of lace
And beaded ceintures.°
10   People are not going
To dream of baboons and periwinkles.°
Only, here and there, an old sailor,
Drunk and asleep in his boots,
Catches tigers
15   In red weather.

                                                      —1923

The Snow Man

One must have a mind of winter
To regard the frost and the boughs

---

9 ceintures sashes   **11 periwinkles** either small sea-snails or blue flowers

Of the pine-trees crusted with snow;

And have been cold a long time
5   To behold the junipers shagged with ice,
The spruces rough in the distant glitter

Of the January sun; and not to think
Of any misery in the sound of the wind,
In the sound of a few leaves,

10   Which is the sound of the land
Full of the same wind
That is blowing in the same bare place

For the listener, who listens in the snow,
And, nothing himself, beholds
15   Nothing that is not there and the nothing that is.

—1923

Sunday Morning

I

Complacencies of the peignoir,° and late
Coffee and oranges in a sunny chair,
And the green freedom of a cockatoo
Upon a rug mingle to dissipate
5   The holy hush of ancient sacrifice.
She dreams a little, and she feels the dark
Encroachment of that old catastrophe,
As a calm darkens among water-lights.
The pungent oranges and bright, green wings
10   Seem things in some procession of the dead,
Winding across wide water, without sound.
The day is like wide water, without sound,
Stilled for the passing of her dreaming feet
Over the seas, to silent Palestine,
15   Dominion of the blood and sepulchre.

II

Why should she give her bounty to the dead?
What is divinity if it can come
Only in silent shadows and in dreams?

---

1 **peignoir** woman's dressing gown

Shall she not find in comforts of the sun,
20   In pungent fruit and bright, green wings, or else
In any balm or beauty of the earth,
Things to be cherished like the thought of heaven?
Divinity must live within herself:
Passions of rain, or moods in falling snow;
25   Grievings in loneliness, or unsubdued
Elations when the forest blooms; gusty
Emotions on wet roads on autumn nights;
All pleasures and all pains, remembering
The bough of summer and the winter branch.
30   These are the measures destined for her soul.

III

Jove° in the clouds had his inhuman birth.
No mother suckled him, no sweet land gave
Large-mannered motions to his mythy mind.
He moved among us, as a muttering king,
35   Magnificent, would move among his hinds,°
Until our blood, commingling, virginal,
With heaven, brought such requital to desire
The very hinds discerned it, in a star.
Shall our blood fail? Or shall it come to be
40   The blood of paradise? And shall the earth
Seem all of paradise that we shall know?
The sky will be much friendlier then than now,
A part of labor and a part of pain,
And next in glory to enduring love,
45   Not this dividing and indifferent blue.

IV

She says, "I am content when wakened birds,
Before they fly, test the reality
Of misty fields, by their sweet questionings;
But when the birds are gone, and their warm fields
50   Return no more, where, then, is paradise?"
There is not any haunt of prophecy,
Nor any old chimera° of the grave,
Neither the golden underground, nor isle
Melodious, where spirits gat them home,
55   Nor visionary south, nor cloudy palm
Remote on heaven's hill, that has endured

---

31 Jove Roman name of Zeus **35 hinds** inferiors or shepherds (see l. 38) **52 chimera** imagined
monster

As April's green endures; or will endure
Like her remembrance of awakened birds,
Or her desire for June and evening, tipped
60   By the consummation of the swallow's wings.

V

She says, "But in contentment I still feel
The need of some imperishable bliss."
Death is the mother of beauty; hence from her,
Alone, shall come fulfilment to our dreams
65   And our desires. Although she strews the leaves
Of sure obliteration on our paths,
The path sick sorrow took, the many paths
Where triumph rang its brassy phrase, or love
Whispered a little out of tenderness,
70   She makes the willow shiver in the sun
For maidens who were wont to sit and gaze
Upon the grass, relinquished to their feet.
She causes boys to pile new plums and pears
On disregarded plate.° The maidens taste
75   And stray impassioned in the littering leaves.

VI

Is there no change of death in paradise?
Does ripe fruit never fall? Or do the boughs
Hang always heavy in that perfect sky,
Unchanging, yet so like our perishing earth,
80   With rivers like our own that seek for seas
They never find, the same receding shores
That never touch with inarticulate pang?
Why set the pear upon those river-banks
Or spice the shores with odors of the plum?
85   Alas, that they should wear our colors there,
The silken weavings of our afternoons,
And pick the strings of our insipid lutes!
Death is the mother of beauty, mystical,
Within whose burning bosom we devise
90   Our earthly mothers waiting, sleeplessly.

VII

Supple and turbulent, a ring of men
Shall chant in orgy on a summer morn

---

74 **plate** dinnerware

Their boisterous devotion to the sun,
Not as a god, but as a god might be,
95 Naked among them, like a savage source.
Their chant shall be a chant of paradise,
Out of their blood, returning to the sky;
And in their chant shall enter, voice by voice,
The windy lake wherein their lord delights,
100 The trees, like serafin,° and echoing hills,
That choir among themselves long afterward.
They shall know well the heavenly fellowship
Of men that perish and of summer morn.
And whence they came and whither they shall go
105 The dew upon their feet shall manifest.

VIII

She hears, upon that water without sound,
A voice that cries, "The tomb in Palestine
Is not the porch of spirits lingering.
It is the grave of Jesus, where he lay."
110 We live in an old chaos of the sun,
Or old dependency of day and night,
Or island solitude, unsponsored, free,
Of that wide water, inescapable.
Deer walk upon our mountains, and the quail
115 Whistle about us their spontaneous cries;
Sweet berries ripen in the wilderness;
And, in the isolation of the sky,
At evening, casual flocks of pigeons make
Ambiguous undulations as they sink,
120 Downward to darkness, on extended wings.

—1923

William Carlos Williams
(1883-1963)

Like his friend Wallace Stevens, Williams followed an unconventional career, working until his death as a pediatrician in Rutherford, New Jersey. Williams is modern poetry's greatest proponent of the American idiom. His plain-spoken poems have been more widely imitated than those of any other American

---

100 serafin seraphim, a type of angel

poet of this century, perhaps because he represents a home-grown modernist alternative to the intellectualized Europeanism of T. S. Eliot and Ezra Pound (a friend of his from college days). In his later years Williams assisted many younger poets, among them Allen Ginsberg, for whose controversial book *Howl* he wrote an introduction.

The Last Words of My English Grandmother

There were some dirty plates
and a glass of milk
beside her on a small table
near the rank, disheveled bed—

5   Wrinkled and nearly blind
she lay and snored
rousing with anger in her tones
to cry for food,

Gimme something to eat—
10 They're starving me—
I'm all right—I won't go
to the hospital. No, no, no

Give me something to eat!
Let me take you
15 to the hospital, I said
and after you are well

you can do as you please.
She smiled, Yes
you do what you please first
20 then I can do what I please—

Oh, oh, oh! she cried
as the ambulance men lifted
her to the stretcher—
Is this what you call

25 making me comfortable?
By now her mind was clear—
Oh you think you're smart
you young people,

she said, but I'll tell you

30 you don't know anything.
   Then we started.
   On the way

—1920

The Red Wheelbarrow

so much depends
upon

a red wheel
barrow

5 glazed with rain
water

beside the white
chickens.

—1923

Spring and All

By the road to the contagious hospital°
under the surge of the blue
mottled clouds driven from the
northeast—a cold wind. Beyond, the
5 waste of broad, muddy fields
brown with dried weeds, standing and fallen

patches of standing water
the scattering of tall trees
All along the road the reddish
10 purplish, forked, upstanding, twiggy
stuff of bushes and small trees
with dead, brown leaves under them
leafless vines—

Lifeless in appearance, sluggish
15 dazed spring approaches—

They enter the new world naked,

---

1 **contagious hospital** a hospital for quarantined patients

cold, uncertain of all
save that they enter. All about them
the cold, familiar wind—

20 Now the grass, tomorrow
the stiff curl of wildcarrot leaf
One by one objects are defined—
It quickens: clarity, outline of leaf

But now the stark dignity of
25 entrance—Still, the profound change
has come upon them: rooted, they
grip down and begin to awaken

—1923

✧   ✧   ✧

D. H. Lawrence
(1885-1930)

The child of a Nottinghamshire coal miner, Lawrence's greatest
fame was as a controversial novelist (*Sons and Lovers*, *Women
in Love*, *The Rainbow*, and *Lady Chatterley's Lover* are among
his best-known works) and as a prophet of liberated sexuality.
He was also a prolific and accomplished poet. Many of his
poems deal with the same themes as his fiction, and they display
a range of formal strategies from traditional forms to free verse.

Piano

Softly, in the dusk, a woman is singing to me;
Taking me back down the vista of years, till I see
A child sitting under the piano, in the boom of the tingling strings
And pressing the small, poised feet of a mother who smiles as she sings.

5 In spite of myself, the insidious mastery of song
Betrays me back, till the heart of me weeps to belong
To the old Sunday evenings at home, with winter outside
And hymns in the cosy parlor, the tinkling piano our guide.

So now it is vain for the singer to burst into clamour
10 With the great black piano appassionato.° The glamour

---

10 appassionato with passion

Of childish days is upon me, my manhood is cast
Down in the flood of remembrance, I weep like a child for the past.

—1918

Ezra Pound
(1885-1972)

Pound was the greatest international proponent of modern poetry. Born in Idaho and reared in Philadelphia, he emigrated to England in 1909, where he befriended Yeats, promoted the early work of Frost, and discovered Eliot. Pound's early promotion of the Imagist movement assisted a number of important poetic principles and reputations, including those of H. D. and, later, William Carlos Williams. Pound's support of Mussolini during World War II, expressed in controversial radio broadcasts, caused him to be held for over a decade after the war as a mental patient in the United States, after which he returned to Italy for the final years of his long and controversial life.

The River-Merchant's Wife: A Letter°

While my hair was still cut straight across my forehead
I played about the front gate, pulling flowers.
You came by on bamboo stilts, playing horse,
You walked about my seat, playing with blue plums.
5   And we went on living in the village of Chokan:
Two small people, without dislike or suspicion.

At fourteen I married My Lord you.
I never laughed, being bashful.
Lowering my head, I looked at the wall.
10   Called to, a thousand times, I never looked back.

At fifteen I stopped scowling,
I desired my dust to be mingled with yours
Forever and forever and forever.
Why should I climb the lookout?

15   At sixteen you departed,
You went into far Ku-tō-en, by the river of swirling eddies,
And you have been gone five months.

The River-Merchant's Wife: A Letter translation of a poem by Li-Po (701-762)

The monkeys make sorrowful noise overhead.

You dragged your feet when you went out.
20   By the gate now, the moss is grown, the different mosses,
Too deep to clear them away!
The leaves fall early this autumn, in wind.
The paired butterflies are already yellow with August
Over the grass in the West garden;
25   They hurt me. I grow older.
If you are coming down through the narrows of the river Kiang,
Please let me know beforehand,
And I will come out to meet you
              As far as Chō-fū-Sa.

                                        —1915

Sestina: Altaforte

LOQUITUR:° En *Bertrans de Born.*°
  Dante Alighieri put this man in hell for that he was a stirrer up of strife.
  Eccovi!°
  Judge ye!
  Have I dug him up again?
The scene is at his castle, Altaforte. "Papiols" is his jongleur.°
"The Leopard," the device *of Richard Cœur de Lion.*°

I

Damn it all! all this our South stinks peace.
You whoreson dog, Papiols, come! Let's to music!
I have no life save when the swords clash.
But ah! when I see the standards gold, vair,° purple, opposing
5   And the broad fields beneath them turn crimson,
Then howl I my heart nigh mad with rejoicing.

II

In hot summer have I great rejoicing
When the tempests kill the earth's foul peace,
And the lightnings from black heav'n flash crimson,
10   And the fierce thunders roar me their music
And the winds shriek through the clouds mad, opposing,
And through all the riven skies God's swords clash.

Loquitur speaker   **Bertrans de Born** Provencal poet and soldier (1140-1209)   **Eccovi!** Behold!
jongleur minstrel   **Richard Coeur de Lion** Richard I of England, the Lion-Hearted (1157-1199)
4 vair fur used in heraldry

III

Hell grant soon we hear again the swords clash!
And the shrill neighs of destriers° in battle rejoicing,
15 Spiked breast to spiked breast opposing!
Better one hour's stour° than a year's peace
With fat boards, bawds, wine and frail music!
Bah! there's no wine like the blood's crimson!

IV

And I love to see the sun rise blood-crimson.
20 And I watch his spears through the dark clash
And it fills all my heart with rejoicing
And pries wide my mouth with fast music
When I see him so scorn and defy peace,
His lone might 'gainst all darkness opposing.

V

25 The man who fears war and squats opposing
My words for stour, hath no blood of crimson
But is fit only to rot in womanish peace
Far from where worth's won and the swords clash
For the death of such sluts I go rejoicing;
30 Yea, I fill all the air with my music.

VI

Papiols, Papiols, to the music!
There's no sound like to swords swords opposing,
No cry like the battle's rejoicing
When our elbows and swords drip the crimson
35 And our charges 'gainst "The Leopard's" rush clash.
May God damn for ever all who cry "Peace!"

VII

And let the music of the swords make them crimson!
Hell grant soon we hear again the swords clash!
Hell blot black for alway the thought "Peace"!

—1909

H. D. (Hilda Doolittle)
(1886-1961)

Born in Bethlehem, Pennsylvania, Hilda Doolittle was a college

---

14 destriers war-horses   **16 stour** combat

friend of both Williams and Pound, and moved to Europe per-
manently in 1911. With her husband Richard Aldington, H.D. was
an important member of the Imagist group promoted by Pound.

Pear Tree

Silver dust,
lifted from the earth,
higher than my arms reach,
you have mounted,
5   O, silver,
higher than my arms reach,
you front us with great mass;

no flower ever opened
so staunch a white leaf,
10 no flower ever parted silver
from such rare silver;

O, white pear,
your flower-tufts
thick on the branch
15 bring summer and ripe fruits
in their purple hearts.

—1916

Siegfried Sassoon
(1886-1967)

A decorated hero who publicly denounced World War I,
Sassoon was a friend and supporter of other British war poets,
including Robert Graves and Wilfred Owen. His sardonic, anti-
heroic war poems owe much to Thomas Hardy, whom he
acknowledged as his chief poetic influence.

The Hero

'Jack fell as he'd have wished,' the Mother said,
And folded up the letter that she'd read.
'The Colonel writes so nicely.' Something broke
In the tired voice that quavered to a choke.
5   She half looked up. 'We mothers are so proud

Of our dead soldiers.' Then her face was bowed.

Quietly the Brother Officer went out.
He'd told the poor old dear some gallant lies
That she would nourish all her days, no doubt.
10 For while he coughed and mumbled, her weak eyes
Had shone with gentle triumph, brimmed with joy,
Because he'd been so brave, her glorious boy.

He thought how 'Jack,' cold-footed, useless swine,
Had panicked down the trench that night the mine
15 Went up at Wicked Corner; how he'd tried
To get sent home, and how, at last, he died,
Blown to small bits. And no one seemed to care
Except that lonely woman with white hair.

                                                    —1918

Robinson Jeffers
(1887-1962)

Jeffers lived with his wife and children for many years in Carmel,
California, in a rock tower that he built by the sea. Many of his
ideas about man's small place in the larger world of nature have
gained in relevance through the years since his death. Largely
forgotten for many years, his poetry, particularly his book-length
verse narratives, is once more regaining the attention of serious
readers.

The Purse-Seine°

Our sardine fishermen work at night in the dark of the moon; daylight or
    moonlight
They could not tell where to spread the net, unable to see the phosphorescence of
    the shoals of fish.
They work northward from Monterey, coasting Santa Cruz; off New Year's
    Point or off Pigeon Point
The look-out man will see some lakes of milk-color light on the sea's night-
    purple; he points, and the helmsman
Turns the dark prow, the motorboat circles the gleaming shoal and drifts out her
5   seine-net. They close the circle

Purse-Seine large circular fishing net; the bottom is closed (or *pursed*) before it is hauled in

and purse the bottom of the net, then with great labor haul it in.

                                                          I cannot tell you
How beautiful the scene is, and a little terrible, then, when the crowded fish
Know they are caught, and wildly beat from one wall to the other of their closing
   destiny the phosphorescent
Water to a pool of flame, each beautiful slender body sheeted with flame, like a
   live rocket
10   A comet's tail wake of clear yellow flame; while outside the narrowing
Floats and cordage of the net great sea-lions come up to watch, sighing in the dark;
   the vast walls of night
Stand erect to the stars.

               Lately I was looking from a night mountain-top
On a wide city, the colored splendor, galaxies of light: how could I help but
   recall the seine-net
Gathering the luminous fish? I cannot tell you how beautiful the city appeared,
   and a little terrible.
I thought, we have geared the machines and locked all together into
15   interdependence; we have built the great cities; now
There is no escape. We have gathered vast populations incapable of free survival,
   insulated
From the strong earth, each person in himself helpless, on all dependent. The
   circle is closed, and the net
Is being hauled in. They hardly feel the cords drawing, yet they shine already. The
   inevitable mass-disasters
Will not come in our time nor in our children's, but we and our children
Must watch the net draw narrower, government take all powers—or revolution,
20   and the new government
Take more than all, add to kept bodies kept souls—or anarchy, the mass-disasters.

               These things are Progress;
Do you marvel our verse is troubled or frowning, while it keeps its reason? Or
   itlets go, lets the mood flow
In the manner of the recent young men into mere hysteria, splintered gleams,
   crackled laughter. But they are quite wrong.
There is no reason for amazement: surely one always knew that cultures decay, and
25   life's end is death.

                                —1937

✧ ✧ ✧

Marianne Moore
(1887-1972)

Moore called her own work poetry—unconventional and

marked with the stamp of a rare personality—because, as she put it, there was no other category for it. For four years she was editor of the *Dial*, one of the chief modernist periodicals. Moore's wide range of reference, which can leap from the commonplace to the wondrous in a single poem, reflects her unique set of personal interests—which can range from natural species to baseball in a single poem.

Poetry

I, too, dislike it: there are things that are important beyond all this fiddle.
   Reading it, however, with a perfect contempt for it, one discovers in
   it after all, a place for the genuine.
      Hands that can grasp, eyes
5   that can dilate, hair that can rise
         if it must, these things are important not because a

high-sounding interpretation can be put upon them but because they are
   useful. When they become so derivative as to become unintelligible,
   the same thing may be said for all of us, that we
10   do not admire what
      we cannot understand: the bat
         holding on upside down or in quest of something to

eat, elephants pushing, a wild horse taking a roll, a tireless wolf under
   a tree, the immovable critic twitching his skin like a horse that feels a flea, the
15   base-
   ball fan, the statistician—
   nor is it valid
      to discriminate against 'business documents and

school-books'; all these phenomena are important. One must make a distinction
20   however: when dragged into prominence by half poets, the result is not poetry,
   nor till the poets among us can be
      'literalists of
      the imagination'—above
         insolence and triviality and can present

25 for inspection, 'imaginary gardens with real toads in them', shall we have
   it. In the meantime, if you demand on the one hand,
   the raw material of poetry in
      all its rawness and
      that which is on the other hand
30   genuine, you are interested in poetry.

                        —1921

Silence

My father used to say,
"Superior people never make long visits,
have to be shown Longfellow's grave
or the glass flowers at Harvard.
5   Self-reliant like the cat—
that takes its prey to privacy,
the mouse's limp tail hanging like a shoelace from its mouth—
they sometimes enjoy solitude
and can be robbed of speech
10 by speech which has delighted them.
The deepest feeling always shows itself in silence;
not in silence, but restraint."
Nor was he insincere in saying, "Make my house your inn."
Inns are not residences.

—1935

T. S. Eliot
(1888-1965)

As the author of "The Waste Land," one of the most famous and difficult modernist poems, Eliot became an international figure. Born in St. Louis and educated at Harvard, he moved to London in 1914, where he remained for the rest of his life, becoming a British subject in 1927. This chief prophet of modern despair turned to the Church of England in later life, and wrote successful dramas on religious themes. As a critic and influential editor, Eliot dominated poetic taste in England and America for over twenty-five years. He was awarded the Nobel Prize in 1948.

Journey of the Magi°

'A cold coming we had of it,
Just the worst time of the year
For a journey, and such a long journey:
The ways deep and the weather sharp,
5   The very dead of winter.'°
And the camels galled, sore-footed, refractory,

Magi Wise Men mentioned in Matthew 2:1-2 **1-5 'A cold . . . winter'** The quotation marks indicated Eliot's source, a sermon by Lancelot Andrewes (1555-1626)

Lying down in the melting snow.
There were times we regretted
The summer palaces on slopes, the terraces,
10 And the silken girls bringing sherbet.
Then the camel men cursing and grumbling
And running away, and wanting their liquor and women,
And the night-fires going out, and the lack of shelters,
And the cities hostile and the towns unfriendly
15 And the villages dirty and charging high prices:
A hard time we had of it.
At the end we preferred to travel all night,
Sleeping in snatches,
With the voices singing in our ears, saying
20 That this was all folly.
Then at dawn we came down to a temperate valley,
Wet, below the snow line, smelling of vegetation;
With a running stream and a water-mill beating the darkness,
And three trees on the low sky.
25 And an old white horse galloped away in the meadow.
Then we came to a tavern with vine-leaves over the lintel,
Six hands at an open door dicing for pieces of silver,
And feet kicking the empty wine-skins.
But there was no information, and so we continued
30 And arrived at evening, not a moment too soon
Finding the place; it was (you may say) satisfactory.

All this was a long time ago, I remember,
And I would do it again, but set down
This° set down
35 This: were we led all that way for
Birth or Death? There was a Birth, certainly,
We had evidence and no doubt. I had seen birth and death,
But had thought they were different; this Birth was
Hard and bitter agony for us, like Death, our death.
40 We returned to our places, these Kingdoms,
But no longer at ease here, in the old dispensation,°
With an alien people clutching their gods.
I should be glad of another death.

—1927

33-34 set down . . . This The Magus is dictating his memoirs to a scribe   **41 old dispensation** world
before the birth of Christ

The Love Song of J. Alfred Prufrock

S' io credessi che mia risposta fosse
A persona che mai tornasse al mondo,
Questa fiamma staria senza più scosse.
Ma perciocchè giammai di questo fondo
Non tornò vivo alcun, s' i' odo il vero,
Senza tema d'infamia ti rispondo.

Let us go then, you° and I,
When the evening is spread out against the sky
Like a patient etherised upon a table;
Let us go, through certain half-deserted streets,
5   The muttering retreats
Of restless nights in one-night cheap hotels
And sawdust restaurants with oyster-shells:
Streets that follow like a tedious argument
Of insidious intent
10   To lead you to an overwhelming question . . .

Oh, do not ask, "What is it?"
Let us go and make our visit.

In the room the women come and go
Talking of Michelangelo.°

15   The yellow fog that rubs its back upon the window panes,
The yellow smoke that rubs its muzzle on the window panes,
Licked its tongue into the corners of the evening,
Lingered upon the pools that stand in drains,
Let fall upon its back the soot that falls from chimneys,
20   Slipped by the terrace, made a sudden leap,
And seeing that it was a soft October night,
Curled once about the house, and fell asleep.

And indeed there will be time
For the yellow smoke that slides along the street,
25   Rubbing its back upon the window panes;
There will be time, there will be time
To prepare a face to meet the faces that you meet;
There will be time to murder and create,

S'io credesse . . . rispondo From Dante's *Inferno*. The speaker is Guido da Montefeltro: "If I thought I spoke to someone who would return to the world, this flame would tremble no longer. But, if what I hear is true, since no one has ever returned alive from this place I can answer you without fear of infamy." **1 you** Eliot said that the auditor of the poem was a male companion of Prufrock.
14 Michelangelo Italian painter and sculptor (1475-1564)

And time for all the works and days of hands
30   That lift and drop a question on your plate:
Time for you and time for me,
And time yet for a hundred indecisions,
And for a hundred visions and revisions,
Before the taking of a toast and tea.

35   In the room the women come and go
Talking of Michelangelo.

And indeed there will be time
To wonder, "Do I dare?" and, "Do I dare?"—
Time to turn back and descend the stair,
40   With a bald spot in the middle of my hair—
(They will say: "How his hair is growing thin!")
My morning coat, my collar mounting firmly to the chin,
My necktie rich and modest, but asserted by a simple pin—
(They will say: "But how his arms and legs are thin!")
45   Do I dare
Disturb the universe?
In a minute there is time
For decisions and revisions which a minute will reverse.

For I have known them all already, known them all:
50   Have known the evenings, mornings, afternoons,
I have measured out my life with coffee spoons;
I know the voices dying with a dying fall
Beneath the music from a farther room.
So how should I presume?

55   And I have known the eyes already, known them all—
The eyes that fix you in a formulated phrase,
And when I am formulated, sprawling on a pin,
When I am pinned and wriggling on the wall,
Then how should I begin
60   To spit out all the butt-ends of my days and ways?
And how should I presume?

And I have known the arms already, known them all—
Arms that are braceleted and white and bare
(But in the lamplight, downed with light brown hair!)
65   Is it perfume from a dress
That makes me so digress?
Arms that lie along a table, or wrap about a shawl.

And should I then presume?
    And how should I begin?
  • • • • •

70   Shall I say, I have gone at dusk through narrow streets,
And watched the smoke that rises from the pipes
Of lonely men in shirtsleeves, leaning out of windows? . . .

I should have been a pair of ragged claws
Scuttling across the floors of silent seas.
  • • • • •

75   And the afternoon, the evening, sleeps so peacefully!
Smoothed by long fingers,
Asleep . . . tired . . . or it malingers,
Stretched on the floor, here beside you and me.
Should I, after tea and cakes and ices,
80   Have the strength to force the moment to its crisis?
But though I have wept and fasted, wept and prayed,
Though I have seen my head (grown slightly bald) brought in upon a platter,
I am no prophet°—and here's no great matter;
I have seen the moment of my greatness flicker,
85   And I have seen the eternal Footman hold my coat, and snicker,
      And in short, I was afraid.

    And would it have been worth it, after all,
After the cups, the marmalade, the tea,
Among the porcelain, among some talk of you and me,
90   Would it have been worth while,
To have bitten off the matter with a smile,
To have squeezed the universe into a ball
To roll it towards some overwhelming question,
To say: "I am Lazarus,° come from the dead,
95   Come back to tell you all, I shall tell you all"—
If one, settling a pillow by her head,
    Should say: "That is not what I meant at all;
      That is not it, at all."

    And would it have been worth it, after all,
100   Would it have been worth while,
After the sunsets and the dooryards and the sprinkled streets,
After the novels, after the teacups, after the skirts that trail along the floor—
And this, and so much more?—

82-83 **my head grown . . . no prophet** allusion to John the Baptist   **94 Lazarus** raised from the dead in John 11:1-44

It is impossible to say just what I mean!
105 But as if a magic lantern° threw the nerves in patterns on a screen:
Would it have been worth while
If one, settling a pillow or throwing off a shawl,
And turning toward the window, should say: "That is not it at all,
    That is not what I meant, at all."
        •   •   •   •   •

110   No! I am not Prince Hamlet, nor was meant to be;
Am an attendant lord, one that will do
To swell a progress, start a scene or two,
Advise the prince; no doubt, an easy tool,
Deferential, glad to be of use,
115 Politic, cautious, and meticulous;
Full of high sentence, but a bit obtuse;
At times, indeed, almost ridiculous—
Almost, at times, the Fool.°

I grow old . . . I grow old . . .
120 I shall wear the bottoms of my trowsers rolled.

    Shall I part my hair behind? Do I dare to eat a peach?
I shall wear white flannel trowsers, and walk upon the beach.
I have heard the mermaids singing, each to each.

I do not think that they will sing to me.

125 I have seen them riding seaward on the waves,
Combing the white hair of the waves blown back
When the wind blows the water white and black.

We have lingered in the chambers of the sea
By sea girls wreathed with seaweed red and brown,
130 Till human voices wake us, and we drown.

                                    —1917

John Crowe Ransom
(1888-1974)

As a professor at Vanderbilt University in Nashville, Ransom

---

105 magic lantern old-fashioned slide projector **110-118 not Prince Hamlet . . . the Fool** The allusion is probably to Polonius, a character in *Hamlet*

began a little magazine called the *Fugitive,* which leant its name
to a group of young southern poets who published in it. Later he
moved to Kenyon College, where he was editor of the *Kenyon
Review* for many years. Ransom was influential as both a poet
and a critic.

Bells for John Whiteside's Daughter

There was such speed in her little body,
And such lightness in her footfall,
It is no wonder her brown study°
Astonishes us all.

5   Her wars were bruited° in our high window.
We looked among orchard trees and beyond
Where she took arms against her shadow,
Or harried unto the pond

The lazy geese, like a snow cloud
10   Dripping their snow on the green grass,
Tricking and stopping, sleepy and proud,
Who cried in goose, Alas,

For the tireless heart within the little
Lady with rod that made them rise
15   From their noon apple-dreams and scuttle
Goose-fashion under the skies!

But now go the bells, and we are ready,
In one house we are sternly stopped
To say we are vexed at her brown study,
20   Lying so primly propped.

—192?

Piazza° Piece

—I am a gentleman in a dustcoat° trying
To make you hear. Your ears are soft and small
And listen to an old man not at all.
They want the young men's whispering and sighing.
5   But see the roses on your trellis dying
And hear the spectral singing of the moon;

---

3 brown study appearance of deep concentration **5 bruited** shouted
Piazza courtyard **1 dustcoat** old-fashioned coat worn while driving an open car

For I must have my lovely lady soon,
I am a gentleman in a dustcoat trying.

—I am a lady young in beauty waiting
10   Until my truelove comes, and then we kiss.
But what grey man among the vines is this
Whose words are dry and faint as in a dream?
Back from my trellis, Sir, before I scream!
I am a lady young in beauty waiting.

                                                        —1927

Edna St. Vincent Millay
(1892-1950)

Millay's poetry was extremely popular in the 1920s, when her
sonnets seemed the ultimate expression of the liberated sex-
uality of what was then called the New Woman. Neglected for
many years, her poems have recently generated renewed
interest, and it seems likely that she will eventually regain her
status as one of the most important female poets of the century.

Sonnet 5

If I should learn, in some quite casual way,
That you were gone, not to return again—
Read from the back-page of a paper, say,
Held by a neighbor in a subway train,
5   How at the corner of this avenue
And such a street (so are the papers filled)
A hurrying man, who happened to be you,
At noon today had happened to be killed—
I should not cry aloud—I could not cry
10   Aloud, or wring my hands in such a place—
I should but watch the station lights rush by
With a more careful interest on my face;
Or raise my eyes and read with greater care
Where to store furs and how to treat the hair.

                                                        —1917

Sonnet 31

Oh, oh, you will be sorry for that word!
Give back my book and take my kiss instead.

Was it my enemy or my friend I heard,
"What a big book for such a little head!"
5   Come, I will show you now my newest hat,
And you may watch me purse my mouth and prink!°
Oh, I shall love you still, and all of that.
I never again shall tell you what I think.
I shall be sweet and crafty, soft and sly;
10 You will not catch me reading any more:
I shall be called a wife to pattern by;
And some day when you knock and push the door,
Some sane day, not too bright and not too stormy,
I shall be gone, and you may whistle for me.

—1923

What Lips My Lips Have Kissed, and Where, and Why

What lips my lips have kissed, and where, and why,
I have forgotten, and what arms have lain
Under my head till morning; but the rain
Is full of ghosts tonight, that tap and sigh
5   Upon the glass and listen for reply,
And in my heart there stirs a quiet pain
For unremembered lads that not again
Will turn to me at midnight with a cry.
Thus in the winter stands the lonely tree,
10 Nor knows what birds have vanished one by one,
Yet knows its boughs more silent than before:
I cannot say what loves have come and gone,
I only know that summer sang in me
A little while, that in me sings no more.

—1923

Archibald MacLeish
(1892-1982)

MacLeish was both a poet and a public servant, serving as an
Under Secretary of State during the Roosevelt administration. He
won Pulitzer prizes, both for his poetry and for his play *J.B.*, a
modern retelling of the Old Testament story of Job.

---

6 prink primp

The End of the World

Quite unexpectedly as Vasserot
The armless ambidextrian was lighting
A match between his great and second toe,
And Ralph the lion was engaged in biting
5   The neck of Madame Sossman while the drum
Pointed, and Teeny was about to cough
In waltz-time swinging Jocko by the thumb—
Quite unexpectedly the top blew off:

And there, there overhead, there, there hung over
10 Those thousands of white faces, those dazed eyes,
There in the starless dark the poise, the hover,
There with vast wings across the canceled skies,
There in the sudden blackness the black pall
Of nothing, nothing, nothing—nothing at all.

—1926

Wilfred Owen
(1893-1918)

Killed in the trenches only a few days before the armistice that
ended World War I, Owen showed more promise than any other
English poet of his generation. A decorated officer whose
nerves broke down after exposure to battle, he met Siegfried
Sassoon at Craiglockhart military hospital. His work was
posthumously collected by Sassoon. A recent novel by Pat
Barker, *Regeneration*, deals with their poetic and personal
relationship.

Dulce et Decorum Est°

Bent double, like old beggars under sacks,
Knock-kneed, coughing like hags, we cursed through sludge,
Till on the haunting flares we turned our backs
And towards our distant rest began to trudge.
5   Men marched asleep. Many had lost their boots
But limped on, blood-shod. All went lame; all blind;

Dulce et Decorum Est (pro patria mori) from the Roman poet Horace: "It is sweet and proper to die for one's country"

Drunk with fatigue; deaf even to the hoots
Of tired, outstripped Five-Nines° that dropped behind.

Gas! GAS! Quick, boys!—An ecstasy of fumbling
10 Fitting the clumsy helmets just in time;
But someone still was yelling out and stumbling
And flound'ring like a man in fire or lime . . .
Dim, through the misty panes and thick green light,°
As under a green sea, I saw him drowning.

15 In all my dreams, before my helpless sight,
He plunges at me, guttering, choking, drowning.

If in some smothering dreams you too could pace
Behind the wagon that we flung him in,
And watch the white eyes writhing in his face,
20 His hanging face, like a devil's sick of sin;
If you could hear, at every jolt, the blood
Come gargling from the froth-corrupted lungs,
Obscene as cancer, bitter as the cud
Of vile, incurable sores on innocent tongues,—
25 My friend,° you would not tell with such high zest
To children ardent for some desperate glory,
The old Lie: Dulce et decorum est
Pro patria mori.

                                                    —1920

Dorothy Parker
(1893-1967)

Humorist, journalist, and poet, Parker was for many years asso-
ciated with the *New Yorker* as both author and critic. Along with
Robert Benchley, James Thurber, and E.B. White she epitomizes
the hard-edged humor that made that magazine unique among
American periodicals.

One Perfect Rose

A single flow'r he sent me, since we met.

---

8 Five-Nines German artillery shells (59 mm)   **13 misty panes and thick green light** i.e., through
the gas mask   **25 my friend** The poem was originally addressed to Jessie Pope, a writer of patriotic
verse

All tenderly his messenger he chose;
Deep-hearted, pure, with scented dew still wet—
One perfect rose.

5   I knew the language of the floweret;
"My fragile leaves," it said, "his heart enclose."
Love long has taken for his amulet
One perfect rose.

Why is it no one sent me yet
10   One perfect limousine, do you suppose?
Ah no, it's always just my luck to get
One perfect rose.

—1926

Résumé

Razors pain you;
Rivers are damp;
Acids stain you;
And drugs cause cramp.
5   Guns aren't lawful;
Nooses give;
Gas smells awful,
You might as well live.

—1926

e. e. cummings
(1894-1962)

The son of a Harvard professor and Unitarian clergyman, Edward Estlin Cummings served as a volunteer ambulance driver in France during World War I. Cummings's experimentation with the typographical aspects of poetry reveals his serious interest in cubist painting, which he studied in Paris in the 1920s. A brilliant satirist, he also excelled as a writer of lyrical poems whose unusual appearance and idiosyncratic grammar, spelling, and punctuation often overshadow their traditional themes.

in Just-

in Just-
spring   when the world is mud-
luscious the little
lame balloonman

5   whistles   far   and wee

and eddieandbill come
running from marbles and
piracies and it's
spring

10   when the world is puddle-wonderful

the queer
old balloonman whistles
far   and   wee
and bettyandisbel come dancing

15   from hop-scotch and jump-rope and
it's
spring
and
    the

20   goat-footed°

ballonMan   whistles
far
and
wee

—1923

Pity This Busy Monster, Manunkind

pity this busy monster,manunkind,

not. Progress is a comfortable disease:
your victim(death and life safely beyond)

---

20 goat-footed allusion to Pan, Roman god of spring

plays with the bigness of his littleness
5   —electrons° deify one razorblade
into a mountainrange;lenses extend

unwish through curving wherewhen till unwish
returns on its unself.
                         A world of made
10   is not a world of born—pity poor flesh

and trees,poor stars and stones,but never this
fine specimen of hypermagical

ultraomnipotence. We doctors know

a hopeless case if—listen:there's a hell
15   of a good universe next door;let's go

                                    —1944

r-p-o-p-h-e-s-s-a-g-r

                   r-p-o-p-h-e-s-s-a-g-r
            who
a)s w(e loo)k
upnowgath
5   PPEGORHRASS
                 eringint(o-
aThe):l
     eA
       !p:
10   S   a
           (r
rIvInG   .gRrEaPsPhOs)
                    to
rea(be)rran(com)gi(e)ngly
15   ,grasshopper;

                                    —1932

Jean Toomer
(1894-1967)

Toomer was born in Washington, D.C., the grandson of a black

---

5 electrons in an electron microscope

man who served as governor of Louisiana during Reconstruction. His only book, *Cane* (1923), is a mixed collection of prose and verse based on his observations of life in rural Georgia, where he was a schoolteacher. A complete edition of his poetry, most of it unpublished during his life, was assembled over twenty years after his death.

Reapers

Black reapers with the sound of steel on stones
Are sharpening scythes. I see them place the hones
In their hip-pockets as a thing that's done,
And start their silent swinging, one by one.
5   Black horses drive a mower through the weeds,
And there, a field rat, startled, squealing bleeds,
His belly close to ground. I see the blade,
Blood-stained, continue cutting weeds and shade.

—1923

Hart Crane
(1899-1933)

Crane is one of the first modernists to make extensive poetic use of the artifacts—advertising slogans, motion picture lore, trade names—of American popular culture. Much of this material surfaces in *The Bridge* (1930) his book-length attempt to write an epic sequence about modern America. Crane committed suicide by leaping from a ship returning from the Yucutan, where he spent his last year on a Guggenheim fellowship, attempting to write an epic poem about the conquest of Mexico.

Chaplinesque°

We make our meek adjustments,
Contented with such random consolations
As the wind deposits
In slithered and too ample pockets.

5   For we can still love the world, who find
A famished kitten on the step, and know
Recesses for it from the fury of the street,

Chaplinesque after Charlie Chaplin, silent-film comedian

Or warm torn elbow coverts.

We will sidestep, and to the final smirk
10 Dally the doom of that inevitable thumb
That slowly chafes its puckered index toward us,
Facing the dull squint with what innocence
And what surprise!

And yet these fine collapses are not lies
15 More than the pirouettes of any pliant cane;
Our obsequies are in a way, no enterprise.
We can evade you, and all else but the heart:
What blame to us if the heart live on.

The game enforces smirks; but we have seen
20 The moon in lonely alleys make
A grail of laughter of an empty ash can,
And through all sound of gaiety and quest
Have heard a kitten in the wilderness.

—1926

Langston Hughes
(1902-1967)

As a leading figure in the Harlem Renaissance of the 1920s,
Hughes became the most famous black writer of his day.
Phrases from his poems and other writings have become deeply
ingrained in the American consciousness. An important experi-
menter with poetic form, Hughes is credited with incorporating
the rhythms of jazz into poetry.

Harlem

What happens to a dream deferred?

Does it dry up
like a raisin in the sun?
Or fester like a sore—
5 And then run?
Does it stink like rotten meat?
Or crust and sugar over—
like a syrupy sweet?

10   Maybe it just sags
     like a heavy load.

     Or does it explode?

                                                    —1951

The Negro Speaks of Rivers

I've known rivers:
I've known rivers ancient as the world and older than the flow of human blood in
     human veins.

My soul has grown deep like the rivers.

     I bathed in the Euphrates when dawns were young.
5   I built my hut near the Congo and it lulled me to sleep.
     I looked upon the Nile and raised the pyramids above it.
     I heard the singing of the Mississippi when Abe Lincoln went down to New
     Orleans, and I've seen its muddy bosom turn all golden in the sunset.

I've known rivers:
Ancient, dusky rivers.

10   My soul has grown deep like the rivers.

                                                    —1926

Countee Cullen
(1903-1946)

Among black writers of the first half of the century, Cullen's poetry
represents a more conservative style than that of his contempo-
rary Hughes. Although he wrote a number of lyrics on poetic
themes, he is best remembered for his eloquent poems on racial
subjects.

Incident

(for Eric Walrond)

Once riding in old Baltimore,
     Heart-filled, head-filled with glee,

I saw a Baltimorean
  Keep looking straight at me.

5 Now I was eight and very small,
  And he was no whit bigger,
And so I smiled, but he poked out
  His tongue, and called me, "Nigger."

I saw the whole of Baltimore
10   From May until December;
Of all the things that happened there
  That's all that I remember.

                                     —1963

Yet Do I Marvel

I doubt not God is good, well-meaning, kind,
And did He stoop to quibble could tell why
The little buried mole continues blind,
Why flesh that mirrors Him must some day die,
5 Make plain the reason tortured Tantalus°
Is baited by the fickle fruit, declare
If merely brute caprice dooms Sisyphus°
To struggle up a never-ending stair.
Inscrutable His ways are, and immune
10 To catechism by a mind too strewn
With petty cares to slightly understand
What awful brain compels His awful hand.
Yet do I marvel at this curious thing:
To make a poet black and bid him sing!

                                     —1963

Richard Eberhart
(1904-)

Born in Austin, Minnesota, and educated at the University of
Minnesota, Dartmouth College, and Cambridge, Eberhart has
worked in business and as a teacher. During World War II, he
served as a naval gunnery instructor. His *Collected Poems*,
containing work from seven decades, was published in 1988.

---

5 Tantalus mythological character tortured by unreachable fruit   **7 Sisyphus** figure in myth who
endlessly rolls a boulder uphill

The Fury of Aerial Bombardment

You would think the fury of aerial bombardment
Would rouse God to relent; the infinite spaces
Are still silent. He looks on shock-pried faces.
History, even, does not know what is meant.

5   You would feel that after so many centuries
God would give man to repent; yet he can kill
As Cain could, but with multitudinous will,
No farther advanced than in his ancient furies.

Was man made stupid to see his own stupidity?
10 Is God by definition indifferent, beyond us all?
Is the eternal truth man's fighting soul
Wherein the Beast ravens° in its own avidity?

Of Van Wettering I speak, and Averill,
Names on a list, whose faces I do not recall
15 But they are gone to early death, who late in school
Distinguished the belt feed lever from the belt holding pawl.°

—1947

✧ ✧ ✧

W. H. Auden
(1907-1973)

Auden was already established as an important younger British poet before he moved to America in 1939 (he later became a U.S. citizen). As an important Transatlantic link between two literary cultures, Auden was one of the most important literary figures and cultural spokespersons in the English-speaking world for almost forty years, giving a name to the postwar era when he dubbed it "The Age of Anxiety" in a poem. In his last years he returned briefly to Oxford, where he occupied the poetry chair.

As I Walked Out One Evening

As I walked out one evening,
  Walking down Bristol Street,
The crowds upon the pavement

---

12 **ravens** devours greedily   16 **belt feed . . . holding pawl** parts of a 50 caliber machine gun; the poet was a naval gunnery instructor during World War II

Were fields of harvest wheat.

5 And down by the brimming river
  I heard a lover sing
Under an arch of the railway:
  "Love has no ending.

"I'll love you, dear, I'll love you
10 Till China and Africa meet,
And the river jumps over the mountain
  And the salmon sing in the street.

"I'll love you till the ocean
  Is folded and hung up to dry,
15 And the seven stars go squawking
  Like geese about the sky.

"The years shall run like rabbits,
  For in my arms I hold
The Flower of the Ages,
20 And the first love of the world."

But all the clocks in the city
  Began to whirr and chime:
"O let not Time deceive you,
  You cannot conquer Time.

25 "In the burrows of the Nightmare
  Where Justice naked is,
Time watches from the shadow
  And coughs when you would kiss.

"In headaches and in worry
30 Vaguely life leaks away,
And Time will have his fancy
  Tomorrow or to-day.

"Into many a green valley
  Drifts the appalling snow;
35 Time breaks the threaded dances
  And the diver's brilliant bow.

"O plunge your hands in water,
  Plunge them in up to the wrist;

Stare, stare in the basin
40   And wonder what you've missed.

"The glacier knocks in the cupboard,
    The desert sighs in the bed,
And the crack in the tea-cup opens
    A lane to the land of the dead.

45 "Where the beggars raffle the banknotes
        And the Giant is enchanting to Jack,
    And the Lily-white Boy is a Roarer,
        And Jill goes down on her back.

"O look, look in the mirror,
50   O look in your distress;
    Life remains a blessing
        Although you cannot bless.

"O stand, stand at the window
    As the tears scald and start;
55 You shall love your crooked neighbor
        With your crooked heart."

It was late, late in the evening,
    The lovers they were gone;
The clocks had ceased their chiming,
60   And the deep river ran on.

                                                            —1940

Musée des Beaux Arts°

About suffering they were never wrong,
The Old Masters: how well they understood
Its human position; how it takes place
5   While someone else is eating or opening a window or just walking dully along;
How, when the aged are reverently, passionately waiting
For the miraculous birth, there always must be
Children who did not specially want it to happen, skating
On a pond at the edge of the wood:
10 They never forgot
That even the dreadful martyrdom must run its course

Musée des Beaux Arts Museum of Fine Arts

Anyhow in a corner, some untidy spot
Where the dogs go on with their doggy life and the torturer's horse
Scratches its innocent behind on a tree.

15   In Brueghel's *Icarus,*° for instance: how everything turns away
Quite leisurely from the disaster; the ploughman may
Have heard the splash, the forsaken cry,
But for him it was not an important failure; the sun shone
As it had to on the white legs disappearing into the green
20   Water; and the expensive delicate ship that must have seen
Something amazing, a boy falling out of the sky,
Had somewhere to get to and sailed calmly on.

—1938

The Unknown Citizen

To JS/07/M/378
This Marble Monument Is Erected by the State

He was found by the Bureau of Statistics to be
One against whom there was no official complaint,
And all the reports on his conduct agree
That, in the modern sense of an old-fashioned word, he was a saint,
5   For in everything he did he served the Greater Community.
Except for the War till the day he retired
He worked in a factory and never got fired,
But satisfied his employers, Fudge Motors Inc.
Yet he wasn't a scab or odd in his views,
10   For his Union reports that he paid his dues,
(Our report on his Union shows it was sound)
And our Social Psychology workers found
That he was popular with his mates and liked a drink.
The Press are convinced that he bought a paper every day
15   And that his reactions to advertisements were normal in every way.
Policies taken out in his name prove that he was fully insured,
And his Health-card shows he was once in hospital but left it cured.
Both Producers Research and High-Grade Living declare
He was fully sensible to the advantages of the Installment Plan
20   And had everything necessary to the Modern Man,
A phonograph, a radio, a car and a frigidaire.
Our researchers into Public Opinion are content
That he held the proper opinions for the time of year;

---

15 Breughel's *Icarus* In this painting (c. 1550) the famous event from Greek myth is almost
inconspicuous among the other details Auden mentions.

When there was peace, he was for peace; when there was war, he went.
25   He was married and added five children to the population,
Which our Eugenist says was the right number for a parent of his generation,
And our teachers report that he never interfered with their education.
Was he free? Was he happy? The question is absurd:
Had anything been wrong, we should certainly have heard.

—1939

Theodore Roethke
(1908-1963)

Born in Michigan, Roethke was an influential teacher of poetry at
the University of Washington for many years. His father was the
owner of a greenhouse, and Roethke's childhood closeness to
the nature was an important influence on his mature poetry. His
periodic nervous breakdowns, the result of bipolar manic-
depression, presaged his early death.

Dolor°

I have known the inexorable sadness of pencils,
Neat in their boxes, dolor of pad and paper-weight,
All of the misery of manilla folders and mucilage,
Desolation in immaculate public places,
5   Lonely reception room, lavatory, switchboard,
The unalterable pathos of basin and pitcher,
Ritual of multigraph, paper-clip, comma,
Endless duplication of lives and objects.
And I have seen dust from the walls of institutions,
10 Finer than flour, alive, more dangerous than silica,°
Sift, almost invisible, through long afternoons of tedium,
Dropping a fine film on nails and delicate eyebrows,
Glazing the pale hair, the duplicate grey standard faces.

—1948

My Papa's Waltz

The whiskey on your breath
Could make a small boy dizzy;

Dolor sadness **9 silica** rock dust, a cause of silicosis, an occupational disease of miners and quarry
workers

But I hung on like death:
Such waltzing was not easy.

5   We romped until the pans
Slid from the kitchen shelf;
My mother's countenance
Could not unfrown itself.

The hand that held my wrist
10 Was battered on one knuckle;
At every step you missed
My right ear scraped a buckle.

You beat time on my head
With a palm caked hard by dirt,
15 Then waltzed me off to bed
Still clinging to your shirt.

—1948

Elizabeth Bishop
(1911-1979)

During most of her life, Bishop was highly regarded as a "poet's poet," winning the Pulitzer prize for *North and South* in 1956, but in the years since her death she has gained a wider readership. She traveled widely and lived in Brazil for a number of years before returning to the United States to teach at Harvard during the last years of her life.

The Fish

I caught a tremendous fish
and held him beside the boat
half out of water, with my hook
fast in a corner of his mouth.
5   He didn't fight.
He hadn't fought at all.
He hung a grunting weight,
battered and venerable
and homely. Here and there
10 his brown skin hung in strips
like ancient wallpaper,

and its pattern of darker brown
was like wallpaper:
shapes like full-blown roses
15   stained and lost through age.
He was speckled with barnacles,
fine rosettes of lime,
and infested
with tiny white sea lice,
20   and underneath two or three
rags of green weed hung down.
While his gills were breathing in
the terrible oxygen
—the frightening gills,
25   fresh and crisp with blood,
that can cut so badly—
I thought of the coarse white flesh
packed in like feathers,
the big bones and the little bones,
30   the dramatic reds and blacks
of his shiny entrails,
and the pink swim-bladder
like a big peony.
I looked into his eyes
35   which were far larger than mine
but shallower, and yellowed,
the irises backed and packed
with tarnished tinfoil
seen through the lenses
40   of old scratched isinglass.°
They shifted a little, but not
to return my stare.
—It was more like the tipping
of an object toward the light.
45   I admired his sullen face,
the mechanism of his jaw,
and then I saw
that from his lower lip
—if you could call it a lip—
50   grim, wet, and weapon like,
hung five old pieces of fish-line,
or four and a wire leader
with the swivel still attached,

---

40 isinglass semi-transparent material made from fish bladders

with all their five big hooks
55 grown firmly in his mouth.
A green line, frayed at the end
where he broke it, two heavier lines,
and a fine black thread
still crimped from the strain and snap
60 when it broke and he got away.
Like medals with their ribbons
frayed and wavering,
a five-haired beard of wisdom
trailing from his aching jaw.
65 I stared and stared
and victory filled up
the little rented boat,
from the pool of bilge
where oil had spread a rainbow
70 around the rusted engine
to the bailer° rusted orange,
the sun-cracked thwarts,
the oarlocks on their strings,
the gunnels°—until everything
75 was rainbow, rainbow, rainbow!
and I let the fish go.

                                                          —1946

One Art

The art of losing isn't hard to master;
so many things seem filled with the intent
to be lost that their loss is no disaster.

Lose something every day. Accept the fluster
5 of lost door keys, the hour badly spent.
The art of losing isn't hard to master.

Then practice losing farther, losing faster:
places, and names, and where it was you meant
to travel. None of these will bring disaster.

10 I lost my mother's watch. And look! my last, or
next-to-last, of three loved houses went.
The art of losing isn't hard to master.

---

71 **bailer** bucket 74 **gunnels** gunwales

I lost two cities, lovely ones. And, vaster,
some realms I owned, two rivers, a continent.
15   I miss them, but it wasn't a disaster.

—Even losing you (the joking voice, a gesture
I love) I shan't have lied. It's evident
the art of losing's not too hard to master
though it may look like *(Write* it!) like disaster.

—1976

Robert Hayden
(1913-1980)

Hayden named Countee Cullen as one of the chief early influ-
ences on his poetry. A native of Michigan, he taught for many
years at Fisk University in Nashville and at the University of
Michigan. Although many of Hayden's poems are on black
subjects, he wished to be considered a poet with strong links to
the mainstream English tradition.

Those Winter Sundays

Sundays too my father got up early
and put his clothes on in the blueblack cold,
then with cracked hands that ached
from labor in the weekday weather made
5   banked fires blaze. No one ever thanked him.

I'd wake and hear the cold splintering, breaking.
When the rooms were warm, he'd call,
and slowly I would rise and dress,
fearing the chronic angers of that house,

10   Speaking indifferently to him,
who had driven out the cold
and polished my good shoes as well.
What did I know, what did I know
of love's austere and lonely offices?°

—1962

---

14 **offices** daily religious ceremonies

Dudley Randall
(1914-)

Randall is the founder of Broadside Press, a black-owned publishing firm that eventually attracted important black writers like Gwendolyn Brooks and Don L. Lee. For most of his life a resident of Detroit, Randall spent many years working in that city's library system before taking a similar position at the University of Detroit.

Ballad of Birmingham

(On the Bombing of a Church in Birmingham, Alabama, 1963)°

"Mother dear, may I go downtown
Instead of out to play,
And march the streets of Birmingham
In a Freedom March today?"

5 "No, baby, no, you may not go,
For the dogs are fierce and wild,
And clubs and hoses, guns and jail
Aren't good for a little child."

"But, mother, I won't be alone.
10 Other children will go with me,
And march the streets of Birmingham
To make our country free."

"No, baby, no, you may not go,
For I fear those guns will fire.
15 But you may go to church instead
And sing in the children's choir."

She has combed and brushed her night-dark hair,
And bathed rose petal sweet,
And drawn white gloves on her small brown hands,
20 And white shoes on her feet.

The mother smiled to know her child

Birmingham, Alabama, 1963 during the height of the civil rights movement

Was in the sacred place,
But that smile was the last smile
To come upon her face.

25 For when she heard the explosion,
Her eyes grew wet and wild.
She raced through the streets of Birmingham
Calling for her child.

She clawed through bits of glass and brick,
30 Then lifted out a shoe.
"O, here's the shoe my baby wore,
But, baby, where are you?"

—1969

William Stafford
(1914-)

One of the most prolific poets of the postwar era, Stafford has
published in virtually every literary magazine in the United States.
Raised as a member of the pacifist Church of the Brethren,
Stafford served in a camp for conscientious objectors during
World War II. His first book did not appear until he was in his for-
ties, but he has published over thirty collections since then.

Traveling through the Dark

Traveling through the dark I found a deer
dead on the edge of the Wilson River road.
It is usually best to roll them into the canyon:
that road is narrow; to swerve might make more dead.

5 By glow of the tail-light I stumbled back of the car
and stood by the heap, a doe, a recent killing;
she had stiffened already, almost cold.
I dragged her off; she was large in the belly.

My fingers touching her side brought me the reason—
10 her side was warm; her fawn lay there waiting,
alive, still, never to be born.
Beside that mountain road I hesitated.

The car aimed ahead its lowered parking lights;
under the hood purred the steady engine.
15 I stood in the glare of the warm exhaust turning red;
around our group I could hear the wilderness listen.

I thought hard for us all—my only swerving— ,
then pushed her over the edge into the river.

—1960

Dylan Thomas
(1914-1953)

Thomas was a legendary performer of his and others' poetry,
and his popularity in the United States led to several collegiate
reading tours, punctuated with outrageous behavior and self-
destructive drinking that led to his early death in New York City,
the victim of what the autopsy report labeled "insult to the brain."
The Wales of his childhood remained a constant source of inspi-
ration for his poetry and for radio dramas like "Under Milk Wood,"
which was turned into a film by fellow Welshman Richard Burton
and his then-wife, Elizabeth Taylor.

Do Not Go Gentle into That Good Night

Do not go gentle into that good night,
Old age should burn and rave at close of day;
Rage, rage against the dying of the light.

Though wise men at their end know dark is right,
5 Because their words had forked no lightning they
Do not go gentle into that good night.

Good men, the last wave by, crying how bright
Their frail deeds might have danced in a green bay,
Rage, rage against the dying of the light.

10 Wild men who caught and sang the sun in flight,
And learn, too late, they grieved it on its way,
Do not go gentle into that good night.

Grave men, near death, who see with blinding sight
Blind eyes could blaze like meteors and be gay,

15   Rage, rage against the dying of the light.

        And you, my father, there on the sad height,
        Curse, bless, me now with your fierce tears, I pray,
        Do not go gentle into that good night.
        Rage, rage against the dying of the light.

                                                              —1952

Fern Hill

        Now as I was young and easy under the apple boughs
        About the lilting house and happy as the grass was green,
                The night above the dingle starry,
                    Time let me hail and climb
5   Golden in the heydays of his eyes,
        And honored among wagons I was prince of the apple towns
        And once below a time I lordly had the trees and leaves
                    Trail with daisies and barley
                Down the rivers of the windfall light.

10   And as I was green and carefree, famous among the barns
        About the happy yard and singing as the farm was home,
                In the sun that is young once only,
                    Time let me play and be
                Golden in the mercy of his means,
15   And green and golden I was huntsman and herdsman, the calves
        Sang to my horn, the foxes on the hills barked clear and cold,
                    And the sabbath rang slowly
                In the pebbles of the holy streams.

        All the sun long it was running, it was lovely, the hay
20   Fields high as the house, the tunes from the chimneys, it was air
                    And playing, lovely and watery
                        And fire green as grass.
                    And nightly under the simple stars
        As I rode to sleep the owls were bearing the farm away,
25   All the moon long I heard, blessed among stables, the night-jars
                    Flying with the ricks, and the horses
                        Flashing into the dark.

        And then to awake, and the farm, like a wanderer white
        With the dew, come back, the cock on his shoulder: it was all
30   Shining, it was Adam and maiden,
                    The sky gathered again

And the sun grew round that very day.
So it must have been after the birth of the simple light
In the first, spinning place, the spellbound horses walking warm
35   Out of the whinnying green stable
            On to the fields of praise.

And honored among foxes and pheasants by the gay house
Under the new made clouds and happy as the heart was long,
            In the sun born over and over,
40   I ran my heedless ways,
            My wishes raced through the house high hay
And nothing I cared, at my sky blue trades, that time allows
In all his tuneful turning so few and such morning songs
            Before the children green and golden
45   Follow him out of grace,

Nothing I cared, in the lamb white days, that time would take me
Up to the swallow thronged loft by the shadow of my hand,
            In the moon that is always rising,
            Nor that riding to sleep
50   I should hear him fly with the high fields
And wake to the farm forever fled from the childless land.
Oh as I was young and easy in the mercy of his means,
            Time held me green and dying
            Though I sang in my chains like the sea.

                                        —1946

Weldon Kees
(1914-1955)

Kees was a multi-talented poet, painter, jazz musician, and film-maker who went from the University of Nebraska to New York to California. His reputation, aided by posthumous publication of his stories, criticism, letters, and novels, has grown steadily since his apparent suicide by leaping from the Golden Gate Bridge.

For My Daughter

Looking into my daughter's eyes I read
Beneath the innocence of morning flesh
Concealed, hintings of death she does not heed.
Coldest of winds have blown this hair, and mesh

5   Of seaweed snarled these miniatures of hands;
The night's slow poison, tolerant and bland,
Has moved her blood. Parched years that I have seen
That may be hers appear; foul, lingering
Death in certain war, the slim legs green.
10   Or, fed on hate, she relishes the sting
Of others' agony; perhaps the cruel
Bride of a syphilitic or a fool.
These speculations sour in the sun.
I have no daughter. I desire none.

—1943

Randall Jarrell
(1914-1965)

Jarrell excelled as both a poet and a (sometimes brutally honest) reviewer of poetry. Ironically, the author of what is perhaps the best-known poem to have emerged from World War II did not see combat during the war: he served as a control tower officer in stateside bases. A native of Nashville, Kentucky, Jarrell studied at Vanderbilt University and followed his mentor, John Crowe Ransom, to Kenyon College in 1937, where he befriended another student, Robert Lowell.

The Death of the Ball Turret Gunner

From my mother's sleep I fell into the State,
And I hunched in its belly till my wet fur froze.
Six miles from earth, loosed from its dream of life,
I woke to black flak and the nightmare fighters.
5   When I died they washed me out of the turret with a hose.

—1945

Margaret Walker
(1915-)

As a black woman poet, Walker has perhaps been overshadowed by Gwendolyn Brooks, even though Walker's receipt of

---

Ball Turret A plexiglass sphere set into the belly of a heavy bomber; Jarrell noted the similarity between the gunner and a fetus in the womb.

the Yale Younger Poets Award in 1942 for *For My People* came some years before Brooks's own recognition. A longtime teacher at Jackson State University, she has influenced several generations of young writers.

For Malcolm X

All you violated ones with gentle hearts;
You violent dreamers whose cries shout heartbreak;
Whose voices echo clamors of our cool capers,
And whose black faces have hollowered pits for eyes.
5   All you gambling sons and hooked children and bowery bums
Hating white devils and black bourgeoisie,
Thumbing your noses at your burning red suns,
Gather round this coffin and mourn your dying swan.

Snow-white moslem head-dress around a dead black face!
10   Beautiful were your sand-papering words against our skins!
Our blood and water pour from your flowing wounds.
You have cut open our breasts and dug scalpels in our brains.
When and Where will another come to take your holy place?
Old man mumbling in his dotage, or crying child, unborn?

—1970

Gwendolyn Brooks
(1917-)

The first black poet to win a Pulitzer Prize for poetry, Brooks has reflected many changes in black culture during her long career, and she has written about the stages of her own life and career candidly in *From the Mecca*, her literary autobiography. The last Poetry Consultant of the Library of Congress before that position became Poet Laureate of the United States, Brooks is among the most honored of living American poets.

The Mother

Abortions will not let you forget.
You remember the children you got that you did not get,
The damp small pulps with a little or with no hair,
The singers and workers that never handled the air.
5   You will never neglect or beat

them, or silence or buy with a sweet.
You will never wind up the sucking-thumb
Or scuttle off ghosts that come.
You will never leave them, controlling your luscious sigh,
10   Return for a snack of them, with gobbling mother-eye.

I have heard in the voices of the wind the voices of my dim killed children.
I have contracted. I have eased
My dim dears at the breasts they could never suck.
I have said, Sweets, if I sinned, if I seized
15   Your luck
And your lives from your unfinished reach,
If I stole your births and your names,
Your straight baby tears and your games,
Your stilted or lovely loves, your tumults, your marriages, aches, and your deaths,
20   If I poisoned the beginnings of your breaths,
Believe that even in my deliberateness I was not deliberate.
Though why should I whine,
Whine that the crime was other than mine?—
Since anyhow you are dead.
25   Or rather, or instead,
You were never made.
But that too, I am afraid,
Is faulty: oh, what shall I say, how is the truth to be said?
You were born, you had body, you died.
30   It is just that you never giggled or planned or cried.

Believe me, I loved you all.
Believe me, I knew you, though faintly, and I loved, I loved you
All.

—1945

We Real Cool

The pool Players.
Seven at the Golden Shovel.

We real cool. We
Left school. We

Lurk late. We
Strike straight. We

5   Sing sin. We

Thin gin. We

Jazz June. We
Die soon.

—1960

Charles Causley
(1917-)

Except for service in the British Royal Navy in World War II,
Causley has spent most of his life teaching in his native Cornwall.
He has written extensively for children, and many of his ballads
display the influence of the popular song. Causley was virtually
unknown in the United States until *Secret Destinations*, a volume
of his selected poems, was published in 1989.

Eden Rock

They are waiting for me somewhere beyond Eden Rock:
My father, twenty-five, in the same suit
Of Genuine Irish Tweed, his terrier Jack
Still two years old and trembling at his feet.

5 My mother, twenty-three, in a sprigged dress
Drawn at the waist, ribbon in her straw hat,
Has spread the stiff white cloth over the grass.
Her hair, the colour of wheat, takes on the light.

She pours tea from a Thermos, the milk straight
10 From an old H.P. sauce-bottle, a screw
Of paper for a cork; slowly sets out
The same three plates, the tin cups painted blue.

The sky whitens as if lit by three suns.
My mother shades her eyes and looks my way
15 Over the drifted stream. My father spins
A stone along the water. Leisurely,

They beckon to me from the other bank.
I hear them call, 'See where the stream-path is!
Crossing is not as hard as you might think.'

20 I had not thought that it would be like this.

—1989

Robert Lowell
(1917-1977)

Because of the immense influence of his nakedly autobiograph-
ical collection of 1959 *Life Studies*, Lowell is noted as one of the
chief confessional poets. His literary career covered many
bases—complex, formal early work; poetic dramas and
translations; statements of a public figure—and he had, as the
scion of one of Boston's oldest families, a ready-made stature
that made him a celebrity for most of his adult life.

For the Union Dead

"Relinquum Omnia Servare Rem Publicam" °

The old South Boston Aquarium stands
in a Sahara of snow now. Its broken windows are boarded.
The bronze weathervane cod has lost half its scales.
The airy tanks are dry.

5 Once my nose crawled like a snail on the glass;
my hand tingled
to burst the bubbles
drifting from the noses of the cowed, compliant fish.

My hand draws back. I often sigh still
10 for the dark downward and vegetating kingdom
of the fish and reptile. On a morning last March,
I pressed against the new barbed and galvanized

fence on the Boston Common. Behind their cage,
yellow dinosaur steamshovels were grunting
15 as they cropped up tons of mush and grass
to gouge their underworld garage.

Parking spaces luxuriate like civics
sandpiles in the heart of Boston.
A girdle of orange, Puritan-pumpkin colored girders
20 braces the tingling Statehouse,

Relinquum . . . Publicam They sacrificed everything to serve the state

shaking over the excavations, as it faces Colonel Shaw °
and his bell-cheeked Negro infantry
on St. Gaudens'° shaking Civil War relief,
propped by a plank splint against the garage's earthquake.

25   Two months after marching through Boston,
half the regiment was dead;
at the dedication,
William James° could almost hear the bronze Negroes breathe.

Their monument sticks like a fishbone
30   in the city's throat.
Its Colonel is as lean
as a compass-needle.

He has an angry wrenlike vigilance,
a greyhound's gentle tautness;
35   he seems to wince at pleasure,
and suffocate for privacy.

He is out of bounds now. He rejoices in man's lovely,
peculiar power to choose life and die—
when he leads his black soldiers to death,
40   he cannot bend his back.

On a thousand small town New England greens,
the old white churches hold their air
of sparse, sincere rebellion; frayed flags
quilt the graveyards of the Grand Army of the Republic.

45   The stone statues of the abstract Union Soldier
grow slimmer and younger each year—
wasp-waisted, they doze over muskets
and muse through their sideburns . . .

Shaw's father wanted no monument
50   except the ditch,
where his son's body was thrown
and lost with his "niggers."

---

21 Colonel Shaw Robert Gould Shaw (1837-1863) led the black troops of the Massachusetts 54th
regiment and died with many of them during the attack on Fort Wagner, S.C. *Glory*, a recent film, was
based on these events.   **23 St. Gaudens** American sculptor (1848-1907)   **28 William James** American
philosopher (1842-1910) who gave a dedication speech for the monument

The ditch is nearer.
There are no statues for the last war here;
55   on Boylston Street, a commercial photograph
shows Hiroshima boiling

over a Mosler Safe, the "Rock of Ages"
that survived the blast. Space is nearer.
When I crouch to my television set,
60   the drained faces of Negro school-children° rise like balloons.

Colonel Shaw
is riding on his bubble,
he waits
for the blessèd break.

65   The Aquarium is gone. Everywhere,
giant finned cars nose forward like fish;
a savage servility
slides by on grease.

                                                —1959

❖ ❖ ❖

Howard Nemerov
(1920-1991)

Nemerov served as Poet Laureate of the United States during
1988 and 1989. A poet of brilliant formal inventiveness, he was
also a skilled satirist and observer of the American scene. His sis-
ter, Diane Arbus, was a famous photographer. His *Collected
Poems* won the Pulitzer prize in 1978.

The Goose Fish°

On the long shore, lit by the moon
To show them properly alone,
Two lovers suddenly embraced
So that their shadows were as one.
5   The ordinary night was graced
For them by the swift tide of blood

---

60 Negro school-children refers to protesters during the early days of the civil-rights movement
Goose Fish anglerfish

That silently they took at flood,
And for a little time they prized
   Themselves emparadised.

10   Then, as if shaken by stage-fright
Beneath the hard moon's bony light,
They stood together on the sand
Embarrassed in each other's sight
But still conspiring hand in hand,
15   Until they saw, there underfoot,
As though the world had found them out,
The goose fish turning up, though dead,
   His hugely grinning head.

There in the china light he lay,
20   Most ancient and corrupt and grey
They hesitated at his smile,
Wondering what it seemed to say
To lovers who a little while
Before had thought to understand,
25   By violence upon the sand,
The only way that could be known
   To make a world their own.

It was a wide and moony grin
Together peaceful and obscene;
30   They knew not what he would express,
So finished a comedian
He might mean failure or success,
But took it for an emblem of
Their sudden, new and guilty love
35   To be observed by, when they kissed,
   That rigid optimist.

So he became their patriarch,
Dreadfully mild in the half-dark.
His throat that the sand seemed to choke,
40   His picket teeth, these left their mark
But never did explain the joke
That so amused him, lying there
While the moon went down to disappear
Along the still and tilted track
45   That bears the zodiac.

   —1955

A Primer of the Daily Round

A peels an apple, while B kneels to God,
C telephones to D, who has a hand
On E's knee, F coughs, G turns up the sod
For H's grave, I do not understand
5   But J is bringing one clay pigeon down
While K brings down a nightstick on L's head,
And M takes mustard, N drives into town,
O goes to bed with P, and Q drops dead,
R lies to S, but happens to be heard
10   By T, who tells U not to fire V
For having to give W the word
That X is now deceiving Y with Z,
     Who happens just now to remember A
     Peeling an apple somewhere far away.

                                                        —1958

Richard Wilbur
(1921-)

Posterity will remember Wilbur as perhaps the most skillful metricist and exponent of wit that American poetry has produced. His highly polished poetry—against the grain of much contemporary writing—is a monument to his craftsmanship and intelligence. Perhaps the most honored of all living American poets, Wilbur served as Poet Laureate of the United States in 1987. His translations of the verse dramas of Molière and Racine are regularly performed throughout the world.

Playboy

High on his stockroom ladder like a dunce
The stock-boy sits, and studies like a sage
The subject matter of one glossy page,
As lost in curves as Archimedes° once.

5   Sometimes, without a glance, he feeds himself.
The left hand, like a mother-bird in flight,

---

4 Archimedes Greek mathematician (287-212 B.C.)

Brings him a sandwich for a sidelong bite,
And then returns it to a dusty shelf.

What so engrosses him? The wild décor
10   Of this pink-papered alcove into which
A naked girl has stumbled, with its rich
Welter of pelts and pillows on the floor,

Amidst which, kneeling in a supple pose,
She lifts a goblet in her farther hand,
15   As if about to toast a flower-stand
Above which hovers an exploding rose

Fired from a long-necked crystal vase that rests
Upon a tasseled and vermillion cloth
One taste of which would shrivel up a moth?
20   Or is he pondering her perfect breasts?

Nothing escapes him of her body's grace
Or of her floodlit skin, so sleek and warm
And yet so strangely like a uniform,
But what now grips his fancy is her face.

25   And how the cunning picture holds her still
At just that smiling instant when her soul,
Grown sweetly faint, and sweet beyond control,
Consents to his inexorable will.

—1969

The Writer

In her room at the prow of the house
Where light breaks, and the windows are tossed with linden,
My daughter is writing a story.

I pause in the stairwell, hearing
5   From her shut door a commotion of typewriter-keys
Like a chain hauled over a gunwale.

Young as she is, the stuff
Of her life is a great cargo, and some of it heavy:
I wish her a lucky passage.

10   But now it is she who pauses,

As if to reject my thought and its easy figure.
A stillness greatens, in which

The whole house seems to be thinking,
And then she is at it again with a bunched clamor
15   Of strokes, and again is silent.

I remember the dazed starling
Which was trapped in that very room, two years ago;
How we stole in, lifted a sash

And retreated, not to affright it;
20   And how for a helpless hour, through the crack of the door,
We watched the sleek, wild, dark

And iridescent creature
Batter against the brilliance, drop like a glove
To the hard floor, or the desk-top.

25   And wait then, humped and bloody,
For the wits to try it again; and how our spirits
Rose when, suddenly sure,

It lifted off from a chair-back,
Beating a smooth course for the right window
30   And clearing the sill of the world.

It is always a matter, my darling,
Of life or death, as I had forgotten. I wish
What I wished you before, but harder.

—1976

Year's End

Now winter downs the dying of the year,
And night is all a settlement of snow;
From the soft street the rooms of houses show
A gathered light, a shapen atmosphere,
5   Like frozen-over lakes whose ice is thin
And still allows some stirring down within.

I've known the wind by water banks to shake
The late leaves down, which frozen where they fell
And held in ice as dancers in a spell

10 Fluttered all winter long into a lake;
    Graved on the dark in gestures of descent,
    They seemed their own most perfect monument.

    There was perfection in the death of ferns
    Which laid their fragile cheeks against the stone
15 A million years. Great mammoths overthrown
    Composedly have made their long sojourns,
    Like palaces of patience, in the gray
    And changeless lands of ice. And at Pompeii°

    The little dog lay curled and did not rise
20 But slept the deeper as the ashes rose
    And found the people incomplete, and froze
    The random hands, the loose unready eyes
    Of men expecting yet another sun
    To do the shapely thing they had not done.

25 These sudden ends of time must give us pause.
    We fray into the future, rarely wrought
    Save in the tapestries of afterthought.
    More time, more time. Barrages of applause
    Come muffled from a buried radio.
30 The New-year bells are wrangling with the snow.

                                                      —1950

Philip Larkin
(1922-1985)

After Auden, Larkin was perhaps the last British poet to establish a significant body of readers in the United States. The general pessimism of his work is mitigated by a wry sense of irony and brilliant formal control. For many years he was a librarian at the University of Hull, and he was also a dedicated fan and critic of jazz.

Next, Please

Always too eager for the future, we
Pick up bad habits of expectancy.

---

18 Pompeii Roman city destroyed by volcanic eruption in 79 A.D.

Something is always approaching; every day
Till then we say,

5   Watching from a bluff the tiny, clear,
Sparkling armada of promises draw near.
How slow they are! And how much time they waste,
Refusing to make haste!

Yet still they leave us holding wretched stalks
10 Of disappointment, for, though nothing balks
Each big approach, leaning with brasswork prinked,
Each rope distinct,

Flagged, and the figurehead with golden tits
Arching our way, it never anchors; it's
15 No sooner present than it turns to past.
Right to the last

We think each one will heave to and unload
All good into our lives, all we are owed
For waiting so devoutly and so long.
20 But we are wrong:

Only one ship is seeking us, a black-
Sailed unfamiliar, towing at her back
A huge and birdless silence. In her wake
No waters breed or break.

                                                        —1951

The Old Fools

What do they think has happened, the old fools,
To make them like this? Do they somehow suppose
It's more grown-up when your mouth hangs open and drools,
And you keep on pissing yourself, and can't remember
5   Who called this morning? Or that, if they only chose,
They could alter things back to when they danced all night,
Or went to their wedding, or sloped arms some September?
Or do they fancy there's really been no change,
And they've always behaved as if they were crippled or tight,
10 Or sat through days of thin continuous dreaming
Watching light move? If they don't (and they can't), it's strange:
                        Why aren't they screaming?

At death, you break up: the bits that were you
Start speeding away from each other for ever
15   With no one to see. It's only oblivion, true:
We had it before, but then it was going to end,
And was all the time merging with a unique endeavour
To bring to bloom the million-petalled flower
Of being here. Next time you can't pretend
20   There'll be anything else. And these are the first signs:
Not knowing how, not hearing who, the power
Of choosing gone. Their looks show that they're for it:
Ash hair, toad hands, prune face dried into lines—
              How can they ignore it?

25   Perhaps being old is having lighted rooms
Inside your head, and people in them, acting.
People you know, yet can't quite name; each looms
Like a deep loss restored, from known doors turning,
Setting down a lamp, smiling from a stair, extracting
30   A known book from the shelves; or sometimes only
The rooms themselves, chairs and a fire burning,
The blown bush at the window, or the sun's
Faint friendliness on the wall some lonely
Rain-ceased midsummer evening. That is where they live:
35   Not here and now, but where all happened once.
              This is why they give

An air of baffled absence, trying to be there
Yet being here. For the rooms grow farther, leaving
Incompetent cold, the constant wear and tear
40   Of taken breath, and them crouching below
Extinction's alp, the old fools, never perceiving
How near it is. This must be what keeps them quiet:
The peak that stays in view wherever we go
For them is rising ground. Can they never tell
45   What is dragging them back, and how it will end? Not at night?
Not when the strangers come? Never, throughout
The whole hideous inverted childhood? Well,
            We shall find out.

                      —1973

This Be The Verse

They fuck you up, your mum and dad.
  They may not mean to, but they do.

They fill you with the faults they had
    And add some extra, just for you.

5   But they were fucked up in their turn
      By fools in old-style hats and coats,
    Who half the time were soppy-stern
      And half at one another's throats.

    Man hands on misery to man.
10   It deepens like a coastal shelf.
    Get out as early as you can,
      And don't have any kids yourself.

—1971

James Dickey
(1923-)

Dickey became a national celebrity with the success of his novel
Deliverance (1970) and the celebrated film version. There was a
long background to Dickey's success, with years spent in the
advertising business before he devoted himself fully to writing.
Born in Atlanta and educated at Clemson, Vanderbilt, and Rice
universities, Dickey has rarely strayed long from the South and
has taught at the University of South Carolina for over two
decades.

Cherrylog Road

Off Highway 106
At Cherrylog Road I entered
The '34 Ford without wheels,
Smothered in kudzu,°
5   With a seat pulled out to run
Corn whiskey down from the hills,

And then from the other side
Crept into an Essex
With a rumble seat of red leather
10   And then out again, aboard
A blue Chevrolet, releasing

---

4 **kudzu** prolific Asian vine widespread in the South

The rust from its other color,

Reared up on three building blocks
None had the same body heat;
15   I changed with them inward, toward
The weedy heart of the junkyard,
For I knew that Doris Holbrook
Would escape from her father at noon

And would come from the farm
20   To seek parts owned by the sun
Among the abandoned chassis,
Sitting in each in turn
As I did, leaning forward
As in a wild stock-car race

25   In the parking lot of the dead.
Time after time, I climbed in
And out the other side, like
An envoy or movie star
Met at the station by crickets.
30   A radiator cap raised its head,

Become a real toad or a kingsnake
As I neared the hub of the yard,
Passing through many states,
Many lives, to reach
35   Some grandmother's long Pierce-Arrow
Sending platters of blindness forth

From its nickel hubcaps
And spilling its tender upholstery
On sleepy roaches,
40   The glass panel in between
Lady and colored driver
Not all the way broken out,

The back-seat phone
Still on its hook.
45   I got in as though to exclaim,
"Let us go to the orphan asylum,
John; I have some old toys
For children who say their prayers."

I popped with sweat as I thought
50   I heard Doris Holbrook scrape
Like a mouse in the southern-state sun
That was eating the paint in blisters
From a hundred car tops and hoods
She was tapping like code,

55   Loosening the screws,
Carrying off headlights,
Sparkplugs, bumpers,
Cracked mirrors and gear-knobs,
Getting ready, already,
60   To go back with something to show

Other than her lips' new trembling
I would hold to me soon, soon,
Where I sat in the ripped back seat
Talking over the interphone,
65   Praying for Doris Holbrook
To come from her father's farm

And to get back there
With no trace of me on her face
To be seen by her red-haired father
70   Who would change, in the squalling barn
Her back's pale skin with a strop,
Then lay for me

In a bootlegger's roasting car
With a string-triggered 12-gauge shotgun
75   To blast the breath from the air.
Not cut by the jagged windshields,
Through the acres of wrecks she came
With a wrench in her hand,

Through dust where the blacksnake dies
80   Of boredom, and the beetle knows
The compost has no more life.
Someone outside would have seen
The oldest car's door inexplicably
Close from within:

85   I held her and held her and held her,
Convoyed at terrific speed

By the stalled, dreaming traffic around us,
So the blacksnake, stiff
With inaction, curved back
90 Into life, and hunted the mouse

With deadly overexcitement,
The beetles reclaimed their field
As we clung, glued together,
With the hooks of the seat springs
95 Working through to catch us red-handed
Amidst the gray breathless batting

That burst from the seat at our backs.
We left by separate doors
Into the changed, other bodies
100 Of cars, she down Cherrylog Road
And I to my motorcycle
Parked like the soul of the junkyard

Restored, a bicycle fleshed
With power, and tore off
105 Up Highway 106, continually
Drunk on the wind in my mouth,
Wringing the handlebar for speed,
Wild to be wreckage forever.

—1964

Alan Dugan
(1923-)

Dugan received the 1961 Yale Younger Poets Award, leading to
the publication of his first collection as he neared forty. His plain-
spoken poetic voice, often with sardonic overtones, is appropri-
ate for the anti-romantic stance of his most characteristic poems.
For many years Dugan has been associated with the Fine Arts
Work Center in Provincetown, Massachusetts, on Cape Cod.

Love Song: I and Thou

Nothing is plumb, level or square:
    the studs are bowed, the joists
are shaky by nature, no piece fits

any other piece without a gap
5   or pinch, and bent nails
dance all over the surfacing
like maggots. By Christ
I am no carpenter. I built
the roof for myself, the walls
10   for myself, the floors
for myself, and got
hung up in it myself. I
danced with a purple thumb
at this house-warming, drunk
15   with my prime whiskey: rage.
Oh I spat rage's nails
into the frame-up of my work:
it held. It settled plumb,
level, solid, square and true
20   for that great moment. Then
it screamed and went on through,
skewing as wrong the other way.
God damned it. This is hell,
but I planned it. I sawed it,
25   I nailed it, and I
will live in it until it kills me.
I can nail my left palm
to the left-hand cross-piece but
I can't do everything myself.
30   I need a hand to nail the right,
a help, a love, a you, a wife.

—1961

Anthony Hecht
(1923-)

Hecht is most often linked with Richard Wilbur as one of the
American poets of the postwar era who have most effectively
utilized traditional poetic forms. The brilliance of Hecht's tech-
nique, however, must be set beside the powerful moral intelli-
gence that informs his poetry. *The Hard Hours*, his second collec-
tion, won the Pulitzer prize for 1968.

"More Light! More Light!"°

For Heinrich Blücher and Hannah Arendt°

Composed in the Tower before his° execution
These moving verses, and being brought at that time
Painfully to the stake, submitted, declaring thus:
"I implore my God to witness that I have made no crime."

5   Nor was he forsaken of courage, but the death was horrible,
The sack of gunpowder failing to ignite.
His legs were blistered sticks on which the black sap
Bubbled and burst as he howled for the Kindly Light.

And that was but one, and by no means one of the worst;
10 Permitted at least his pitiful dignity;
And such as were by made prayers in the name of Christ,
That shall judge all men, for his soul's tranquility.

We move now to outside a German wood°
Three men are there commanded to dig a hole
15 In which the two Jews are ordered to lie down
And be buried by the third, who is a Pole.

Not light from the shrine at Weimar° beyond the hill
Nor light from heaven appeared. But he did refuse.
A Lüger° settled back deeply in its glove.
20 He was ordered to change places with the Jews.

Much casual death had drained away their souls.
The thick dirt mounted toward the quivering chin.
When only the head was exposed the order came
To dig him out again and to get back in.

25 No light, no light in the blue Polish eye.
When he finished a riding boot packed down the earth.
The Lüger hovered lightly in its glove.
He was shot in the belly and in three hours bled to death.

No prayers or incense rose up in those hours

More Light! More Light! reputed last words of Johann Wolfgang von Goethe (1749-1832), greatest
German poet **Heinrich Blücher and Hannah Arendt** husband and wife who escaped from Germany
in 1941; Arendt wrote several books on the Holocaust **1 his** a fictional English religious martyr (c.
1550), a composite of several actual cases **13 German wood** Buchenwald ("beechen wood") was the
site of a concentration camp **17 shrine at Weimar** Goethe's home **19 Lüger** German military pistol

30   Which grew to be years, and every day came mute
      Ghosts from the ovens, sifting through crisp air,
      And settled upon his eyes in a black soot.

                                                    —1967

In Memory of David Kalstone°

who died of AIDS

      Lime-and-mint mayonnaise and salsa verde
      Accompanied poached fish that Helen° made
      For you and J.M.° when you came to see us
      Just at the salmon season. Now a shade,

5   A faint blurred absence who before had been
      Funny, intelligent, kindness itself,
      You leave behind, beside the shock of death,
      Three of the finest books upon my shelf.

      "Men die from time to time," said Rosalind,°
10   "But not," she said, "for love." A lot she knew!
      From the green world of Africa the plague
      Wiped out the Forest of Arden,° the whole crew

      Of innocents, of which. poor generous ghost,
      You were among the liveliest. Your friend
15   Scattered upon the calm Venetian tides
      Your sifted ashes so they might descend

      Even to the bottom of the monstrous world
      Or lap at marble steps and pass below
      The little bridges, whirl and eddy through
20   A liquified Palazzo Barbaro.

      That mirrored splendor briefly entertains
      Your passing as the whole edifice trembles
      Within the waters of the Grand Canal,
      And writhes and twists, wrinkles and reassembles.

                                                    —1990

David Kalstone American literary critic   **2 Helen** Hecht's wife   **3 J.M.** poet James Merrill
9 Rosalind character in Shakespeare's *As You Like It*   **12 Forest of Arden** setting of *As You Like It*
20-23 Palazzo Barbaro . . . Grand Canal locations in Venice

Denise Levertov
(1923-)

Levertov was as an outspoken opponent of U.S. involvement in the Vietnam War , an activity that has tended to overshadow her accomplishments as a lyric poet. Born of Jewish and Welsh parents in England, she emigrated to the United States during World War II.

The Ache of Marriage

The ache of marriage:

thigh and tongue, beloved,
are heavy with it,
it throbs in the teeth

5   We look for communion
and are turned away, beloved,
each and each

It is leviathan° and we
in its belly
10 looking for joy, some joy
not to be known outside it

two by two in the ark of
the ache of it.

                —1964

Louis Simpson
(1923-)

Born in Jamaica to a colonial lawyer and an American mother, Simpson came to the United States in his teens and served in the U.S. Army in World War II. He won the Pulitzer prize in 1964 for *At the End of the Open Road*, a volume that attempts to reexamine

---

8 leviathan great sea-creature mentioned in book of Job

Walt Whitman's nineteenth century definitions of the American experience. Subsequent collections have continued to demonstrate Simpson's unsentimental view of American suburban life.

American Classic

It's a classic American scene—
a car stopped off the road
and a man trying to repair it.

The woman who stays in the car
5   in the classic American scene
stares back at the freeway traffic.

They look surprised, and ashamed
to be so helpless . . .
let down in the middle of the road!

10   To think that their car would do this!
They look like mountain people
whose son has gone against the law.

But every night they set out food
and the robber goes skulking back to the trees.
15   That's how it is with the car . . .

it's theirs, they're stuck with it.
Now they know what it's like to sit
and see the world go whizzing by.

In the fume of carbon monoxide and dust
20   they are not such good Americans
as they thought they were.

The feeling of being left out
through no fault of your own, is common.
That's why I say, an American classic.

—1980

My Father in the Night Commanding No

My father in the night commanding No
Has work to do. Smoke issues from his lips;

He reads in silence.
The frogs are croaking and the street lamps glow.

5   And then my mother winds the gramophone:
The Bride of Lammermoor° begins to shriek—
   Or reads a story
About a prince, a castle, and a dragon.

The moon is glittering above the hill.
10   I stand before the gateposts of the King—
   So runs the story—
Of Thule, at midnight when the mice are still.

And I have been in Thule! It has come true—
The journey and the danger of the world,
15   All that there is
To bear and to enjoy, endure and do.

Landscapes, seascapes . . . Where have I been led?
The names of cities—Paris, Venice, Rome—
   Held out their arms.
20   A feathered god, seductive, went ahead.

Here is my house. Under a red rose tree
A child is swinging; another gravely plays.
   They are not surprised
That I am here; they were expecting me.

25   And yet my father sits and reads in silence,
My mother sheds a tear, the moon is still,
   And the dark wind
Is murmuring that nothing ever happens.

Beyond his jurisdiction as I move,
30   Do I not prove him wrong? And yet, it's true
   They will not change
There, on the stage of terror and of love.

The actors in that playhouse always sit
In fixed positions—father, mother, child
35   With painted eyes.
How sad it is to be a little puppet!

---

6 Bride of Lammermoor *Lucia di Lammermoor*, opera by Donizetti

Their heads are wooden. And you once pretended
To understand them! Shake them as you will,
    They cannot speak.
40   Do what you will, the comedy is ended.

Father, why did you work? Why did you weep,
Mother? Was the story so important?
    "Listen!" the wind
Said to the children, and they fell asleep.

                          —1963

Vassar Miller
(1924-)

A lifelong resident of Houston, Texas, and a victim of cerebral
palsy since birth, Miller has published both traditional devotional
verse and a large amount of poetry in open form. *If I Had
Wheels or Love*, her collected poems, appeared in 1990.

Subterfuge

I remember my father, slight,
staggering in with his Underwood,°
bearing it in his arms like an awkward bouquet

for his spastic child who sits down
5   on the floor, one knee on the frame
of the typewriter, and holding her left wrist

with her right hand, in that precision known
to the crippled, pecks at the keys
with a sparrow's preoccupation.

10 Falling by chance on rhyme, novel and curious bubble
blown with a magic pipe, she tries them over and over,
spellbound by life's clashing in accord or against itself,

pretending pretense and playing at playing,
she does her childhood backward as children do,

---

2 **Underwood** popular brand of manual typewriter

15   her fun a delaying action against what she knows.

My father must lose her, his runaway on her treadmill,
will lose the terrible favor that life has done him
as she toils at tomorrow, tensed at her makeshift toy.

                                                    —1981

Donald Justice
(1925-)

A Floridian who returned to his native state to serve as poet-in-residence at the University of Florida, Justice has published more selectively than most of his contemporaries. His Pulitzer prize-winning volume of selected poems displays considerable literary sophistication and reveals the poet's familiarity with contemporary European and Latin American poetry.

Counting the Mad

This one was put in a jacket,
This one was sent home,
This one was given bread and meat
But would eat none,
5   And this one cried No No No No
All day long.

This one looked at the window
As though it were a wall,
This one saw things that were not there,
10   This one things that were,
And this one cried No No No No
All day long.

This one thought himself a bird,
This one a dog,
15   And this one thought himself a man,
An ordinary man,
And cried and cried No No No No
All day long.

                                                    —1959

Carolyn Kizer
(1925-)

Kizer's fascinating career includes a year's study in Taiwan and another year in Pakistan, where she worked for the U.S. State Department. Her first collection, *The Ungrateful Garden* (1961), demonstrates an equal facility with formal and free verse, but her subsequent books (including the Pulitzer prize-winning *Yin* of 1985) have tended more toward the latter. A committed feminist, Kizer anticipated many of today's women's issues as early as the mid 1950s, just as "The Ungrateful Garden" was published and a decade before "ecology" became a household word.

The Ungrateful Garden

Midas watched the golden crust
That formed over his streaming sores,
Hugged his agues, loved his lust,
But damned to hell the out-of-doors

5   Where blazing motes of sun impaled
The serried° roses, metal-bright.
"Those famous flowers," Midas wailed,
"Have scorched my retina with light."

This gift, he'd thought, would gild his joys,
10   Silt up the waters of his grief;
His lawns a wilderness of noise,
The heavy clang of leaf on leaf.

Within, the golden cup is good
To heft, to sip the yellow mead.
15   Outside, in summer's rage, the rude
Gold thorn has made his fingers bleed.

"I strolled my halls in golden shift,
As ruddy as a lion's meat.
Then I rushed out to share my gift,
20   And golden stubble cut my feet."

---

6 serried crowded in rows

Dazzled with wounds, he limped away
To climb into his golden bed.
Roses, roses can betray.
"Nature is evil," Midas said.

—1961

Maxine Kumin
(1925-)

Born in Philadelphia and educated at Radcliffe, Kumin was an
early literary ally and friend of Anne Sexton, with whom she co-
authored several children's books. The winner of the 1973 Pulitzer
prize, Kumin has preferred a rural life raising horses for some
years. Her increased interest in the natural world has paralleled
the environmental awareness of many of her readers.

Noted in the *New York Times*
Lake Buena Vista, Florida, June 16, 1987

Death claimed the last pure dusky seaside sparrow
today, whose coastal range was narrow,
as narrow as its two-part buzzy song.
From hummocks lost to Cape Canaveral
5   this mouselike skulker in the matted grass,
a six-inch bird, plain brown, once thousands strong,
sang *toodle-raeee azhee*, ending on a trill
before the air gave way to rocket blasts.

It laid its dull white eggs (brown specked) in small
10   neat cups of grass on plots of pickleweed,
bulrushes, or salt hay. It dined
on caterpillars, beetles, ticks, the seeds
of sedges. Unremarkable
the life it lead with others of its kind.

15   Tomorrow we can put it on a stamp,
a first-day cover with Key Largo rat,
Schaus swallowtail, Florida swamp
crocodile, and fading cotton mouse.
How simply symbols replace habitat!
20   The tower frames of Aerospace

quiver in the flush of another shot
where, once indigenous, the dusky sparrow
soared trilling twenty feet above its burrow.

—1989

Robert Creeley
(1926-)

Educated at Harvard, Creeley is one of several important con-
temporary poets (Denise Levertov is another) to be associated
with Black Mountain College, a small experimental school in North
Carolina that attracted writers and artists during the 1950s.

Oh No

If you wander far enough
you will come to it
and when you get there
they will give you a place to sit

5   for yourself only, in a nice chair,
and all your friends will be there
with smiles on their faces
and they will likewise all have places.

—1962

Allen Ginsberg
(1926-)

Ginsberg, the chief poetic spokesman of the Beat Generation,
has remained a force—as poet and celebrity—who continues to
outrage and delight four decades after the appearance of
Howl, the monumental poem describing how Ginsberg saw: "the
best minds of my generation destroyed by madness."
Ginsberg's poems are cultural documents key to understanding
the radical changes in American life, particularly among youth,
that began in the mid 1950s.

A Supermarket in California

What thoughts I have of you tonight, Walt Whitman, for I walked down the streets under the trees with a headache self-conscious looking at the full moon.

In my hungry fatigue, and shopping for images, I went into the neon fruit su-
permarket, dreaming of your enumerations!

5   What peaches and what penumbras?° Whole families shopping at night! Aisles
full of husbands! Wives in the avocados, babies in the tomatoes!—and you, García
Lorca,° what were you doing down by the watermelons?

I saw you, Walt Whitman, childless, lonely old grubber, poking among the
meats in the refrigerator and eyeing the grocery boys.

10 I heard you asking questions of each: Who killed the pork chops? What price
bananas? Are you my Angel?

I wandered in and out of the brilliant stacks of cans following you, and fol-
lowed in my imagination by the store detective.

We strode down the open corridors together in our solitary fancy tasting arti-
15 chokes, possessing every frozen delicacy, and never passing the cashier.

Where are we going, Walt Whitman? The doors close in an hour. Which way
does your beard point tonight?

(I touch your book and dream of our odyssey in the supermarket and feel
absurd.)

20 Will we walk all night through solitary streets? The trees add shade to shade,
lights out in the houses, we'll both be lonely.

Will we stroll dreaming of the lost America of love past blue automobiles in
driveways, home to our silent cottage?

Ah, dear father, graybeard, lonely old courage-teacher, what America did you
25 have when Charon° quit poling his ferry and you got out on a smoking bank and
stood watching the boat disappear on the black waters of Lethe?°

—1956

James Merrill
(1926-)

The Changing Light at Sandover, a long poem that resulted from
many years of sessions with a Ouija board, is Merrill's major work
and, among many other things, a straightforward memoir of a
long-term gay relationship. "Investiture at Cecconi's" is
addressed to David Kalstone, the literary critic who is also the
subject of an elegy by Anthony Hecht.

---

5 penumbras shadows   **6-7 García Lorca** Federico García Lorca, Spanish poet (1899-1936)
25 Charon ferryman of Hades   **26 Lethe** river in Hades

Casual Wear

Your average tourist: Fifty. 2.3
Times married. Dressed, this year, in Ferdi Plinthbower°
Originals. Odds 1 to 9¹⁰°
Against her strolling past the Embassy

5   Today at noon. Your average terrorist:
Twenty-five. Celibate. No use for trends,
At least in clothing. Mark, though, where it ends.
People have come forth made of colored mist

Unsmiling on one hundred million screens
10   To tell of his prompt phone call to the station,
"Claiming responsibility"—devastation
Signed with a flourish, like the dead wife's jeans.

                                    —1984

Investiture at Cecconi's°
for David Kalstone°

Caro, that dream (after the diagnosis)
found me losing patience outside the door of
"our" Venetian tailor. I wanted evening
clothes for the new year.

5   Then a bulb went on. The old woman, she who
stitches dawn to dusk in his back room, opened
one suspicious inch, all the while exclaiming
over the late hour—

Fabrics? patterns? those the proprietor must
10   show by day, not now—till a lightning insight
cracks her face wide: *Ma! the Signore's here to
try on his new robe!*

Robe? She nods me onward. The mirror triptych
summons three bent crones she diffracted into
15   back from no known space. They converge by magic,
arms full of moonlight.

---

2 Ferdi Plinthbower a fictional designer **3 1 to 9**¹⁰ pronounced "one to nine to the tenth power"
Cecconi's the tailor shop in l. 3 **David Kalstone** see note to Hecht's "For David Kalstone"

Up my own arms glistening sleeves are drawn. Cool
silk in grave, white folds—Oriental mourning—
sheathes me, throat to ankles. I turn to face her,
20   uncomprehending.

Thank your friend, she cackles, *the Professore!*
Wonderstruck I sway, like a tree of tears. You—
miles away, sick, fearful—have yet arranged this
heartstopping present.

—1988

W. D. Snodgrass
(1926-)

Snodgrass won the Pulitzer prize for his first collection, *Heart's Needle*, and is generally considered one of the first important confessional poets. However, in his later career he has turned away from autobiographical subjects, writing a long sequence of dramatic monologues spoken by leading Nazis during the final days of the Hitler regime.

Mementos, I

Sorting out letters and piles of my old
      Canceled checks, old clippings, and yellow note cards
That meant something once, I happened to find
      Your picture. *That* picture. I stopped there cold,
5   Like a man raking piles of dead leaves in his yard
            Who has turned up a severed hand.

Still, that first second, I was glad: you stand
      Just as you stood—shy, delicate, slender,
In that long gown of green lace netting and daisies
10   That you wore to our first dance. The sight of you stunned
Us all. Well, our needs were different, then,
            And our ideals came easy.

Then through the war and those two long years
      Overseas, the Japanese dead in their shacks
15   Among dishes, dolls, and lost shoes; I carried
      This glimpse of you, there, to choke down my fear,
Prove it had been, that it might come back.

That was before we got married.

—Before we drained out one another's force
20   With lies, self-denial, unspoken regret
And the sick eyes that blame; before the divorce
    And the treachery. Say it: before we met. Still,
I put back your picture. Someday, in due course,
    I will find that it's still there.

                                        —1968

Frank O'Hara
(1926-1966)

O'Hara's untimely death in a dune buggy accident on Fire Island
robbed American poetry of one its most refreshing talents. An
authority on modern art, O'Hara incorporates many of the spon-
taneous techniques of abstract painting in his own poetry, which
was often written as an immediate reaction to the events of his
daily life.

The Day Lady° Died

It is 12:20 in New York a Friday
three days after Bastille day,° yes
it is 1959 and I go get a shoeshine
because I will get off the 4:19 in Easthampton
5   at 7:15 and then go straight to dinner
and I don't know the people who will feed me

I walk up the muggy street beginning to sun
and have a hamburger and a malted and buy
an ugly NEW WORLD WRITING to see what the poets
10   in Ghana are doing these days
            I go on to the bank
and Miss Stillwagon (first name Linda I once heard)
doesn't even look up my balance for once in her life
and in the GOLDEN GRIFFIN I get a little Verlaine
15   for Patsy with drawings by Bonnard although I do
think of Hesiod, trans. Richmond Lattimore or
Brendan Behan's new play or *Le Balcon* or *Les Nègres*

Lady Billie Holiday (1915-1959), blues singer   **2 Bastille day** July 14

of Genet, but I don't, I stick with Verlaine
after practically going to sleep with quandariness

20 and for Mike I just stroll into the PARK LANE
Liquor Store and ask for a bottle of Strega and
then I go back where I came from to 6th Avenue
and the tobacconist in the Ziegfield Theatre and
casually ask for a carton of Gauloises and a carton
25 of Picayunes, and a NEW YORK POST with her face on it

and I am sweating a lot by now and thinking of
leaning on the john door in the 5 SPOT
while she whispered a song along the keyboard
to Mal Waldron° and everyone and I stopped breathing.

                                                        —1964

John Ashbery
(1927-)

Ashbery was born in Rochester, New York, and educated at
Harvard University. His first full-length book, *Some Trees*, was cho-
sen by W.H. Auden as winner of the Yale Younger Poets Award in
1956. His enigmatic poems have intrigued readers for so long
that much contemporary literary theory seems to have been
created expressly for explicating his poems. Impossible to dis-
miss, Ashbery is now seen as the chief inheritor of the symbolist
tradition brought to American locales by Wallace Stevens.

Paradoxes and Oxymorons

The poem is concerned with language on a very plain level.
Look at it talking to you. You look out a window
Or pretend to fidget. You have it but you don't have it.
You miss it, it misses you. You miss each other.

5   The poem is sad because it wants to be yours, and cannot.
What's a plain level? It is that and other things,
Bringing a system of them into play. Play?
Well, actually, yes, but I consider play to be

---

29 Mal Waldron Holiday's accompanist.

A deeper outside thing, a dreamed role-pattern,
10 As in the division of grace these long August days
Without proof. Open-ended. And before you know
It gets lost in the steam and chatter of typewriters.

It has been played once more. I think you exist only
To tease me into doing it, on your level, and then you aren't there
15 Or have adopted a different attitude. And the poem
Has set me softly down beside you. The poem is you.

—1981

What Is Poetry

The medieval town, with frieze
Of boy scouts from Nagoya?° The snow

That came when we wanted it to snow?
Beautiful images? Trying to avoid

5 Ideas, as in the poem? But we
Go back to them as to a wife, leaving

The mistress we desire? Now they
Will have to believe it

As we believe it. In school
10 All the thought got combed out:

What was left was like a field.
Shut your eyes, and you can feel it for miles around.

Now open them on a thin vertical path.
It might give us—what?—some flowers soon?

—1977

W. S. Merwin
(1927-)

In recent years Merwin's environmental concerns have come to

---

2 **Nagoya** city in Japan

dominate his poetry, but even in earlier work his fears of the
results of uncontrolled destruction of the environment are pre-
sented allegorically. Born in New York City, he currently resides in
Hawaii.

For the Anniversary of My Death

Every year without knowing it I have passed the day
When the last fires will wave to me
And the silence will set out
Tireless traveller
5   Like the beam of a lightless star
Then I will no longer
find myself in life as in a strange garment
surprised at the earth
And the love of one woman
10 And then shamelessness of men
As today writing after three days of rain
Hearing the wren sing and the falling cease
And bowing not knowing to what

—1969

The Last One

Well they'd make up their minds to be everywhere because why not.
Everywhere was theirs because they thought so.
They with two leaves they whom the birds despise.
In the middle of stones they made up their minds.
5   They started to cut.

Well they cut everything because why not.
Everything was theirs because they thought so.
It fell into its shadows and they took both away.
Some to have some for burning.

10 Well cutting everything they came to the water.
They came to the end of the day there was one left standing.
They would cut it tomorrow they went away.
The night gathered in the last branches.
The shadow of the night gathered in the shadow on the water.
15 The night and the shadow put on the same head.
And it said Now.

Well in the morning they cut the last one.

Like the others the last one fell into its shadow.
It fell into its shadow on the water.
20   They took it away its shadow stayed on the water.

Well they shrugged they started trying to get the shadow away.
They cut right to the ground the shadow stayed whole.
They laid boards on it the shadow came out on top.
They shone lights on it the shadow got blacker and clearer.
25   They exploded the water the shadow rocked.
They built a huge fire on the roots.
They sent up black smoke between the shadow and the sun.
The new shadow flowed without changing the old one.
They shrugged they went away to get stones.

30   They came back the shadow was growing.
They started setting up stones it was growing.
They looked the other way it went on growing.
They decided they would make a stone out of it.
They took stones to the water they poured them into the shadow.
35   They poured them in they poured them in the stones vanished.
The shadow was not filled it went on growing.
That was one day.

The next day was just the same it went on growing.
They did all the same things it was just the same.
40   They decided to take its water from under it.
They took away water they took it away the water went down.
The shadow stayed where it was before.
It went on growing it grew onto the land.
They started to scrape the shadow with machines.
45   When it touched the machines it stayed on them.
They started to beat the shadow with sticks.
Where it touched the sticks it stayed on them.
They started to beat the shadow with hands.
Where it touched the hands it stayed on them.
50   That was another day.

Well the next day started about the same it went on growing.
They pushed lights into the shadow.
Where the shadow got onto them they went out.
They began to stomp on the edge it got their feet.
55   And when it got their feet they fell down.
It got into eyes the eyes went blind.
The ones that fell down it grew over and they vanished.

The ones that went blind and walked into it vanished.
The ones that could see and stood still
60   It swallowed their shadows.
Then it swallowed them too and they vanished.
Well the others ran.

The ones that were left went away to live if it would let them.
They went as far as they could.
65   The lucky ones with their shadows.

—1969

James Wright
(1927-1980)

Wright's compassion for losers and underdogs of all types is everywhere in his poetry. A native of Martins Ferry, Ohio, he often described lives of quiet desperation in the blue-collar towns of his youth. Like many poets of his generation, Wright wrote formal verse in his early career and shifted to open forms during the 1960s.

Autumn Begins in Martins Ferry, Ohio 1963

In the Shreve High football stadium,
I think of Polacks nursing long beers in Tiltonsville,
And gray faces of Negroes in the blast furnace at Benwood,
And the ruptured night watchman of Wheeling Steel,
5   Dreaming of heroes.

All the proud fathers are ashamed to go home.
Their women cluck like starved pullets,
Dying for love.

Therefore,
10   Their sons grow suicidally beautiful
At the beginning of October,
And gallop terribly against each other's bodies.

—1963

Saint Judas

When I went out to kill myself, I caught

A pack of hoodlums beating up a man.
Running to spare his suffering, I forgot
My name, my number, how my day began,
5   How soldiers milled around the garden stone
And sang amusing songs; how all that day
Their javelins measured crowds; how I alone
Bargained the proper coins, and slipped away.

Banished from heaven, I found this victim beaten,
10   Stripped, kneed, and left to cry. Dropping my rope
Aside, I ran, ignored the uniforms:
Then I remembered bread my flesh had eaten,
The kiss that ate my flesh. Flayed without hope,
I held the man for nothing in my arms.

—1959

Philip Levine
(1928-)

Born in Detroit, Michigan, Levine is one of many contemporary
poets to hold a degree from the University of Iowa Writers'
Workshop. The gritty urban landscapes and characters trapped
in dead-end industrial jobs that provide Levine subjects for many
poems match exactly with his unadorned, informal idiom. Like the
deceptively simple William Carlos Williams, Levine has influenced
many younger poets.

Genius

Two old dancing shoes my grandfather
gave the Christian Ladies,
an unpaid water bill, the rear license
of a dog that messed on your lawn,
5   a tooth I saved for the good fairy
and which is stained with base metals
and plastic filler. With these images
and your black luck and my bad breath
a bright beginner could make a poem
10   in fourteen rhyming lines about the purity
of first love or the rose's many thorns
or dew that won't wait long enough
to stand my little gray wren a drink.

—1981

Donald Petersen
(1928-)

Born in Minneapolis, Minnesota, Petersen has taught for many years at the State University College in Oneonta, New York. One of Petersen's first appearances was in *New Poets of England and America*, a popular and influential anthology of the early 1960s.

The Ballad of Dead Yankees

Where's Babe Ruth,° the King of Swat,
Who rocked the heavens with his blows?
Grabowski, Pennock, and Malone—
Mother of mercy, where are those?

5   Where's Tony (Poosh 'em up) Lazzeri,
The quickest man that ever played?
Where's the gang that raised the roof
In the house that Colonel Ruppert made?

Where's Lou Gehrig, strong and shy,
10   who never missed a single game?
Where's Tiny Bonham, where's Jake Powell
And many another peerless name?

Where's Steve Sundra, good but late,
Who for a season had his fling?
15   Where are the traded, faded ones?
Lord, can they tell us anything?

Where's the withered nameless dwarf
Who sold us pencils at the gate?
Hurled past the clamor of our cheers?
20   Gone to rest with the good and great?

Where's the swagger, where's the strut,
Where's the style that was the hitter?
Where's the pitcher's swanlike motion?

---

1 **Babe Ruth** This and the names that follow are those of former players for the New York Yankees

What in God's name turned life bitter?

25 For strong-armed Steve, who lost control
And weighed no more than eighty pounds,
No sooner benched than in his grave,
Where's the cleverness that confounds?

For Lou the man, erect and clean,
30 Wracked with a cruel paralysis,
Gone in his thirty-seventh year,
Where's the virtue that was his?

For nimble Tony, cramped in death,
God knows why and God knows how,
35 Shut in a dark and silent house,
Where's the squirrel quickness now?

For big brash Babe in an outsize suit,
Himself grown thin and hoarse with cancer,
Still autographing balls for boys,
40 Mother of mercy, what's the answer?

Is there a heaven with rainbow flags,
Silver trophies hung on walls,
A horseshoe grandstand, mobs of fans,
Webbed gloves and official balls?

45 Is there a power in judgment there
To stand behind the body's laws,
A stern-faced czar whose slightest word
Is righteous as Judge Kenesaw's?°

And if there be no turnstile gate
50 At that green park, can we get in?
Is the game suspended or postponed,
And do the players play to win?

Mother of mercy, if you're there,
Pray to the high celestial czar
55 For all of these, the early dead,
Who've gone where no ovations are.

—1964

---

48 Judge Kenesaw Kenesaw Mountain Landis (1866-1945), the first commissioner of organized baseball

Anne Sexton
(1928-1974)

Sexton, with her tortured history of mental illness and family trou-
bles, is the model of the confessional poet. A housewife with two
small daughters, she began writing poetry as the result of a pro-
gram on public television, later taking a workshop from Robert
Lowell in which Sylvia Plath was a fellow student. For fifteen years
until her suicide, she was a vibrant, exciting presence in American
poetry. A controversial biography of Sexton by Diane Wood
Middlebrook appeared in 1991.

The Truth the Dead Know

For my mother, born March 1902, died March 1959
and my father, born February 1900, died June 1959

Gone, I say and walk from church,
refusing the stiff procession to the grave,
letting the dead ride alone in the hearse.
It is June. I am tired of being brave.

5   We drive to the Cape. I cultivate
myself where the sun gutters from the sky,
where the sea swings in like an iron gate
and we touch. In another country people die.

My darling, the wind falls in like stones
10   from the whitehearted water and when we touch
we enter touch entirely. No one's alone.
Men kill for this, or for as much.

And what of the dead? They lie without shoes
in their stone boats. They are more like stone
15   than the sea would be if it stopped. They refuse
to be blessed, throat, eye and knucklebone.

—1962

Wanting to Die

Since you ask, most days I cannot remember.
I walk in my clothing, unmarked by that voyage.

Then the almost unnameable lust returns.

Even then I have nothing against life.
5   I know well the grass blades you mention,
the furniture you have placed under the sun.

But suicides have a special language.
Like carpenters they want to know *which tools*.
They never ask *why build*.

10   Twice I have so simply declared myself,
have possessed the enemy, eaten the enemy,
have taken on his craft, his magic.

In this way, heavy and thoughtful,
warmer than oil or water,
15   I have rested, drooling at the mouth-hole.

I did not think of my body at needle point.
Even the cornea and the leftover urine were gone.
Suicides have already betrayed the body.

Still-born, they don't always die,
20   but dazzled, they can't forget a drug so sweet
that even children would look on and smile.

To thrust all that life under your tongue!—
that, all by itself, becomes a passion.
Death's a sad bone; bruised, you'd say,

25   and yet she waits for me, year after year,
to so delicately undo an old wound,
to empty my breath from its bad prison.

Balanced there, suicides sometimes meet,
raging at the fruit, a pumped-up moon,
30   leaving the bread they mistook for a kiss,

leaving the page of the book carelessly open,
something unsaid, the phone off the hook
and the love, whatever it was, an infection.

—1966

John Hollander
(1929-)

A prolific author of poetry and criticism, Hollander's wit and formal originality mark him as one of the chief contemporary heirs of W. H. Auden. A native of New York City, he was educated at Columbia and served as a Junior Fellow at Harvard University. He has taught at Yale University for many years.

Adam's Task

"And Adam gave names to all cattle, and to the fowl of the air, and to every beast of the field..."—Gen. 2:20

Thou, paw-paw-paw; thou, glurd; thou, spotted
   Glurd; thou, whitestap, lurching through
The high-grown brush; thou, pliant-footed,
   Implex; thou, awagabu.

5 Every burrower, each flier
   Came for the name he had to give:
Gay, first work, ever to be prior,
   Not yet sunk to primitive.

Thou, verdle; thou, McFleery's pomma;
10 Thou; thou; thou—three types of grawl;
Thou, flisket; thou, kabasch; thou, comma-
   Eared mashawk; thou, all; thou, all.

Were, in a fire of becoming,
   Laboring to be burned away,
15 Then work, half-measuring, half-humming,
   Would be as serious as play.

Thou, pambler; thou, rivarn; thou, greater
   Wherret, and thou, lesser one;
Thou, sproal; thou, zant; thou, lily-eater.
20 Naming's over. Day is done.

—1971

X. J. Kennedy
(1929-)

Kennedy is one the few contemporary American poets who has not been attracted by free verse, preferring to remain what he calls a "dinosaur," one of those poets who continues to write in meter. He is also rare among his contemporaries in his commitment to writing poems with strong ties to song. Kennedy is also the author of *Literature: An Introduction to Fiction, Poetry, and Drama*, perhaps the most widely used college literature text ever written.

In a Prominent Bar in Secaucus One Day
To the tune of "The Old Orange Flute"
or the tune of "Sweet Betsy from Pike"

In a prominent bar in Secaucus one day
Rose a lady in skunk with a topheavy sway,
Raised a knobby red finger—all turned from their beer—
While with eyes bright as snowcrust she sang high and clear:

5 "Now who of you'd think from an eyeload of me
That I once was a lady as proud as could be?
Oh I'd never sit down by a tumbledown drunk
If it wasn't, my dears, for the high cost of junk.

"All the gents used to swear that the white of my calf
10 Beat the down of the swan by a length and a half.
In the kerchief of linen I caught to my nose
Ah, there never fell snot, but a little gold rose.

"I had seven gold teeth and a toothpick of gold,
My Virginia cheroot° was a leaf of it rolled
15 And I'd light it each time with a thousand in cash—
Why the bums used to fight if I flicked them an ash.

"Once the toast of the Biltmore, the belle of the Taft,
I would drink bottle beer at the Drake, never draft,
And dine at the Astor on Salisbury steak
20 With a clean tablecloth for each bite I did take.

---

14 cheroot a thin cigar

"In a car like the Roxy I'd roll to the track,
A steel-guitar trio, a bar in the back,
And the wheels made no noise, they turned over so fast,
Still it took you ten minutes to see me go past.

25   "When the horses bowed down to me that I might choose,
I bet on them all, for I hated to lose.
Now I'm saddled each night for my butter and eggs
And the broken threads race down the backs of my legs.

"Let you hold in mind, girls, that your beauty must pass
30   Like a lovely white clover that rusts with its grass.
Keep your bottoms off barstools and marry you young
Or be left—an old barrel with many a bung.

"For when time takes you out for a spin in his car
You'll be hard-pressed to stop him from going too far
35   And be left by the roadside, for all your good deeds,
Two toadstools for tits and a face full of weeds."

All the house raised a cheer, but the man at the bar
Made a phonecall and up pulled a red patrol car
And she blew us a kiss as they copped her away
40   From that prominent bar in Secaucus, N.J.

                                                 —1961

Adrienne Rich
(1929-)

A winner of the Yale Younger Poets competition for her first book,
Rich has evolved over the years from a careful formalist to one
of the chief spokespersons of the feminist movement. Her sup-
port of various social causes is apparent in her poetry, and she
often seems well in advance of her readers in the turns her life
has taken. Oddly, some of the nation's major awards have
eluded her, a reflection perhaps of the controversy that her
words often engender.

Aunt Jennifer's Tigers

Aunt Jennifer's tigers prance across a screen,
Bright topaz denizens of a world of green.

They do not fear the men beneath the tree;
They pace in sleek chivalric certainty.

5   Aunt Jennifer's fingers fluttering through her wool
Find even the ivory needle hard to pull.
The massive weight of Uncle's wedding band
Sits heavily upon Aunt Jennifer's hand.

When Aunt is dead, her terrified hands will lie
10 Still ringed with ordeals she was mastered by.
The tigers in the panel that she made
Will go on prancing, proud and unafraid.

                                        —1984

Diving into the Wreck

First having read the book of myths,
and loaded the camera,
and checked the edge of the knife-blade,
I put on
5   the body-armor of black rubber
the absurd flippers
the grave and awkward mask.
I am having to do this
not like Cousteau° with his
10 assiduous team
aboard the sun-flooded schooner
but here alone.

There is a ladder.
The ladder is always there
15 hanging innocently
close to the side of the schooner.
We know what it is for,
we who have used it.
Otherwise
20 it is a piece of maritime floss
some sundry equipment.

I go down.
Rung after rung and still
the oxygen immerses me

---

9 Cousteau Jacques-Yves Cousteau (b. 1910), underwater explorer and inventor of the SCUBA tank

25   the blue light
     the clear atoms
     of our human air.
     I go down.
     My flippers cripple me,
30   I crawl like an insect down the ladder
     and there is no one
     to tell me when the ocean
     will begin.

     First the air is blue and then
35   it is bluer and then green and then
     black I am blacking out and yet
     my mask is powerful
     it pumps my blood with power
     the sea is another story
40   the sea is not a question of power
     I have to learn alone
     to turn my body without force
     in the deep element.

     And now: it is easy to forget
45   what I came for
     among so many who have always
     lived here
     swaying their crenellated fans
     between the reefs
50   and besides
     you breathe differently down here.

     I came to explore the wreck.
     The words are purposes.
     The words are maps.
55   I came to see the damage that was done
     and the treasures that prevail.
     I stroke the beam of my lamp
     slowly along the flank
     of something more permanent
60   than fish or weed

     the thing I came for:
     the wreck and not the story of the wreck
     the thing itself and not the myth
     the drowned face always staring

65   toward the sun
      the evidence of damage
      worn by salt and sway into this threadbare beauty
      the ribs of the disaster
      curving their assertion
70   among the tentative haunters.

      This is the place.
      And I am here, the mermaid whose dark hair
      streams black, the merman in his armored body.
      We circle silently
75   about the wreck
      we dive into the hold.
      I am she: I am he

      whose drowned face sleeps with open eyes
      whose breasts still bear the stress
80   whose silver, copper, vermeil cargo lies
      obscurely inside barrels
      half-wedged and left to rot
      we are the half-destroyed instruments
      the once held to a course
85   the water-eaten log
      the fouled compass

      We are, I am, you are
      by cowardice or courage
      the one who find our way
90   back to this scene
      carrying a knife, a camera
      a book of myths
      in which
      our names do not appear.

                                                    —1973

Rape

There is a cop who is both prowler and father:
he comes from your block, grew up with your brothers,
had certain ideals.
You hardly know him in his boots and silver badge,
5   on horseback, one hand touching his gun.

You hardly know him but you have to get to know him:

he has access to machinery that could kill you.
He and his stallion clop like warlords among the trash,
his ideals stand in the air, a frozen cloud

10 from between his unsmiling lips.

And so, when the time comes, you have to turn to him,
the maniac's sperm still greasing your thighs,
your mind whirling like crazy. You have to confess
to him, you are guilty of the crime

15 of having been forced.

And you see his blue eyes, the blue eyes of all the family
whom you used to know, grow narrow and glisten,
his hand types out the details
and he wants them all

20 but the hysteria in your voice pleases him best.

You hardly know him but now he thinks he knows you:
he has taken down your worst moment
on a machine and filed it in a file.
He knows, or thinks he knows, how much you imagined;

25 he knows, or thinks he knows, what you secretly wanted.
He has access to machinery that could get you put away;
and if, in the sickening light of the precinct,
and if, in the sickening light of the precinct,
your details sound like a portrait of your confessor,

30 will you swallow, will you deny them, will you lie your way home?

—1972

✧ ✧ ✧

Ted Hughes
(1930-)

A native of Yorkshire, England, Hughes has never ventured far
from the natural world of his childhood for his subject matter.
Hughes was married to Sylvia Plath until her death in 1966, and
has served as her literary executor. He is currently Poet Laureate
of England.

Pike

Pike, three inches long, perfect
Pike in all parts, green tigering the gold.

Killers from the egg: the malevolent aged grin.
They dance on the surface among the flies.

5   Or move, stunned by their own grandeur,
Over a bed of emerald, silhouette
Of submarine delicacy and horror.
A hundred feet long in their world.

In ponds, under the heat-struck lily pads—
10 Gloom of their stillness:
Logged on last year's black leaves, watching upwards.
Or hung in an amber cavern of weeds

The jaw's hooked clamp and fangs
Not to be changed at this date;
15 A life subdued to its instrument;
The gills kneading quietly, and the pectorals.

Three we kept behind glass,
Jungled in weed: three inches, four,
And four and a half: fed fry to them—
20 Suddenly there were two. Finally one

With a sag belly and the grin it was born with.
And indeed they spare nobody.
Two, six pounds each over two feet long,
High and dry and dead in the willow-herb—

25 One jammed past its gills down the other's gullet:
The outside eye stared: as a vice locks—
The same iron in this eye
Though its film shrank in death.

A pond I fished, fifty yards across,
30 Whose lilies and muscular tench°
Had outlasted every visible stone
Of the monastery that planted them—

Stilled legendary depth:
It was as deep as England. It held
35 Pike too immense to stir, so immense and old
That past nightfall I dared not cast

---

30 tench European freshwater fish

But silently cast and fished
With the hair frozen on my head
For what might move, for what eye might move.
40 The still splashes on the dark pond,

Owls hushing the floating woods
Frail on my ear against the dream
Darkness beneath night's darkness had freed,
That rose slowly towards me, watching.

—1960

The Thought-Fox

I imagine this midnight moment's forest:
Something else is alive
Beside the clock's loneliness
And this lank page where my fingers move.

5 Through the window I see no star;
Something more near
Though deeper within darkness
Is entering the loneliness:

Cold, delicately as the dark snow,
10 A fox's nose touches twig, leaf;
Two eyes serve a movement, that now
And again now, and now, and now

Sets neat prints into the snow
Between trees, and warily a lame
15 Shadow lags by stump and in hollow
Of a body that is bold to come

Across clearings, an eye,
A widening deepening greenness,
Brilliantly, concentratedly,
20 Coming about its own business

Till, with a sudden sharp hot stink of fox
It enters the dark hole of the head.
The window is starless still; the clock ticks,
The page is printed.

—1957

Gary Snyder
(1930-)

Snyder was deeply involved in poetic activity in his hometown,
San Francisco, when that city became the locus of the Beat
Generation in the mid-1950s. Yet Snyder, whose studies in Zen
Buddhism and Oriental cultures preceded his acquaintance with
Allen Ginsberg and Jack Kerouac, has always exhibited a seri-
ousness of purpose that sets him apart from his peers. His long
familiarity with the mountains of the Pacific Northwest date from
his jobs with logging crews during his college days.

A Walk

Sunday the only day we don't work:
Mules farting around the meadow,
                                    Murphy fishing,
The tent flaps in the warm
5   Early sun: I've eaten breakfast and I'll
                                    take a walk
To Benson Lake. Packed a lunch,
Goodbye. Hopping on creekbed boulders
Up the rock throat three miles
10   Piute Creek—
In steep gorge glacier-slick rattlesnake country
Jump, land by a pool, trout skitter,
The clear sky. Deer tracks.
Bad place by a falls, boulders big as houses,
15 Lunch tied to belt,
I stemmed up a crack and almost fell
But rolled out safe on a ledge
                                and ambled on.
Quail chicks freeze underfoot, color of stone
20 Then run cheep! away, hen quail fussing.
Craggy west end of Benson Lake—after edging
Past dark creek pools on a long white slope—
Lookt down in the ice-black lake
                                lined with cliff
25 From far above: deep shimmering trout.
A lone duck in a gunsightpass
                                steep side hill

Through slide-aspen and talus, to the east end
Down to grass, wading a wide smooth stream
30 Into camp. At last.
                    By the rusty three-year-
Ago left-behind cookstove
Of the old trail crew,
Stoppt and swam and ate my lunch.

—1968

Derek Walcott
(1930-)

Walcott, a native of the tiny Caribbean island of St. Lucia in the West Indies, combines a love of the tradition of English poetry with the exotic surfaces of tropical life. In many ways, his life and career have constituted a study in divided loyalties, which are displayed in his ambivalent poems about life in the United States, where he has lived and taught for many years. Walcott was awarded the Nobel Prize in 1992.

Central America

Helicopters are cutlassing the wild bananas.
Between a nicotine thumb and forefinger
brittle faces crumble like tobacco leaves.
Children waddle in vests, their legs bowed,
5   little shrimps curled under their navels.
The old men's teeth are stumps in a charred forest.
Their skins grate like the iguana's.
Their gaze like slate stones.
Women squat by the river's consolations
10 where children wade up to their knees,
and a stick stirs up a twinkling of butterflies.
Up there, in the blue acres
of forest, flies circle their fathers.
In spring, in the upper provinces
15 of the Empire, yellow tanagers
float up through the bare branches.
There is no distinction in these distances.

—1987

Sea Canes

Half my friends are dead.
I will make you new ones, said earth.

No, give me them back, as they were, instead,
with faults and all, I cried.

5 Tonight I can snatch their talk
from the faint surf's drone
through the canes, but I cannot walk

on the moonlit leaves of ocean
down that white road alone,
10 or float with the dreaming motion

of owls leaving earth's load.
O earth, the number of friends you keep
exceeds those left to be loved.

The sea-canes by the cliff flash green and silver;
15 they were the seraph lances of my faith,
but out of what is lost grows something stronger

that has the rational radiance of stone,
enduring moonlight, further than despair,
strong as the wind, that through dividing canes

20 brings those we love before us, as they were,
with faults and all, not nobler, just there.

—1985

Miller Williams
(1930-)

Williams won the Poets' Prize in 1990 for *Living on the Surface,* a
volume of selected poems. A skillful translator of both Giuseppe
Belli, a Roman poet of the early nineteenth century, and of
Nicanor Parra, a contemporary Chilean, Williams has written
many poems about his travels throughout the world yet has
retained the relaxed idiom of his native Arkansas.

The Book

I held it in my hands while he told the story.

He had found it in a fallen bunker,
a book for notes with all the pages blank.
He took it to keep for a sketchbook and diary.

5   He learned years later, when he showed the book
to an old bookbinder, who paled, and stepped back
a long step and told him what he held,
what he had laid the days of his life in.
It's bound, the binder said, in human skin.

10   I stood turning it over in my hands,
turning it in my head. Human skin.

What child did this skin fit? What man, what woman?
Dragged still full of its flesh from what dream?

Who took it off the meat? Some other one
15   who stayed alive by knowing how to do this?

I stared at the changing book and a horror grew,
I stared and a horror grew, which was, which is,
how beautiful it was until I knew.

—1989

Linda Pastan
(1932-)

Linda Pastan is Poet Laureate of Maryland, where she has lived
and taught for many years. Her first book, *A Perfect Circle of
Sun*, appeared in 1971, and four more collections have been
published since.

Crocuses

They come
by stealth, spreading
the rumor of spring—
near the hedge . . .

5   by the gate . . .
    at our chilly feet . . .
    mothers of saffron, fathers
    of insurrection, purple
    and yellow scouts
10 of an army still massing
    just to the south.

                                                    —1991

Sylvia Plath
(1932-1963)

Plath's troubled personal life is often difficult to separate from her poetry, which is almost always read as autobiographical and confessional. A brilliant and precocious poet, she served a long apprenticeship to the tradition of modern poetry before attaining her mature style in the final two years of her life. Only one collection, *The Colossus*, appeared in her lifetime, and her fame has mainly rested on her posthumous books of poetry and the success of her lone novel, *The Bell Jar*. She committed suicide in 1963. Plath has been the subject of a half-dozen biographical studies, reflecting the intense interest that readers, especially women, have in her life and work.

Daddy

    You do not do, you do not do
    Any more, black shoe
    In which I have lived like a foot
    For thirty years, poor and white,
5   Barely daring to breathe or Achoo.

    Daddy, I have had to kill you.
    You died before I had time—
    Marble-heavy, a bag full of God,
    Ghastly statue with one gray toe
10 Big as a Frisco seal

    And a head in the freakish Atlantic
    Where it pours bean green over blue
    In the waters off beautiful Nauset.

I used to pray to recover you.
15 Ach, du.°

In the German tongue, in the Polish town
Scraped flat by the roller
Of wars, wars, wars.
But the name of the town is common.
20 My Polack friend

Says there are a dozen or two.
So I never could tell where you
Put your foot, your root,
I never could talk to you.
25 The tongue stuck in my jaw.

It stuck in a barb wire snare.
Ich, ich, ich, ich,°
I could hardly speak.
I thought every German was you.
30 And the language obscene

An engine, an engine
Chuffing me off like a Jew.
A Jew to Dachau, Auschwitz, Belsen.°
I began to talk like a Jew.
35 I think I may well be a Jew.

The snows of the Tyrol, the clear beer of Vienna
Are not very pure or true.
With my gypsy ancestress and my weird luck
And my Taroc pack and my Taroc pack
40 I may be a bit of a Jew.

I have always been scared of *you,*
With your Luftwaffe,° your gobbledygoo.
And your neat mustache
And your Aryan eye, bright blue.
45 Panzer-man, panzer-man, O You—

Not God but a swastika
So black no sky could squeak through.

---

15 **Ach, du** Oh, you   27 **Ich, ich, ich, ich** I, I, I, I   33 **Dachau, Auschwitz, Belsen** German
concentration camps   42 **Luftwaffe** German Air Force

Every woman adores a Fascist,
The boot in the face, the brute
50   Brute heart of a brute like you.

You stand at the blackboard, daddy,
In the picture I have of you,
A cleft in your chin instead of your foot
But no less a devil for that, no not
55   Any less the black man who

Bit my pretty red heart in two.
I was ten when they buried you.
At twenty I tried to die
And get back, back, back to you.
60   I thought even the bones would do.

But they pulled me out of the sack,
And they stuck me together with glue.
And then I knew what to do.
I made a model of you,
65   A man in black with a Meinkampf° look

And a love of the rack and the screw.
And I said I do, I do.
So daddy, I'm finally through.
The black telephone's off at the root,
70   The voices just can't worm through.

If I've killed one man, I've killed two—
The vampire who said he was you
And drank my blood for a year,
Seven years, if you want to know.
75   Daddy, you can lie back now.

There's a stake in your fat black heart
And the villagers never liked you.
They are dancing and stamping on you.
They always *knew* it was you.
80   Daddy, daddy, you bastard, I'm through.

—1966

---

65 **Meinkampf** title of Hitler's autobiography ("My Struggle")

Edge

The woman is perfected.
Her dead

Body wears the smile of accomplishment,
The illusion of a Greek necessity

5   Flows in the scrolls of her toga,
Her bare

Feet seem to be saying:
We have come so far, it is over.

Each dead child coiled, a white serpent,
10   One at each little

Pitcher of milk, now empty.
She has folded

Them back into her body as petals
Of a rose close when the garden

15   Stiffens and odors bleed
From the sweet, deep throats of the night flower.

The moon has nothing to be sad about,
Staring from her hood of bone.

She is used to this sort of thing.
20   Her blacks crackle and drag.

—1965

Metaphors

I'm a riddle in nine syllables,
An elephant, a ponderous house,
A melon strolling on two tendrils.
O red fruit, ivory, fine timbers!
5   This loaf's big with its yeasty rising.
Money's new-minted in this fat purse.
I'm a means, a stage, a cow in calf.

I've eaten a bag of green apples,
Boarded the train there's no getting off.

—1960

Etheridge Knight
(1933-1991)

Born in Corinth, Mississippi, and seriously wounded during the
Korean War, Etheridge Knight wrote his first poems while serving a
six-year term of imprisonment for robbery. His first book, *Poems
from Prison*, was published in 1968, making him one of the chief
figures in the black renaissance of the 1960s and 1970s.

For Black Poets Who Think of Suicide

Black Poets should live—not leap
From steel bridges (like the white boys do).

Black Poets should *live*—not lay
Their necks on railroad tracks (like the white boys do).
5 Black Poets should seek, but not search
Too much in sweet dark caves
Or hunt for snipes down psychic trails—
(Like the white boys do).

For Black Poets belong to Black People.
10 Are the flutes of Black Lovers—Are
The organs of Black Sorrows—Are
The trumpets of Black Warriors.
Let all Black Poets die as trumpets,
And be buried in the dust of marching feet.

—1966

Mark Strand
(1934-)

The deceptive simplicity of Strand's best poems reveals the
influence of Spanish-language poets like Nicanor Parra, the
father of "anti-poetry," and Rafael Alberti, whom Strand has
translated. Strand was named U.S. poet laureate in 1990.

The Marriage

The wind comes from opposite poles,
traveling slowly.

She turns in the deep air.
He walks in the clouds.

5   She readies herself,
shakes out her hair,

makes up her eyes,
smiles.

The sun warms her teeth,
10   the tip of her tongue moistens them.

He brushes the dust from his suit
and straightens his tie.

He smokes.
Soon they will meet.

15   The wind carries them closer.
They wave.

Closer, closer.
They embrace.

She is making a bed.
20   He is pulling off his pants.

They marry
and have a child.

The wind carries them off
in different directions.

25   The wind is strong, he thinks
as he straightens his tie.

I like this wind, she says
as she puts on her dress

The wind unfolds.
30   The wind is everything to them.

                                              —1968

Mary Oliver
(1935-)

Mary Oliver was born in Cleveland, Ohio, and educated at Ohio
State and Vassar. She has served as a visiting professor at a
number of universities and at the Fine Arts Center in
Provincetown, Massachusetts. She has won both the Pulitzer prize
and the National Book Award for her work, which first appeared
in *No Voyage and Other Poems* in 1965.

The Black Walnut Tree

My mother and I debate:
we could sell
the black walnut tree
to the lumberman,
5   and pay off the mortgage.
Likely some storm anyway
will churn down its dark boughs,
smashing the house. We talk
slowly, two women trying
10 in a difficult time to be wise.
Roots in the cellar drains,
I say, and she replies
that the leaves are getting heavier
every year, and the fruit
15 harder to gather away.
But something brighter than money
moves in our blood—an edge
sharp and quick as a trowel
that wants us to dig and sow.
20 So we talk, but we don't do
anything. That night I dream
of my fathers out of Bohemia
filling the blue fields
of fresh and generous Ohio
25 with leaves and vines and orchards.
What my mother and I both know

is that we'd crawl with shame
in the emptiness we'd made
in our own and our fathers' backyard.
30 So the black walnut tree
swings through another year
of sun and leaping winds,
of leaves and bounding fruit,
and, month after month, the whip-
35 crack of the mortgage.

—1979

Fred Chappell
(1936-)

The immense achievement of Chappell's epic-length poem
Midquest (1981) was belatedly recognized when he was
awarded the Bollingen Prize in 1985. A four-part poem written
over a decade, *Midquest* uses the occasion of the poet's thirty-
fifth birthday as a departure for a complex sequence of auto-
biographical poems that are heavily indebted to Dante for their
formal structure. A versatile writer of both poetry and prose,
Chappell displays his classical learning brilliantly and in unusual
contexts.

Narcissus and Echo°

Shall the water not remember *Ember*
my hand's slow gesture, tracing above *of*
its mirror my half-imaginary *airy*
portrait? My only belonging *longing;*
5 is my beauty, which I take *ache*
away and then return, as love *of*
teasing playfully the one being *unbeing.*
whose gratitude I treasure *Is your*
moves me. I live apart *heart*
10 from myself, yet cannot *not*
live apart. In the water's tone, *stone?*
that brilliant silence, a flower *Hour,*
whispers my name with such slight *light:*
moment, it seems filament of air, *fare*
15 the world become cloudswell. *well.*

—1985

Narcissus and Echo In the myth, the vain Narcissus drowned attempting to embrace his own
reflection in the water. Echo, a nymph who loved him, pined away until only her voice remained

Lucille Clifton
(1936-)

Clifton, a native of Depew, New York, was educated at SUNY—
Fredonia and Howard University and has taught at several
colleges, including the American University in Washington, D.C.
About her own work, she has commented succinctly, "I am a
Black woman poet, and I sound like one." Clifton performed
"homage to my hips" on a 1992 edition of *Nightline* devoted to
contemporary American poetry.

homage to my hips

these hips are big hips.
they need space to
move around in.
they don't fit into little
5   petty places. these hips
are free hips.
they don't like to be held back.
these hips have never been enslaved,
they go where they want to go
10 they do what they want to do.
these hips are mighty hips.
these hips are magic hips.
i have known them
to put a spell on a man and
15 spin him like a top!

—1991

Marge Piercy
(1936-)

A political radical during her student days at the University of
Michigan, Piercy has continued to be outspoken on political,
cultural, and sexual issues. Her phrase "to be of use" has
become a key measure by which feminist writers and critics
have gauged the meaning of their own life experiences.

Barbie Doll

This girlchild was born as usual
and presented dolls that did pee-pee
and miniature GE stoves and irons
and wee lipsticks the color of cherry candy.
5 Then in the magic of puberty, a classmate said:
You have a great big nose and fat legs.

She was healthy, tested intelligent
possessed strong arms and back,
abundant sexual drive and manual dexterity.
10 She went to and fro apologizing.
Everyone saw a fat nose on thick legs.

She was advised to play coy,
exhorted to come on hearty,
exercise, diet, smile and wheedle.
15 Her good nature wore out
like a fan belt.
So she cut off her nose and her legs
and offered them up.

In the casket displayed on satin she lay
20 with the undertaker's cosmetics painted on,
a turned-up putty nose,
dressed in a pink and white nightie.
Doesn't she look pretty? everyone said.
Consummation at last.
25 To every woman a happy ending.

—1982

Nancy Willard
(1936-)

The author of eight collections of poetry, Willard has also written
a novel and an award-winning book of poems for children, *A
Visit to William Blake's Inn*. About her whimsical work Donald Hall
has said, "She imagines with a wonderful concreteness. But also,
she takes real language and by literal-mindedness turns it into the
structure of dream."

A Hardware Store as Proof of the Existence of God

I praise the brightness of hammers pointing east
like the steel woodpeckers of the future,
and dozens of hinges opening brass wings,
and six new rakes shyly fanning their toes,
5   and bins of hooks glittering into bees,

and a rack of wrenches like the long bones of horses,
and mailboxes sowing rows of silver chapels,
and a company of plungers waiting for God
to claim their thin legs in their big shoes
10   and put them on and walk away laughing.

In a world not perfect but not bad either
let there be glue, glaze, gum, and grabs,
caulk also, and hooks, shackles. cables, and slips,
and signs so spare a child may read them,
15   *Men, Women, In, Out, No Parking, Beware the Dog.*

In the right hands, they can work wonders.

                                                                —1989

Tony Harrison
(1937-)

Harrison—poet, translator, playwright—has become the chief
poetic spokesman for the English working class. Born in the indus-
trial city of Leeds, he published *The School of Eloquence*, an
autobiographical sequence of sixteen-line "sonnets" in 1981. His
unapologetic use of dialect has been rare in English poetry for
most of this century.

Self Justification

Me a poet! My daughter with maimed limb
became a more than tolerable sprinter.
And Uncle Joe. Impediment spurred him,
the worst stammerer I've known, to be a printer.

5   He handset type much faster than he spoke.
Those cruel consonants, *ms, ps,* and *bs*

on which his jaws and spirit almost broke
flicked into order with sadistic ease.

It seems right that Uncle Joe, 'b-buckshee°
10   from the works', supplied those scribble pads
on which I stammered my first poetry
that made me seem a cissy° to the lads.

Their aggro° towards me, my need of them 's
what keeps my would-be mobile tongue still tied—

15   aggression, struggle, loss, blank printer's ems°
by which all   eloquence   gets justified.

                              —1981

Betty Adcock
(1938-)

Born in San Augustine, Texas, Adcock has lived for many years in
Raleigh, North Carolina, where she is poet-in-residence at
Meredith College. Many of her poems express her strong ties to
the regions where she has lived.

Digression on the Nuclear Age

In some difficult part of Africa, a termite tribe
builds elaborate tenements that might be called
cathedrals, were they for anything so terminal
as Milton's God. Who was it said
5   the perfect arch will always separate
the civilized from the not? Never mind.
These creatures are quite blind and soft
and hard at labor chemically induced.
Beginning with a dish-like hollow, groups
10 of workers pile up earthen pellets.
A few such piles will reach a certain height;
fewer still, a just proximity.
That's when direction changes, or a change
directs: the correct two bands of laborers

---

9 b-buckshee/from the works' "Buckshee," from the Indian "bakshee," means "free"; i.e. stolen from
the printshop **12 cissy** sissy **13 aggro** aggravation **15 printer's ems** blank types used for spaces

15   will make their towers bow toward each other.
      Like saved and savior, they will meet in air.
      It is unambiguously an arch and it will serve,
      among the others rising and the waste,
      an arch's purposes. Experts are sure
20   a specific moment comes when the very structure
      triggers the response that will perfect it.

      I've got this far and don't know what
      termites can be made to mean. Or this poem:
      a joke, a play on arrogance, nothing
25   but language? Untranslated, the world gets on
      with dark, flawless constructions rising,
      rising even where we think we are. And think
      how we must hope convergences will fail this time,
      that whatever it is we're working on won't work.

                                                    —1988

Gary Gildner
(1938-)

Gildner was born in West Branch, Michigan and attended
Michigan State University. He teaches at Drake University. "First
Practice" is the title poem of his first collection, published in 1969
A volume of Gildner's selected poems appeared in 1984.

First Practice

      After the doctor checked to see
      we weren't ruptured,
      the man with the short cigar took us
      under the grade school,
5   where we went in case of attack
      or storm, and said
      he was Clifford Hill, he was
      a man who believed dogs
      ate dogs, he had once killed
10   for his country, and if
      there were any girls present
      for them to leave now.
                          No one
      left. OK, he said, he said I take

that to mean you are hungry
15 men who hate to lose as much
as I do. OK. Then
he made two lines of us
facing each other,
and across the way, he said,
20 is the man you hate most
in the world,
and if we are to win
that title I want to see how.
But I don't want to see
25 any marks when you're dressed,
he said. He said, *Now*.

—1969

Charles Simic
(1938-)

Simic was born in Yugoslavia and came with his parents to
Chicago in 1949. Educated at New York University, he teaches at
the University of New Hampshire. *The World Doesn't End*, a col-
lection of prose poems, won the Pulitzer prize in 1990.

My Shoes

Shoes, secret face of my inner life:
Two gaping toothless mouths,
Two partly decomposed animal skins
Smelling of mice-nests.

5 My brother and sister who died at birth
Continuing their existence in you,
Guiding my life
Toward their incomprehensible innocence.

What use are books to me
10 When in you it is possible to read
The Gospel of my life on earth
And still beyond, of things to come?

I want to proclaim the religion
I have devised for your perfect humility

15   And the strange church I am building
       With you as the altar.

       Ascetic and maternal, you endure:
       Kin to oxen, to Saints, to condemned men,
       With your mute patience, forming
20   The only true likeness of myself.

                                                              —1971

Margaret Atwood
(1939-)

The leading woman writer of Canada, Atwood excels at both
poetry and prose fiction. Among her six novels, *The Handmaid's
Tale* is perhaps the best known, becoming a best seller in the
United States and the subject of a motion picture. Atwood's
Selected Poems appeared in 1976.

Siren° Song

       This is the one song everyone
       would like to learn: the song
       that is irresistible:

       the song that forces men
5   to leap overboard in squadrons
       even though they see the beached skulls

       the song nobody knows
       because anyone who has heard it
       is dead, and the others can't remember.

10   Shall I tell you the secret
       and if I do, will you get me
       out of this bird suit?

       I don't enjoy it here
       squatting on this island
15   looking picturesque and mythical

Siren in Greek myth, one of the women whose irresistible song lured sailors onto the rocks

with these two feathery maniacs,
I don't enjoy singing
this trio, fatal and valuable.

I will tell the secret to you,
20 to you, only to you.
Come closer. This song

is a cry for help: Help me!
Only you, only you can,
you are unique

25 at last. Alas
it is a boring song
but it works every time.

—1974

Stephen Dunn
(1939-)

A graduate of the creative writing program at Syracuse University, Dunn teaches at Stockton State College in Pomona, New Jersey. His attempt to blend ordinary experience with larger significance is illustrated in the duality of book titles like *Full of Lust and Good Usage*, *Work and Love*, and *Between Angels*.

The Sacred

After the teacher asked if anyone had
    a sacred place
and the students fidgeted and shrank

in their chairs, the most serious of them all
5   said it was his car,
being in it alone, his tape deck playing

things he'd chosen, and others knew the truth
        had been spoken
and began speaking about their rooms,

10 their hiding places, but the car kept coming up,
        the car in motion,

music filling it, and sometimes one other person

who understood the bright altar of the dashboard
        and how far away
15   a car could take him from the need

to speak, or to answer, the key
        in having a key
and putting it in, and going.

—1989

Seamus Heaney
(1939-)

Born in the troubled country of Northern Ireland, Heaney has
largely avoided the type of political divisions that have divided
his homeland. Instead, he has chosen to focus on the landscape
of the rural Ireland he knew while growing up as a farmer's son.
Since 1982, Heaney has taught part of the year at Harvard
University.

Digging

Between my finger and my thumb
The squat pen rests; snug as a gun.

Under my window, a clean rasping sound
When the spade sinks into gravelly ground:
5   My father, digging. I look down

Till his straining rump among the flowerbeds
Bends low, comes up twenty years away
Stooping in rhythm through potato drills °
Where he was digging.

10   The coarse boot nestled on the lug, the shaft
Against the inside knee was levered firmly.
He rooted out tall tops, buried the bright edge deep
To scatter new potatoes that we picked
Loving their cool hardness in our hands.

---

8 drills furrows

15 By God, the old man could handle a spade.
Just like his old man.

My grandfather cut more turf in a day
Than any other man on Toner's bog.
Once I carried him milk in a bottle
20 Corked sloppily with paper. He straightened up
To drink it, then fell to right away

Nicking and slicing neatly, heaving sods
Over his shoulder, going down and down
For the good turf. Digging.

25 The cold smell of potato mould, the squelch and slap
Of soggy peat, the curt cuts of an edge
Through living roots awaken in my head.
But I've no spade to follow men like them.

Between my finger and my thumb
30 The squat pen rests.
I'll dig with it.

—1980

Pattiann Rogers
(1940-)

Rogers is unique among contemporary poets in her breadth of
knowledge of the species of the natural world. In many of her
philosophical poems, she reflects a modern-day version of
Emersonian Transcendentalism.

Concepts and Their Bodies
(The Boy in the Field Alone)

Staring at the mud turtle's eye
Long enough, he sees *concentricity* there
For the first time, as if it possessed
Pupil and iris and oracular lid,
5 As if it grew, forcing its own gene of circularity.
The concept is definitely

The cellular arrangement of sight.

The five amber grasses maintaining their seedheads
In the breeze against the sky
10 Have borne *latitude* from the beginning,
Secure *civility* like leaves in their folds.
He discovers *persistence* in the mouth
Of the caterpillar in the same way
As he discovers clear syrup
15 On the broken end of the dayflower,
Exactly as he comes accidentally upon
The mud crown of the crawfish.
The spotted length of the bullfrog leaping
Lakeward just before the footstep
20 Is not bullfrog, spread and sailing,
But the body of *initiative* with white glossy belly.
Departure is the wing let loose
By the dandelion, and it does possess
A sparse down and will not be thought of,
25 Even years later, even in the station
At midnight among the confusing lights,
As separate from that white twist
Of filament drifting.

Nothing is sharp enough to disengage
30 The butterfly's path from *erraticism*.
And *freedom* is this September field
Covered this far by tree shadows
Through which this child chooses to run
Until he chooses to stop,
35 And it will be so hereafter.

                                                    —1981

James Welch
(1940-)

Welch is a member of the Montana Blackfeet tribe, and many of
his poems and pieces of fiction detail the collision of white and
Native American cultures in the contemporary West. Educated
at the University of Montana, he still resides in Missoula.

Christmas Comes to Moccasin Flat°

Christmas comes like this: Wise men
unhurried, candles bought on credit (poor price
for calves), warriors face down in wine sleep.
Winds cheat to pull heat from smoke.

5   Friends sit in chinked cabins, stare out
plastic windows and wait for commodities.
Charlie Blackbird, twenty miles from church
and bar, stabs his fire with flint.

When drunks drain radiators for love
10   or need, chiefs eat snow and talk of change,
an urge to laugh pounding their ribs.
Elk play games in high country.

Medicine Woman, clay pipe and twist tobacco,
calls each blizzard by name and predicts
15   five o'clock by spitting at her television.
Children lean into her breath to beg a story:

Something about honor and passion,
warriors back with meat and song,
a peculiar evening star, quick vision of birth.
20   Blackbird feeds his fire. Outside, a quick 30 below.

—1979

Robert Hass
(1941-)

Hass was born and reared in San Francisco, and teaches at
Berkeley. His first book, *Field Guide*, was chosen for the Yale
Series of Younger Poets in 1973. Recently he has collaborated
with Nobel Prize winner Czeslaw Milosz on English translations of
the latter's poetry.

Moccasin Flat reservation town in Montana

Picking Blackberries with a Friend Who Has Been Reading Jacques Lacan°

August dust is here. Drought
stuns the road,
but juice gathers in the berries.

We pick them in the hot
5   slow-motion of midmorning.
Charlie is exclaiming:

for him it is twenty years ago
and raspberries and Vermont.
We have stopped talking

10   about *L'Histoire de la verite,*°
about subject and object
and the mediation of desire.

Our ears are stoppered
in the bee-hum. And Charlie,
15   laughing wonderfully,

beard stained purple
by the word *juice,*
goes to get a bigger pot.

—1979

Jonathan Holden
(1941-)

One of the most knowledgeable critics of contemporary American poetry, Holden is also a poet who manages to absorb and transmute the influences of American popular culture—from baseball to celebrities—in his poetry. *The Fate of American Poetry,* a critical work, appeared in 1992.

Liberace°

It took generations to mature

Jacques Lacan French psychoanalyst and literary theorist   10 *L' Histoire de la verite The History of Truth,* by Lacan
Liberace American pianist and popular entertainer (1919-1987)

this figure. Every day it
had to be caught sneaking off
to its piano lesson and beaten up.
5   Every day it came back
for more. It would have been
trampled underground, but
like a drop of mercury, it was
too slippery. Stamped on,
10   it would divide, squirt away
and gather somewhere else, it was
insoluble, it had nowhere to go.
All it could do was gather again,
a puddle in the desert, festering
15   until the water had gone punk, it
was no good for anything anymore.
It wears rubies on its fingers now.
Between its dimples, its leer is
fixed. Its cheeks are
20   chocked, its eyes twinkle. It
knows. Thank you, it breathes
with ointment in its voice,
Thank you very much.

—1984

Gibbons Ruark
(1941-)

A native of North Carolina, Ruark is the author of five collections
of poetry. He teaches at the University of Delaware.

The Visitor

Holding the arm of his helper, the blind
Piano tuner comes to our piano.
He hesitates at first, but once he finds
The keyboard, his hands glide over the slow
5   Keys, ringing changes finer than the eye
Can see. The dusty wires he touches, row
On row, quiver like bowstrings as he
Twists them one notch tighter. He runs his
Finger along a wire, touches the dry

10   Rust to his tongue, breaks into a pure bliss
And tells us, "One year more of damp weather
Would have done you in, but I've saved it this
Time. Would one of you play now, please? I hear
It better at a distance." My wife plays
15   *Stardust.* The blind man stands and smiles in her
Direction, then disappears into the blaze
Of new October. Now the afternoon,
The long afternoon that blurs in a haze
Of music . . . Chopin nocturnes, *Clair de Lune,*
20   All the old familiar, unfamiliar
Music-lesson pieces, *Papa's Haydn's*
Dead and gone, gently down the stream . . . Hours later,
After the latest car has doused its beams.
Has cooled down and stopped its ticking, I hear
25   Our cat, with the grace of animals free
To move in darkness. strike one key only,
And a single lucid drop of water stars my dream.

—1971

Gladys Cardiff
(1942-)

Gladyss Cardiff is a member of the Cherokee nation. "Combing"
is taken from her first collection *To Frighten a Storm* which was
originally published in 1976.

Combing

Bending, I bow my head
And lay my hand upon
Her hair, combing, and think
How women do this for
5   Each other. My daughter's hair
Curls against the comb,
Wet and fragrant—orange
Parings. Her face, downcast,
Is quiet for one so young.

10   I take her place. Beneath

My mother's hands I feel
The braids drawn up tight
As a piano wire and singing,
Vinegar-rinsed. Sitting
15 Before the oven I hear
The orange coils tick
The early hour before school.

She combed her grandmother
Mathilda's hair using
20 A comb made out of bone.
Mathilda rocked her oak wood
Chair, her face downcast,
Intent on tearing rags
In strips to braid a cotton
25 Rug from bits of orange
and brown. A simple act,

Preparing hair. Something
Women do for each other,
Plaiting the generations.

—1976

✧ ✧ ✧

Charles Martin
(1942-)

A lifelong resident of New York City, Martin has taught English as a
second language for many years at Queensborough College.
"E.S.L" appeared as a prefatory poem to Martin's sequence
"Passages from Friday," an ironic retelling of the Robinson
Crusoe story from his servant's point of view.

E.S.L.°

My frowning students carve
Me monsters out of prose:
This one—a gargoyle—thumbs its contemptuous nose
At how, in English, subject must agree
5 With verb—for any such agreement shows
Too great a willingness to serve,

E.S.L. English as a Second Language

A docility

Which wiry Miss Choi
· Finds un-American.
10 She steals a hard look at me. I wink. Her grin
Is my reward. *In his will, our peace, our Pass:*
Gargoyle erased, subject and verb now in
    Agreement, reach object, enjoy
        Temporary truce.

15   Tonight my students must
      Agree or disagree:
America is still a land of opportunity.
The answer is always, uniformly, *Yes*—even though
"It has no doubt that here were to much free,"
20   As Miss Torrico will insist.
        She and I both know

      That Language binds us fast,
      And those of us without
Are bound and gagged by those within. Each fledgling
25 Polyglot must shake old habits: tapping her sneakered feet,
Miss Choi exorcises incensed ancestors, flout-
    ing the ghosts of her Chinese past.
        Writhing in the seat

      Next to Miss Choi, Mister
30   Fedakis, in anguish
Labors to express himself in a tongue which
Proves *Linear B* to me, when I attempt to read it
Later. They're here for English as a Second Language,
    Which I'm teaching this semester.
35   God knows they need it,

      And so, thank God, do they.
      The night's made easier
By our agreement: I am here to help deliver
Them into the good life they write me papers about.
40 English is pre-requisite for that endeavor,
    Explored in their nightly essays
        Boldly setting out

      To reconnoiter the fair
      New World they would enter:

45 Suburban Paradise, the endless shopping center
Where one may browse for hours before one chooses
Some new necessity—gold-flecked magenta
    Wallpaper to re-do the spare
        Bath no one uses,

50   Or a machine which can,
        In seven seconds, crush
A newborn calf into such seamless mush
As a *mousse* might be made of—or our true sublime:
The gleaming counters where frosted cosmeticians brush
55   Decades from the allotted span,
            Abrogating Time

        As the spring tide brushes
        A single sinister
Footprint from the otherwise unwrinkled shore
60 Of America the Blank. In absolute confusion
Poor Mister Fedakis rumbles with despair
    And puts the finishing smutches
        To his conclusion

        While Miss Choi erases:
65   One more gargoyle routed.
Their pure, erroneous lines yield an illuminated
Map of the new found land. We will never arrive there,
Since it exists only in what we say about it,
    As all the rest of my class is
70   Bound to discover.

                                        —1987

Sharon Olds
(1942-)

Olds's candor in dealing with the intimacies of family romance
covering three generations has made her, along with Stephen
Dunn, one of the chief contemporary heirs of the confessional
tradition. A powerful and dramatic reader, she is much in
demand on the lecture circuit. Born in San Francisco, she currently
resides in New York City.

The One Girl at the Boys Party

When I take my girl to the swimming party

I set her down among the boys. They tower and
bristle, she stands there smooth and sleek,
her math scores unfolding in the air around her.
5   They will strip to their suits, her body hard and
indivisible as a prime number,
they'll plunge into the deep end, she'll subtract
her height from ten feet, divide it into
hundreds of gallons of water, the numbers
10 bouncing in her mind like molecules of chlorine
in the bright blue pool. When they climb out,
her ponytail will hang its pencil lead
down her back, her narrow silk suit
with hamburgers and french fries printed on it
15 will glisten in the brilliant air, and they will
see her sweet face, solemn and
sealed, a factor of one, and she will
see their eyes, two each,
their legs, two each, and the curves of their sexes,
20 one each, and in her head she'll be doing her
wild multiplying, as the drops
sparkle and fall to the power of a thousand from her body.

                                                                    —1983

James Tate
(1943-)

Tate's unique brand of comic surrealism has remained a con-
stant throughout his career. *The Lost Pilot* won the Yale Younger
Poets Award in 1966. Tate's *Selected Poems* was the recipient of
the Pulitzer prize in 1992.

Teaching the Ape to Write Poems

They didn't have much trouble
teaching the ape to write poems:
first they strapped him into the chair,
then tied the pencil around his hand
5   (the paper had already been nailed down).
Then Dr. Bluespire leaned over his shoulder
and whispered into his ear:
"You look like a god sitting there.
Why don't you try writing something?"

                                                                    —1991

Ellen Bryant Voight
(1943-)

A native of Virginia, Voight was trained as a concert pianist before earning her creative writing degree from the University of Iowa. She has taught poetry at a number of colleges in New England and the South.

Daughter

There is one grief worse than any other.

When your small feverish throat clogged, and quit,
I knelt beside the chair on the green rug
and shook you and shook you,
5   but the only sound was mine shouting you back,
the delicate curls at your temples,
the blue wool blanket,
your face blue,
your jaw clamped against remedy—

10   how could I put a knife to that white neck?
With you in my lap,
my hands fluttering like flags,
I bend instead over your dead weight
to administer a kiss so urgent, so ruthless,
15   pumping breath into your stilled body,
counting out the rhythm for how long until
the second birth, the second cry
oh Jesus that sudden noisy musical inhalation
that leaves me stunned
20   by your survival.

                                        —1983

Robert Morgan
(1944-)

A native of the mountains of North Carolina, Morgan has always

retained a large degree of regionalism in his poetry. A recent
collection, *Sigodlin*, takes its title from an Appalachian word for
things that are built slightly out of square.

Mountain Bride

They say Revis found a flatrock
on the ridge just
perfect for a natural hearth,
and built his cabin with a stick

5   and clay chimney right over it.
On their wedding night he lit
the fireplace to dry away the mountain
chill of late spring, and flung on

applewood to dye
10   the room with molten color while
he and Martha that was a Parrish
warmed the sheets between the tick

stuffed with leaves and its feather
cover. Under that wide hearth
15   a nest of rattlers,
they'll knot a hundred together,

had wintered and were coming awake.
The warming rock
flushed them out early.
20   It was she

who wakened to their singing near
the embers and roused him to go look.
Before he reached the fire
more than a dozen struck

25   and he died yelling her to stay
on the big four-poster.
Her uncle coming up the hollow
with a gift bearham two days later

found her shivering there
30   marooned above a pool
of hungry snakes,

and the body beginning to swell.

—1979

Craig Raine
(1944-)

Raine's brand of comic surrealism was responsible for so many imitations that critic James Fenton dubbed him the founder of the "Martian School" of contemporary poetry. Born in Bishop Auckland, England, and educated at Oxford, Raine is an editor with the prestigious publishing firm of Faber & Faber.

A Martian Sends a Postcard Home

Caxtons° are mechanical birds with many wings
and some are treasured for their markings—

they cause the eyes to melt
or the body to shriek without pain.

5 I have never seen one fly, but
sometimes they perch on the hand.

Mist is when the sky is tired of flight
and rests its soft machine on ground:

then the world is dim and bookish
10 like engravings under tissue paper.

Rain is when the earth is television.
It has the property of making colours darker.

Model T is a room with the lock inside—
a key is turned to free the world

15 for movement, so quick there is a film
to watch for anything missed.

But time is tied to the wrist
or kept in a box, ticking with impatience.

---

1 **Caxtons** i.e., books; after William Caxton (1422-1491), first English printer

In homes, a haunted apparatus sleeps,
20   that snores when you pick it up.

If the ghost cries, they carry it
to their lips and soothe it to sleep

with sounds. And yet, they wake it up
deliberately, by tickling with a finger.

25   Only the young are allowed to suffer
openly. Adults go to a punishment room

with water but nothing to eat.
They lock the door and suffer the noises

alone. No one is exempt
30   and everyone's pain has a different smell.

At night, when all the colours die,
they hide in pairs

and read about themselves—
in colour, with their eyelids shut.

                                                                    —1978

Enid Shomer
(1944-)

Shomer grew up in Washington, D.C., and has lived for a number of years in Gainesville, Florida. Her first collection, *Stalking the Florida Panther* (1987), explored both the Jewish traditions of her childhood and her adult attachment to her adopted state. A second book, *This Close to the Earth*, appeared in 1992.

Women Bathing at Bergen-Belsen°

April 24, 1945

Twelve hours after the Allies arrive

Bergen-Belsen German concentration camp in WWII

there is hot water, soap. Two women bathe
in a makeshift, open-air shower while nearby
fifteen thousand are flung naked into mass graves
5   by captured SS guards. Clearly legs and arms
are the natural handles of a corpse. The bathers,
taken late in the war, still have flesh
on their bones, still have breasts. Though nudity was
a death sentence here, they have undressed,
10   oblivious to the soldiers and the cameras.
The corpses push through the limed earth like upended
headstones. The bathers scrub their feet, bending
in beautiful curves, mapping the contours
of the body, that kingdom to which they've returned.

—1987

Alice Walker
(1944-)

As the author of *The Color Purple* and other novels, Alice Walker
is a leading black American writer. Less well-known as a poet,
she won the Pulitzer prize for fiction in 1983. Her most recent nov-
els combine her concerns with both racial and feminist issues.

Even as I Hold You

Even as I hold you
I think of you as someone gone
far, far away. Your eyes the color
of pennies in a bowl of dark honey
5   bringing sweet light to someone else
your black hair slipping through my fingers
is the flash of your head going
around a corner
your smile, breaking before me,
10   the flippant last turn
of a revolving door,
emptying you out, changed,
away from me.

Even as I hold you
15   I am letting go.

—1979

Leon Stokesbury
(1945-)

Governor's Square Mall is located in Tallahassee, Florida, where the poet attended graduate school in the early 1980s. Stokesbury has remarked that this poem began as his attempt to write a contemporary American version of Wordsworth's "Tintern Abbey." The author of two collections, Stokesbury has also edited anthologies of contemporary Southern poetry and the poetry of World War II.

Day Begins at Governor's Square Mall

Here, newness is all. Or almost all. And like
a platterful of pope's noses° at a White House dinner,
I exist apart. But these trees now—
how do you suppose they grow this high in here?
5   They look a little like the trees I sat beneath in 1959
waiting with my cheesecloth net for butterflies.
It was August and it was hot. Late summer,
yes, but already the leaves in trees were
flecked with ochers and the umbers of the dead.
10 I sweated there for hours, so driven,
so immersed in the forest's shimmering life,
that I could will my anxious self not move
for half a day—just on the imagined chance
of making some slight part of it my own.
15 Then they came. One perfect pair of just-hatched
black-and-white striped butterflies. The white
lemon-tipped with light, in shade
then out, meandering. Zebra swallowtails,
floating, drunk in the sun, so rare to find
20 their narrow, fragile, two-inch tails intact.
At that moment I could only drop my net and stare.
The last of August. 1959. But these trees, now,
climb up through air and concrete never hot or cold.
And I suspect the last lepidoptera that found
25 themselves in here were sprayed then swept away.
Everyone is waiting though, as before a storm—

---

2 **pope's noses** rumps of cooked chickens

anticipating something. Do these leaves never fall?

Now, and with a mild surprise, faint
music falls. But no shop breaks open yet.
30 The people, like myself, range aimlessly;
the air seems thick and still. Then, lights blink on;
the escalators jerk and hum. And in the center, at
the exact center of the mall, a jet of water spurts
twenty feet straight up, then drops and spatters
35 in a shallow pool where signs announce that none
may ever go. O bright communion! O new cathedral!
where the appetitious, the impure, the old, the young,
the bored, the lost, the dumb, with wide dilated eyes
advance with offerings to be absolved and be made clean.
40 Now, the lime-lit chainlink fronts from over one hundred
pleasant and convenient stalls and stores are rolled away.
Now, odors of frying won tons come wafting up from
Lucy Ho's Bamboo Garden. And this music, always
everywhere, yet also somehow strangely played as if
45 not to be heard, pours its soft harangue down now.
The people wander forward now. And the world begins.

—1986

Marilyn Nelson Waniek
(1946-)

Waniek's book *The Homeplace* is a sequence of poems on
family history, perhaps, like Rita Dove's *Thomas and Beulah*, a
poetic manifestation of the *"Roots"* phenomenon in black
American literary culture. *The Homeplace* is remarkable for its
sensitive exploration of the mixed white and black bloodlines in a
southern family tree.

The Ballad of Aunt Geneva

Geneva was the wild one.
Geneva was a tart.
Geneva met a blue-eyed boy
and gave away her heart.

5   Geneva ran a roadhouse.
Geneva wasn't sent

to college like the others:
Pomp's pride her punishment.

She cooked out on the river,
watching the shore slide by,
her lips pursed into hardness,
her deep-set brown eyes dry.

They say she killed a woman
over a good black man
by braining the jealous heifer
with an iron frying pan.

They say, when she was eighty,
she got up late at night
and sneaked her old, white lover in
to make love, and to fight.

First, they heard the tell-tale
singing of the springs,
then Geneva's voice rang out:
I need to buy some things,

So next time, bring more money.
And bring more moxie, too.
I ain't got no time to waste
on limp white mens like you.

Oh yeah? Well, Mister White Man,
it sure might be stone-white,
but my thing's white as it is.
And you know damn well I'm right.

Now listen: take your heart pills
and pay the doctor mind.
If you up and die on me,
I'll whip your white behind.

They tiptoed through the parlor
on heavy, time-slowed feet.
She watched him, from her front door,
walk down the dawnlit street.

Geneva was the wild one.

Geneva was a tart.
Geneva met a blue-eyed boy
and gave away her heart.

—1990

Ai
(1947-)

Ai's realistic dramatic monologues often reveal the agonies of
characters trapped in unfulfilling or even dangerous lives. With
her gallery of social misfits, she is the contemporary heir of the
tradition begun by Robert Browning.

Child Beater

Outside, the rain, pinafore of gray water, dresses the town
and I stroke the leather belt,
as she sits in the rocking chair,
holding a crushed paper cup to her lips.
5   I yell at her, but she keeps rocking;
back, her eyes open, forward, they close.
Her body, somehow fat, though I feed her only once a day,
reminds me of my own just after she was born.
It's been seven years, but I still can't forget how I felt.
10   How heavy it feels to look at her.

I lay the belt on a chair
and get her dinner bowl.
I hit the spoon against it, set it down
and watch her crawl to it,
15   pausing after each forward thrust of her legs
and when she takes her first bite,
I grab the belt and beat her across the back
until her tears, beads of salt-filled glass, falling,
shatter on the floor.

20   I move off. I let her eat,
while I get my dog's chain leash from the closet.
I whirl it around my head.
O daughter, so far, you've only had a taste of icing,
are you ready now for some cake?

—1973

Jim Hall
(1947-)

Hall, one of the most brilliantly inventive comic poets in recent years, has also written a successful series of crime novels set in his native south Florida, beginning with *Under Cover of Daylight* in 1987.

Maybe Dats Your Pwoblem Too

All my pwoblems,
who knows, maybe evwybody's pwoblems
is due to da fact, due to da awful twuth
dat I am SPIDERMAN.

5   I know, I know. All da dumb jokes:
No flies on you, ha ha,
and da ones about what do I do wit all
doze extwa legs in bed. Well, dat's funny yeah.
But you twy being
10   SPIDERMAN for a month or two. Go ahead.

You get doze cwazy calls fwom da
Gubbener askin you to twap some booglar who's
only twying to wip off color T.V. sets.
Now, what do I cawre about T.V. sets?
15   But I pull on da suit, da stinkin suit,
wit da sucker cups on da fingers,
and get my wopes and wittle bundle of
equipment and den I go flying like cwazy
acwoss da town fwom woof top to woof top.

20   Till der he is. Some poor dumb color T.V. slob
and I fall on him and we westle a widdle
until I get him all woped. So big deal.

You tink when you SPIDERMAN
der's sometin big going to happen to you.
25   Well, I tell you what. It don't happen dat way.
Nuttin happens. Gubbener calls, I go.
Bwing him to powice, Gubbener calls again,

like dat over and over.

I tink I twy sometin diffunt. I tink I twy
30 sometin excitin like wacing cawrs. Sometin to make
my heart beat at a difwent wate.
But den you just can't quit being sometin like
SPIDERMAN.
You SPIDERMAN for life. Fowever. I can't even
35 buin my suit. It won't buin. It's fwame wesistent.
So maybe dat's youwr pwoblem too, who knows.
Maybe dat's da whole pwoblem wif evwytin.
Nobody can buin der suits, dey all fwame wesistent.
Who knows?

—1980

✧   ✧   ✧

Yusef Komunyakaa
(1947-)

A native of Bogalusa, Louisiana, Komunyakaa has written memorably on a wide range of subjects, including jazz and his military service during the Vietnam War. *Copacetic*, his first collection of poems, appeared in 1984.

Facing It

My black face fades,
hiding inside the black granite.
I said I wouldn't,
dammit: No tears.
5 I'm stone. I'm flesh.
My clouded reflection eyes me
like a bird of prey, the profile of night
slanted against morning. I turn
this way—the stone lets me go.
10 I turn this way—I'm inside
the Viet Nam Veterans Memorial
again, depending on the light
to make a difference.
I go down the 58,022 names,
15 half-expecting to find
my own in letters like smoke.
I touch the name Andrew Johnson;

I see the booby trap's white flash.
Names shimmer on a woman's blouse
20 but when she walks away
the names stay on the wall.
Brushstrokes flash, a red bird's
wings cutting across my stare.
The sky. A plane in the sky.
25 A white vet's image floats
closer to me, then his pale eyes
look through mine. I'm a window.
He's lost his right arm
inside the stone. In the black mirror
30 a woman's trying to erase names:
No, she's brushing a boy's hair.

—1988

Timothy Steele
(1948-)

Steele, who has written a successful scholarly study of the rise of
free verse, *Missing Measures*, is perhaps the most skillful crafts-
man of the contemporary New Formalist poets. Born in Vermont,
he has lived for a number of years in Los Angeles, where he
teaches at California State University.

Sapphics° Against Anger

Angered, may I be near a glass of water;
May my first impulse be to think of Silence,
Its deities (who are they? do, in fact, they
            Exist? etc.).

5 May I recall what Aristotle says of
The subject: to give vent to rage is not to
Release it but to be increasingly prone
            To its incursions.

May I imagine being in the *Inferno*,
10 Hearing it asked: "Virgilio mio,° who's

Sapphics stanza form named after Sappho (c. 650 B.C.)   **10 Virgilio mio** Dante is addressing Virgil,
his guide through hell

That sulking with Achilles there?" and hearing
       Virgil say: "Dante,

That fellow, at the slightest provocation,
Slammed phone receivers down, and waved his arms like
15   A madman. What Attila did to Europe,
       What Genghis Khan did

To Asia, that poor dope did to his marriage."
May I, that is, put learning to good purpose,
Mindful that melancholy is a sin, though
20   Stylish at present.

Better than rage is the post-dinner quiet,
The sink's warm turbulence, the streaming platters,
The suds rehearsing down the drain in spirals
       In the last rinsing.

25   For what is, after all, the good life save that
Conducted thoughtfully, and what is passion
If not the holiest of powers, sustaining
       Only if mastered.

                      —1986

✧ ✧ ✧

David Bottoms
(1949-)

Born in Canton, Georgia, Bottoms is the author both of collections
of poetry and successful novels. His first book, *Shooting Rats at
Bibb County Dump*, was a winner of the Walt Whitman Award of
the Academy of American Poets. He is the co-editor, with Dave
Smith, of *The Morrow Anthology of Younger American Poets*.

Sign for My Father, Who Stressed the Bunt

On the rough diamond,
the hand-cut field below the dog lot and barn,
we rehearsed the strict technique
of bunting. I watched from the infield,
5   the mound, the backstop
as your left hand climbed the bat, your legs
and shoulders squared toward the pitcher.

You could drop it like a seed
down either base line. I admired your style,
10   but not enough to take my eyes off the bank
that served as our center-field fence.

Years passed, three leagues of organized ball,
no few lives. I could homer
into the left-field lot of Carmichael Motors,
15   and still you stressed the same technique,
the crouch and spring, the lead arm absorbing
just enough impact. That whole tiresome pitch
about basics never changing,
and I never learned what you were laying down.

20   Like a hand brushed across the bill of a cap,
let this be the sign
I'm getting a grip on the sacrifice.

—1983

James Fenton
(1949-)

Born in Lincoln, England, and educated at Oxford, Fenton has
worked extensively as a book and drama critic. A brilliant satiri-
cal poet, he has also written lyrics for *Les Misérables*, the musical
version of Victor Hugo's novel, and has served as a journalist in
Asia.

God, a Poem

A nasty surprise in a sandwich,
A drawing-pin caught in your sock.
The limpest of shakes from a hand which
You'd thought would be firm as a rock.

5   A serious mistake in a nightie,
A grave disappointment all around
Is all that you'll get from th'Almighty.
Is all that you'll get underground.

Oh, he *said:* 'If you lay off the crumpet°

---

9 crumpet vulgar British slang for women

10 I'll see you alright in the end.
Just hand on until the last trumpet.
Have faith in me, chum—I'm your friend.'

But if you remind him, he'll tell you:
I'm sorry, I must have been pissed—°
15 Though your name rings a sort of a bell. You
Should have guessed that I do not exist.

'I didn't exist at Creation,
I didn't exist at the Flood.
And I won't be around for Salvation
20 To sort out the sheep from the cud—

'Or whatever the phrase is. The fact is
In soteriological° terms
I'm a crude existential malpractice
And you are a diet of worms.

25 'You're a nasty surprise in a sandwich,
You're a drawing-pin caught in my sock.
You're the limpest of shakes from a hand which
I'd have thought would be firm as a rock,

'You're a serious mistake in a nightie,
30 You're a grave disappointment all round—
'That's all that you are,' says th'Almighty,
'And that's all that you'll be underground.'

—1983

Carolyn Forché
(1950-)

Forché won the Yale Younger Poets Award for her first collection,
Gathering the Tribes (1975). *The Country Between Us*, Forché's
second collection, contains poems based on the poet's experi-
ences in the war-torn country of El Salvador in the early 1980s.

---

14 pissed drunk   **22 soteriological** relation to salvation

The Colonel

What you have heard is true. I was in his house.° His wife carried a tray of coffee
and sugar. His daughter filed her nails, his son went out for the night. There were
daily papers, pet dogs, a pistol on the cushion beside him The moon swung bare
on its black cord over the house. On the television was a cop show. it was in
5   English. Broken bottles were embedded in the walls around the house to scoop the
kneecaps from a man's legs or cut his hands to lace. On the windows there were
gratings like those in liquor stores. We had dinner, rack of lamb, good wine, a
gold bell was on the table for calling the maid. The maid brought green
mangoes, salt, a type of bread. I was asked how I enjoyed the country. There was a
10 brief commercial in Spanish. His wife took everything away. There was some
talk then of how difficult it had become to govern. The parrot said hello on the
terrace. The colonel told it to shut up, and pushed himself from the table. My
friend said to me with his eyes: say nothing. The colonel returned with a sack used
to bring groceries home. He spilled many human ears on the table. They were like
15 dried peach halves. There is no other way to say this. He took one of them in his
hands, shook it in our faces, dropped it into a water glass. It came alive there. I am
tired of fooling around he said. As for the rights of anyone, tell your people they
can go fuck themselves. He swept the ears to the floor with his arm and held the
last of his wine in the air. Something for your poetry, no? he said. Some of the
20 ears on the floor caught this scrap of his voice. Some of the ears on the floor were
pressed to the ground.

—May 1978

Dana Gioia
(1950-)

Gioia, who grew up in the suburbs of Los Angeles, took a grad-
uate degree in English from Harvard but made a successful
career in business. He is usually mentioned as one of the leading
New Formalist poets and as an influential critic of contemporary
poetry whose essay "Can Poetry Matter?" stimulated much dis-
cussion when it appeared in The Atlantic in 1991.

Cruising with the Beachboys

So strange to hear that song again tonight
Travelling on business in a rented car
Miles from anywhere I've been before.

---

1 **his house** in El Salvador

And now a tune I haven't heard for years
5 Probably not since it last left the charts
Back in L.A. in 1969.
I can't believe I know the words by heart
And can't think of a girl to blame them on.

Every lovesick summer has its song,
10 And this one I pretended to despise,
But if I was alone when it came on,
I turned it up full-blast to sing along—
A primal scream in croaky baritone,
The notes all flat, the lyrics mostly slurred
15 No wonder I spent so much time alone
Making the rounds in Dad's old Thunderbird.

Some nights I drove down to the beach to park
And walk along the railings of the pier.
The water down below was cold and dark,
20 The waves monotonous against the shore.
The darkness and the mist, the midnight sea
The flickering lights reflected from the city—
A perfect setting for a boy like me,
The Cecil B. DeMille° of my self-pity.

25 I thought by now I'd left those nights behind,
Lost like the girls that I could never get,
Gone with the years, junked with the old T-Bird.
But one old song, a stretch of empty road,
Can open up a door and let them fall
30 Tumbling like boxes from a dusty shelf,
Tightening my throat for no reason at all
Bringing on tears shed only for myself.

—1986

Rodney Jones
(1950-)

Born in Alabama, Jones received important national attention
when *Transparent Gestures* won the Poets' Prize in 1990. Like
many younger southern poets, he often deals with the difficult

---

24 Cecil B. DeMille American director of spectacular films like *The Ten Commandments*

legacy of racism and the adjustments that a new era have
forced on both whites and blacks.

Winter Retreat: Homage to Martin Luther King, Jr.

There is a hotel in Baltimore where we came together,
we black and white educated and educators,
for a week of conferences, for important counsel
sanctioned by the DOE° and the Carter administration,
5   to make certain difficult inquiries, to collate notes
on the instruction of the disabled, the deprived,
the poor, who do not score well on entrance tests,
who, failing school, must go with mop and pail
skittering across the slick floors of cafeterias,
10   or climb dewy girders to balance high above cities,
or, jobless, line up in the bone cold. We felt
substantive burdens lighter if we stated it right.
Very delicately, we spoke in turn. We walked
together beside the still waters of behaviorism.
15   Armed with graphs and charts, with new strategies
to devise objectives and determine accountability,
we empathetic black and white shone in seminar rooms.
We enunciated every word clearly and without accent.
We moved very carefully in the valley of the shadow
20   of the darkest agreement error. We did not digress.
We ascended the trunk of that loftiest cypress
of Latin grammar the priests could never
successfully graft onto the rough green chestnut
of the English language. We extended ourselves
25   with that sinuous motion of the tongue that is half
pain and almost eloquence. We black and white
politely reprioritized the parameters of our agenda
to impact equitably on the Seminole and the Eskimo.
We praised diversity and involvement, the sacrifices
30   of fathers and mothers. We praised the next white
Gwendolyn Brooks° and the next black Robert Burns.°
We deep made friends. In that hotel we glistened
over the *pommes au gratin* ° and the *poitrine de veau* .°
The morsels of lamb flamed near where we talked.
35   The waiters bowed and disappeared among the ferns.
And there is a bar there, there is a large pool.

---

4 DOE Department of Education   **31 Gwendolyn Brooks** black American poet (b. 1917)   **Robert
Burns** Scottish poet (1759-1796)   **33 *pommes au gratin*** potatoes baked with cheese   ***poitrine de
veau*** brisket of veal

Beyond the tables of the drinkers and raconteurs,
beyond the hot tub brimming with Lebanese tourists
and the women in expensive bathing suits doing laps,
40   if you dive down four feet, swim out far enough,
and emerge on the other side, it is sixteen degrees.
It is sudden and very beautiful and colder
than thought, though the air frightens you at first,
not because it is cold, but because it is visible,
45   almost palpable, in the fog that rises from difference.
While I stood there in the cheek-numbing snow,
all Baltimore was turning blue. And what I remember
of that week of talks is nothing the record shows,
but the revelation outside, which was the city
50   many came to out of the fields, then the thought
that we had wanted to make the world kinder,
but, in speaking proudly, we had failed a vision.

                                                        —1989

Joy Harjo
(1951-)

A member of the Creek tribe, Harjo is one of the leading voices
of contemporary Native-American poetry. She is a powerful
performer and was one of the poets featured on Bill Moyers's
television series, *The Power of the Word.*

Song for the Deer and Myself to Return On

This morning when I looked out the roof window
before dawn and a few stars were still caught
in the fragile weft of ebony night
I was overwhelmed. I sang the song Louis taught me:
5   a song to call the deer in Creek,° when hunting,
and I am certainly hunting something as magic as deer
in this city far from the hammock of my mother's belly.
It works, of course, and deer came into this room
and wondered at finding themselves
10   in a house near downtown Denver.
Now the deer and I are trying to figure out a song
to get them back, to get all of us back,

---

5 **Creek** Native-American tribal language

because if it works I'm going with them.
And it's too early to call Louis
15   and nearly too late to go home.

—1990

Garrett Hongo
(1951-)

Of Japanese ancestry, Garrett Kaoru Hongo was born in Hawaii
and educated at Pomona College and the University of
California at Irvine. His books include *Yellow Light* (1982) and *The
River of Heaven* (1988).

Crossing Ka'ū Desert°

from under the harpstring shade of tree ferns
and the blue trumpets of morning glories
          beside the slick road,
the green creep of davallia and club moss
5   (their tiny hammers
                              staffed quarter-notes
                    and fiddlenecks on the forest floor),
spider lilies and ginger flowers like paper cranes
          furling in the tongues of overgrowth,
10   in the sapphired arpeggios of rain

to the frozen, shale-colored sea,
          froth, swirls, bleak dithyrambs of glass,
a blizzard of cinderrock and singed amulets,
warty spires and pipelines,
15   threnodies of surf whirling on the lava land—
our blue car the last note of color
driving a black channel
                    through hymnless ground

—1988

Andrew Hudgins
(1951-)

Reared in Montgomery, Alabama, Hudgins has demonstrated

Ka'ū Desert on the island of Hawaii

his poetic skills in a wide variety of poems, including a book-length sequence of dramatic monologues, *After the Lost War*, in the voice of Sidney Lanier, the greatest southern poet of the late 19th century.

Air View of an Industrial Scene

There is a train at the ramp, unloading people
who stumble from the cars and toward the gate.
The building's shadows tilt across the ground
and from each shadow juts a longer one
5   and from that shadow crawls a shadow of smoke
black as just-plowed earth. Inside the gate
is a small garden and someone on his knees.
Perhaps he's fingering the yellow blooms
to see which ones have set and will soon wither,
10 clinging to a green tomato as it swells.
The people hold back, but are forced to the open gate,
and when they enter they will see the garden
and some, gardeners themselves, will yearn
to fall to their knees there, untangling vines,
15 plucking at weeds, cooling their hands in damp earth.
They're going to die soon, a matter of minutes.
Even from our height, we see in the photograph
the shadow of the plane stamped dark and large
on Birkenau,° one black wing shading the garden.
20 We can't tell which are guards, which prisoners.
We're watchers. But if we had bombs we'd drop them.

—1985

✧   ✧   ✧

Rita Dove
(1952-)

Dove won the Pulitzer prize in 1987 for *Thomas and Beulah*, a sequence of poems about her grandparents' lives in Ohio. She is one of the most important voices of the younger generation of black American poets.

Adolescence—III

With Dad gone, Mom and I worked

---

19 **Birkenau** German concentration camp in WWII

The dusky rows of tomatoes.
As they glowed orange in sunlight
And rotted in shadow, I too
5   Grew orange and softer, swelling out
Starched cotton slips.

The texture of twilight made me think of
Lengths of Dotted Swiss.° In my room
I wrapped scarred knees in dresses
10   That once went to big-band dances;
I baptized my earlobes with rosewater.
Along the window-sill, the lipstick stubs
Glittered in their steel shells.

Looking out at the rows of clay
15   And chicken manure, I dreamed how it would happen:
He would meet me by the blue spruce,
A carnation over his heart, saying,
"I have come for you, Madam;
I have loved you in my dreams."
20   At his touch, the scabs would fall away.
Over his shoulder, I see my father coming toward us:
He carries his tears in a bowl,
And blood hangs in the pine-soaked air.

—1980

✧ ✧ ✧

Naomi Shihab Nye
(1952-)

A dedicated world traveler and humanitarian, Nye has read her
poetry in Bangladesh and the Middle East. Many of her poems
are informed by her Lebanese ancestry, and she has translated
contemporary Arabic poetry.

The Traveling Onion

"It is believed that the onion originally came from India. In Egypt it was an object of
worship—why I haven't been able to find out. From Egypt the onion entered Greece
and on to Italy, thence into all of Europe." *Better Living Cookbook*

When I think how far the onion has traveled

---

8 **Dotted Swiss** type of sheer fabric

5   just to enter my stew today, I could kneel and praise
all small forgotten miracles,
crackly paper peeling on the drainboard,
pearly layers in smooth agreement,
the way knife enters onion
10 and onion falls apart on the chopping block,
a history revealed.

And I would never scold the onion
for causing tears.
It is right that tears fall
15 for something small and forgotten.
How at meal, we sit to eat,
commenting on texture of meat or herbal aroma
but never on the translucence of onion,
now limp, now divided,
20 or its traditionally honorable career:
For the sake of others,
disappear.

—1986

Alberto Ríos
(1952-)

Born in Nogales, Arizona, the son of a Mexican-American father
and an English-born mother, Ríos won the Walt Whitman Award of
the Academy of American Poets for his first book, *Whispering to
Fool the Wind* (1982). He has also written a collection of short sto-
ries, *The Iguana Killer: Twelve Stories of the Heart*, which won the
Western States Book Award in 1984.

The Purpose of Altar Boys

Tonio told me at catechism
the big part of the eye
admits good, and the little
black part is for seeing
5 evil—his mother told him
who was a widow and so
an authority on such things.
That's why at night
the black part gets bigger.
10 That's why kids can't go out

at night, and at night
girls take off their clothes
and walk around their
bedrooms or jump on their
15 beds or wear only sandals
and stand in their windows.
I was the altar boy
who knew about these things,
whose mission on some Sundays
20 was to remind people of
the night before as they
knelt for Holy Communion.
To keep Christ from falling
I held the metal plate
25 under chins,
while on the thick
red carpet of the altar
I dragged my feet
and waited for the precise
30 moment: plate to chin
I delivered without expression
the Holy Electric Shock,
the kind that produces
a really large swallowing
35 and makes people think.
I thought of it as justice.
But on other Sundays the fire
in my eyes was different,
my mission somehow changed.
40 I would hold the metal plate
a little too hard
against those certain same
nervous chins, and I
I would look
45 with authority down
the tops of white dresses.

                                              —1982

Gary Soto
(1952-)

A professor of Chicano Studies at the University of California at
Berkeley, Soto grew up in Fresno. His poetry collections *The
Elements of San Joaquin* (1977) and *The Tale of Sunlight* (1978)
appeared in the 1970s. A prose book, *Living Up the Street*

(1984), is a memoir of his urban childhood.

How Things Work

Today it's going to cost us twenty dollars
To live. Five for a softball. Four for a book,
A handful of ones for coffee and two sweet rolls,
Bus fare, rosin for your mother's violin.
5   We're completing our task. The tip I left
For the waitress filters down
Like rain, wetting the new roots of a child
Perhaps, a belligerent cat that won't let go
Of a balled sock until there's chicken to eat.
10 As far as I can tell, daughter, it works like this:
You buy bread from a grocery, a bag of apples
From a fruit stand, and what coins
Are passed on helps others buy pencils, glue,
Tickets to a movie in which laughter
15 Is thrown into their faces.
If we buy a goldfish, someone tries on a hat.
If we buy crayons, someone walks home with a broom.
A tip, a small purchase here and there,
And things just keep going. I guess.

—1985

Cathy Song
(1955-)

Song was born in Honolulu, Hawaii, and holds degrees from Wellesley College and Boston University. Her first book, *Picture Bride*, won the Yale Series of Younger Poets Award in 1983, and a second collection, *Frameless Windows, Squares of Light*, followed in 1988.

Stamp Collecting

The poorest countries
have the prettiest stamps
as if impracticality were a major export
shipped with the bananas, t-shirts, and coconuts.
5 Take Tonga,° where the tourists,
expecting a dramatic waterfall replete with birdcalls,

---

5 **Tonga** island in southwestern Pacific

are taken to see the island's peculiar mystery:
hanging bats with collapsible wings
like black umbrellas swing upside down from fruit trees.
10   The Tongan stamp is a fruit.
The banana stamp is scalloped like a butter-varnished seashell.
The pineapple resembles a volcano, a spout of green on top,
and the papaya, a tarnished goat skull.

They look impressive,
15   these stamps of countries without a thing to sell
except for what is scraped, uprooted and hulled
from their mule-scratched hills.
They believe in postcards,
in portraits of progress: the new dam;
20   a team of young native doctors
wearing stethoscopes like exotic ornaments;
the recently constructed "Facultad de Medicina,"°
a building as lack-lustre as an American motel.

The stamps of others are predictable.
25   Lucky is the country that possesses indigenous beauty.
Say a tiger or a queen.
The Japanese can display to the world
their blossoms: a spray of pink on green.
Like pollen, they drift, airborne.
30   But pity the country that is bleak and stark.

Beauty and whimsey are discouraged as indiscreet.
Unbreakable as their climate, a monument of ice,
they issue serious statements, commemorating
factories, tramways and aeroplanes;
35   athletes marbled into statues.
They turn their noses upon the world, these countries,
and offer this: an unrelenting procession
of a grim, historic profile.

—1988

---

2 **Facultad de Medicina** Medical Faculty (building)

Li-Young Lee
(1957-)

Born in Indonesia to parents who emigrated to the United States, Lee combines a rich heritage of traditional Chinese poetry with many western influences, including Christian teachings he learned from his father, a Presbyterian minister. *Rose*, his first collection, appeared in 1986.

Eating Together

In the steamer is the trout
seasoned with slivers of ginger,
two sprigs of green onion, and sesame oil.
We shall eat it with rice for lunch,
5   brothers, sister, my mother who will
taste the sweetest meat of the head,
holding it between her fingers
deftly, the way my father did
weeks ago. Then he lay down
10 to sleep like a snow-covered road
winding through pines older than him,
without any travelers, and lonely for no one.

—1985

Appendix 1

Poems Grouped by Genre, Technique, or Subject

Since it is possible to classify the poems in the anthology in many different ways, the following appendix is not exhaustive. It should, however, provide suggestions for reading and writing about poems that share some similarities. Some poems appear in more than one category.

ADOLESCENCE

AGING (See also CARPE DIEM)

ALLEGORICAL AND SYMBOLIC POETRY

ANIMALS

ART: IMMORTALITY OF ART (ARS LONGA VITA BREVIS)

CARPE DIEM

CONCEIT AND EXTENDED METAPHOR

Appendix 2

Traditional Stanza and Fixed Forms

BALLAD STANZA (AND VARIANTS)

Anonymous: Bonny Barbara Allan 37
Anonymous: Sir Patrick Spens 38
Auden, W.H.: As I Walked Out One Evening 206
Hollander, John: Adam's Task 263
Housman, A.E.: Is My Team Plowing? 157
Keats, John: La Belle Dame sans Merci 106
Petersen, Donald: The Ballad of Dead Yankees 259
Plath, Sylvia: Daddy 276
Roethke, Theodore: My Papa's Waltz 210
Rossetti, Christina: Up-Hill 149
Waniek, Marilyn Nelson: The Ballad of Aunt Geneva 309

BLANK VERSE

Coleridge, Samuel Taylor: Frost at Midnight 96
Frost, Robert: Home Burial 167
Hudgins, Andrew: Air View of an Industrial Scene 323
Ruark, Gibbons: The Visitor 297
Stafford, William: Traveling Through the Dark 216
Stevens, Wallace: Sunday Morning 174
Tennyson, Alfred, Lord: Ulysses 126
Wordsworth, William: Lines (Composed a Few Miles Above Tintern Abbey . . . 86
Yeats, William Butler: The Second Coming 161

COMMON MEASURE

Anonymous: Western Wind 37
Burns, Robert: A Red, Red Rose 83
Cullen, Countee: Incident 204
Dickinson, Emily: Because I Could Not Stop for Death 146
Dickinson, Emily: I Died for Beauty— But Was Scarce 147

Dickinson, Emily: I Heard a Fly Buzz— When I Died 147
Dickinson, Emily: My Life Closed Twice Before Its Close 148
Dickinson, Emily: A Narrow Fellow in the Grass 148
Dickinson, Emily: The Soul Selects Her Own Society 149
Herrick, Robert: To the Virgins, to Make Much of Time 57
Lovelace, Richard: To Lucasta, Going to the Wars 64

FOURTEENERS

Southwell, Robert: The Burning Babe 44

HEROIC COUPLETS

Bradstreet, Anne: The Author to Her Book 63
Bradstreet, Anne: To My Dear and Loving Husband 63
Browning, Robert: My Last Duchess 129
Dryden, John: Epigram on Milton 66
Jonson, Ben: On My First Son 56
Pope, Alexander: An Essay on Criticism (selection) 70
Rich, Adrienne: Aunt Jennifer's Tigers 265
Swift, Jonathan: A Description of a City Shower 68
Toomer, Jean: Reapers 201

IN MEMORIAM STANZA

Tennyson, Alfred, Lord: In Memoriam A.H.H., 54 125

LONG MEASURE

Emerson, Ralph Waldo: Concord Hymn 112
Kizer, Carolyn: The Ungrateful Garden 246
Landor, Walter Savage: Mother, I Cannot 100

Index
to
Poets, Titles, and First Lines

Alphabetical List of Terms Found in the Introduction

Acknowledgments

Betty Adcock, "Digression on the Nuclear Age" reprinted by permission of Louisiana State University Press from *Beholdings* by Betty Adcock. Copyright © 1988 by Betty Adcock.

Ai, "Child Beater", from *Cruelty* by Ai. Copyright © 1970, 1973 by Ai. Reprinted by permission of Houghton Mifflin Company. All rights reserved.

John Ashbery, "Paradoxes and Oxymorons" from *Shadow Train* by John Ashbery (New York: Viking Penguin, 1981). Reprinted by permission of Georges Borchardt, Inc. for the author. Copyright © 1980, 1981 by John Ashbery. "What is Poetry" from *Houseboat Days* by John Ashbery (New York: Viking, 1977). Reprinted by permission of Georges Borchardt, Inc. for the author. Copyright © 1975, 1976, 1977 by John Ashbery.

Margaret Atwood, "Siren Song" from *You Are Happy*, reprinted in *Selected Poems 1965-1975* and *Selected Poems 1966-1984* by Margaret Atwood. Copyright © 1976 by Margaret Atwood, copyright © Margaret Atwood 1990. Reprinted by permission of Houghton Mifflin Company and Oxford University Press Canada. All rights reserved.

W.H. Auden, "As I Walked Out One Evening," "Musee des Beaux Arts," and "The Unknown Citizen." From *W.H. Auden: Collected Poems* by W.H. Auden, ed. by Edward Mendelson. Copyright 1940 and renewed 1968 by W.H. Auden. Reprinted by permission of Random House, Inc. and Faber and Faber Ltd.

Elizabeth Bishop, "The Fish" and "One Art" from *The Complete Poems 1927-1979* by Elizabeth Bishop. Copyright © 1979, 1983 by Alice Helen Methfessel. Reprinted by permission of Farrar, Straus & Giroux, Inc.

David Bottoms, "Sign for My Father Who Stressed the Bunt. Copyright © 1983 David Bottoms. From *In a U-Haul North of Damascus* published by William Morrow and Company, Inc., New York. Reprinted by permission of Maria Carvainis Agency.

Anne Bradstreet, "The Author to Her Book" and "To My Dear and Loving Husband." Reprinted by permission of the publishers from *The Works of Anne Bradstreet* edited by Jeannine Hensley, Cambridge, Mass.: Harvard University Press, Copyright ©1967 by the President and Fellows of Harvard College.

Gwendolyn Brooks, "the mother" and "We Real Cool" from *Blacks* by Gwendolyn Brooks. Copyright © 1991 by Gwendolyn Brooks. Reprinted by permission of the author.

Gladys Cardiff, "Combing." Copyright © 1971 by Gladys Cardiff. Reprinted from *To Frighten a Storm* (Copper Canyon Press, 1976) by permission of the author.

Charles Causley, "Eden Rock" from *Secret Destinations: Selected Poems 1977-1988* by Charles Causley. Copyright © 1989 by Charles Causley. Reprinted by permission of David R. Godine, Publisher.

Fred Chappell, "Narcissus and Echo" reprinted by permission of Lousiana State University Press from *Source* by Fred Chappell. Copyright ©1985 by Fred Chappell.

Lucille Clifton, "homage to my hips" from *two-headed woman* by Lucille Clifton (University of Massachusetts Press, 1980). Reprinted by permission of Curtis Brown, Ltd. Copyright © 1980 by Lucille Clifton.

Hart Crane, "Chaplinesque" is reprinted from from *The Poems of Hart Crane*, Edited by Marc Simon, by permission of Liveright Publishing Corporation. Copyright © 1986 by Marc Simon.

Robert Creeley, "Oh No" from *Collected Poems of Robert Creeley 1945-1975.* Copyright © 1983 The Regents of the University of California. Reprinted by permission of the Regents of the University of California and the University of California Press.

Gountee Cullen, "Incident" and "Yet Do I Marvel." Reprinted by permission of GRM Associates, Inc., Agents for the Estate of Ida M. Cullen. From the book *Color* by Countee Cullen. Copyright 1925 by Harper & Brothers; copyright renewed 1953 by Ida M. Cullen.

E.E. Cummings, "in Just-", "pity this busy monster, manukind", and "r-p-o-p-h-e-s-s-a-g-r". Reprinted from *Complete Poems, 1913-1962* by E.E. Cummings, by permission of Liveright Publishing Corporation. Copyright 1923, 1925, 1931, 1935, 1938, 1939, 1940, 1944, 1945, 1946, 1947, 1948, 1949, 1950, 1951, 1952, 1953, 1954, © 1955, 1956, 1957, 1958, 1959, 1960, 1961, 1962 by the Trustees for the E.E. Cummings Trust. Copyright © 1961, 1963, 1968 by Marion Morehouse Cummings.

James Dickey, "Cherrylog Road" from *Poems 1957-1967* by James Dickey, copyright 1963 by James Dickey, Wesleyan University Press by permission of University Press of New England.

Emily Dickinson, "Because I could not stop for Death," "I died for Beauty," "I heard a Fly buzz—when I died," "My life closed twice before its close," "A narrow Fellow in the Grass," and "The Soul selects her own Society." Reprinted by permission of the publishers and the Trustees of Amherst College from *The Poems of Emily Dickinson*, Thomas H. Johnson, ed., Cambridge, Mass.: The Belknap Press of Harvard University Press. Copyright 1951, © 1955, 1979, 1983 by the President and Fellows of Harvard College.

H.D. (Hilda Doolittle), "Pear Tree" from H.D.: *Collected Poems 1912-1944.* Copyright © 1982 by The Estate of Hilda Doolittle. Reprinted by permission of New Directions Publishing Corporation.

Rita Dove, "Adolescence—III." Reprinted from *The Yellow House on the Corner* by Rita Dove. Copyright © 1980 by Rita Dove. By permission of Carnegie Mellon University Press.

Alan Dugan, "Love Song: I and Thou" © 1961, 1962, 1968, 1972, 1973, 1974, 1983 by Alan Dugan. From *New and Collected Poems 1961-1983* by Alan Dugan, first published by The Ecco Press in 1983. Reprinted by permission.

Stephen Dunn, "The Sacred" is reprinted from *Between Angels*, Poems by Stephen Dunn, by permission of W.W. Norton & Company, Inc. Copyright © 1989 by Stephen Dunn.

Richard Eberhart, "The Fury of Aerial Bombardment." From *Collected Poems 1930-1986* by Richard Eberart. Copyright © 1988 by Richard Eberhart. Reprinted by permission of Oxford University Press, Inc.

T.S. Eliot, "Journey of the Magi" from *Collected Poems 1909-1962* by T.S. Eliot, copyright 1936 by Harcourt Brace Jovanovich, Inc., copyright © 1964, 1963 by T.S. Eliot, reprinted by permission of the publishers, Harcourt Brace & Company, and Faber and Faber Ltd. "The Love Song of J. Alfred Prufrock" appeared in the June 1915 issue of *Poetry* Magazine. Reprinted from *Collected Poems 1909-1962* by T.S. Eliot by permission of Faber and Faber Ltd.

James Fenton, "God: A Poem." From *Children in Exile* by James Fenton. Copyright ©1972, 1978, 1980, 1981, 1982, 1983 by James Fenton. Reprinted by permission of Random House, Inc.

Carolyn Forche, "The Colonel" from *The Country Between Us* by Carolyn Forche. Copyright ©1980 by Carolyn Forche. Reprinted by permission of HarperCollins Publishers.

Robert Frost, "Design" and "Stopping by Woods on a Snowy Evening." Copyright 1923, © 1969 by Holt, Rinehart and Winston. Copyright 1936, 1951 by Robert Frost. Copyright ©1964 by Lesley Frost

Ballantine. "Acquainted with the Night." Copyright 1928, © 1956 by Robert Frost. Copyright © 1969 by Holt, Rinehart and Winston. "Home Burial," "The Road Not Taken," Copyright 1916, 1930, 1939, © 1969 by Holt, Rinehart and Winston. Copyright 1944, © 1958 by Robert Frost. Copyright 1967 by Lesley Frost Ballantine. Lines from "The Oven Bird" Copyright 1916, © 1969 by Henry Holt and Company, Inc. Copyright 1944 by Robert Frost. From *The Poetry of Robert Frost* edited by Edward Connery Lathem. Reprinted by permission of Henry Holt and Company, Inc.

Gary Gildner, "First Practice." Reprinted from *First Practice*, by Gary Gildner, by permission of the University of Pittsburgh Press. © 1969 by the University of Pittsburgh Press.

Allen Ginsberg, "A Supermarket in California." Copyright © 1955 by Allen Ginsberg. From *Collected Poems 1947-1980*. Reprinted by permission of HarperCollins Publishers.

Dana Gioia, "Cruising with the Beachboys" copyright 1986 by Dana Gioia. Reprinted from *Daily Horoscope* with the permission of Graywolf Press, St. Paul, Minnesota.

Jim Hall, "Maybe Dat's Your Pwoblem Too." Reprinted from *The Mating Reflex* by Jim Hall. Copyright © 1980 by Jim Hall. By permission of Carnegie Mellon University Press.

Joy Harjo, "Song for the Deer and Myself to Return On" from *In Mad Love and War* by Joy Harjo, copyright 1990 by Joy Harjo, Wesleyan University Press by permission of University Press of New England.

Tony Harrison, "Self Justification." From *Selected Poems* by Tony Harrison. Copyright © 1987 by Tony Harrison. Reprinted by permission of Random House, Inc.

Robert Hass, "Picking Blackberries with a Friend Who Has Been Reading Jacques Lacan" © 1974, 1975, 1976, 1977, 1978, 1979 by Robert Hass. From *Praise* by Robert Hass, first published in 1979 by The Ecco Press. Reprinted by permission.

Robert Hayden, "Those Winter Sundays" is reprinted from *Collected Poems* of Robert Hayden, Edited by Frederick Glaysher, by permission of Liveright Publishing Corporation. Copyright ©1985 by Erma Hayden.

Seamus Heaney, "Digging" from *Selected Poems 1966-1987* by Seamus Heaney. Copyright © 1990 by Seamus Heaney. Reprinted by permission of Farrar, Straus & Giroux, Inc. and Faber and Faber Ltd.

Anthony Hecht, "'More Light, More Light!'." From *Collected Earlier Poems* by Anthony Hecht. Copyright © 1990 by Anthony Hecht. "In Memory of David Kalstone." From *The Transparent Man* by Anthony Hecht. Copyright © 1990 by Anthony Hecht. Reprinted by permission of Alfred A. Knopf, Inc.

Jonathan Holden, "Liberace." Reprinted from *Falling from Stardom* by Jonathan Holden. Copyright © 1984 by Jonathan Holden. By permission of Carnegie Mellon University Press.

John Hollander, "Adam's Task." From *Selected Poetry* by John Hollander. Copyright © 1993 by John Hollander. Reprinted by permission of Alfred A. Knopf, Inc.

Garrett Hongo, "Crossing Ka'u Desert." From *The River of Heaven* by Garrett Hongo. Copyright ©1988 by Garrett Hongo. Reprinted by permission of Alfred A. Knopf, Inc.

A.E. Housman, "Eight O'Clock." From *Last Poems* by A.E. Housman. Copyright 1922 by Holt, Rinehart and Winston. Copyright 1950 by Barclays Bank Ltd. From *The Collected Poems of A.E. Housman*. Copyright 1939, 1940, © 1964 by Holt, Rinehart and Winston. Copyright © 1967. 1968 by Robert E. Symons. Reprinted by permission of Henry Holt and Co., Inc.

Andrew Hudgins, "Air View of an Industrial Scene", from *Saints and Strangers* by Andrew Hudgins. Copyright © 1985 by Andrew Hudgins. Reprinted by permission of Houghton Mifflin Company. All rights reserved. First published in *Poetry*.

Langston Hughes, "Dream Deferred" ("Harlem"). From *The Panther and the Lash* by Langston Hughes. Copyright 1951 by Langston Hughes. Reprinted by permission of Alfred A. Knopf, Inc. "The Negro Speaks of Rivers." From *Selected Poems* by Langston Hughes. Copyright 1926 by Alfred A. Knopf, Inc. and renewed 1954 by Langston Hughes. Reprinted by permission of the publisher.

Ted Hughes, "Pike" from *Selected Poems 1957-1981* by Ted Hughes. Copyright ©1959 by Ted Hughes. Reprinted by permission of HarperCollins Publishers and Faber and Faber Ltd. Ted Hughes, "The Thought-Fox" from *New Selcted Poems* by Ted Hughes. First Published in *The New Yorker*. Copyright © 1957, 1982 by Ted Hughes. Reprinted by permission of HarperCollins Publishers and Faber and Faber, Ltd.

Randall Jarrell, "The Death of the Ball Turret Gunner" from *The Complete Poems* by Randall Jarrell. Copyright ©1945, 1969 by Mrs. Randall Jarrell. Reprinted by permission of Farrar, Straus & Giroux, Inc.

Robinson Jeffers, "The Purse-Seine." From *The Selected Poetry of Robinson Jeffers* by Robinson Jeffers. Copyright 1937 and renewed 1965 by Donnan Jeffers and Garth Jeffers. Reprinted by permission of Random House, Inc.

Rodney Jones, "Winter Retreat: Homage to Martin Luther King, Jr." from *Transparent Gestures* by Rodney Jones. Copyright © 1989 by Rodney Jones. Reprinted by permission of Houghton Mifflin Company. All rights reserved. Originally published in *The Missouri Review*.

Donald Justice, "Counting the Mad" from *The Summer Anniversaries* by Donald Justice, copyright 1981 by Donald Justice, Wesleyan University Press by permission of University Press of New England.

Weldon Kees, "For My Daughter." Reprinted from *The Collected Poems of Weldon Kees*, edited by Donald Justice, by permission of the University of Nebraska Press. Copyright ©1975 by the University of Nebraska Press.

X.J. Kennedy, "In a Prominent Bar in Secaucus One Day" from *Cross Ties: Selected Poems* by X.J. Kennedy. Copyright © 1985 by X.J. Kennedy. Reprinted by permission of The University of Georgia Press.

Carolyn Kizer, "The Ungrateful Garden" from *Midnight Was My Cry: New & Selected Poems*. Copyright © 1961 by Carolyn Kizer. Reprinted by permission of the author.

Etheridge Knight, "For Black Poets Who Think of Suicide." Reprinted from *The Essential Etheridge Knight*, by Etheridge Knight, by permission of the University of Pittsburgh Press. © 1986 by Etheridge Knight.

Yusef Komunyakaa, "Facing It" from *Dien Cai Dau* by Yusef Komunyakaa, copyright 1988 by Yusef Komunyakaa, Wesleyan University Press by permission of University Press of New England.

Maxine Kumin, "Noted in *The New York Times*", from *Nurture* by Maxine Kumin. Copyright © 1989 by Maxine Kumin. Used by permission of Viking Penguin, a division of Penguin Books USA Inc.

Philip Larkin, "Next, Please" is reprinted from *The Less Deceived* by permission of The Marvell Press, England and Australia. Copyright © The Marvell Press 1955. "The Old Fools" and "This Be the Verse" from *High Windows* by Philip Larkin. Copyright © 1974 by Philip Larkin. Reprinted by permssion of Farrar, Straus & Giroux, Inc. and Faber and Faber Ltd.

D.H. Lawrence, "Piano" from *The Complete Poems of D.H. Lawrence* by D.H. Lawrence. Copyright © 1964, 1971 by Angelo Ravagli and C.M. Weekely, Executors of the Estate of Frieda Lawrence Ravagli. Used by permission of Viking Penguin, a division of Penguin Books USA Inc.

Li-Young Lee, "Eating Together" copyright © 1986 by Li-Young Lee. Reprinted from *Rose* by Li-Young Lee with the permission of BOA Editions, Ltd., 92 Park Ave., Brockport, NY 14420.

Denise Levertov, "The Ache of Marriage" from Denise Levertov: *Poems 1960-1967*. Copyright © 1964 by Denise Levertov Goodman. Reprinted by permission of New Directions Publishing Corporation.

Philip Levine, "Genius." From *New Selected Poems* by Philip Levine. Copyright ©1991 by Philip Levine. Reprinted by permission of Alfred A. Knopf, Inc.

Robert Lowell, "For the Union Dead" from *For the Union Dead* by Robert Lowell. Copyright © 1964 by Robert Lowell. Reprinted by permission of Farrar, Straus & Giroux, Inc.

Claude McKay, lines from "If We Must Die." From *Selected Poems of Claude McKay*, published by Harcourt Brace Jovanovich, 1981. By permission of The Archives of Claude McKay: Carl Cowl, Administrator.

Archibald MacLeish, "The End of the World", from *Collected Poems 1917-1982* by Archibald MacLeish. Copyright © 1985 by the Estate of Archibald MacLeish. Reprinted by permission of Houghton Mifflin Company. All rights reserved.

Charles Martin, "E.S.L." From *Steal the Bacon* by Charles Martin, © 1987 The Johns Hopkins University Press. Reprinted by permission of the publisher.

James Merrill, "Casual Wear" (Part I of "Topics") from *Selected Poems 1946-1985* by James Merrill. Copyright © 1992 by James Merrill. "Investiture at Cecconi's" from *The Inner Room* by James Merrill. Copyright © 1988 by James Merrill. Reprinted by permission of Alfred A. Knopf, Inc.

W.S. Merwin, "For the Anniversary of My Death" from *The Lice* by W.S. Merwin. Copyright © 1967 by R.S. Gwynn. Reprinted by permission of Georges Borchardt, Inc.

Edna St. Vincent Millay, "If I should learn, in some quite casual way," "Oh, oh, you will be sorry for that word!" and "What lips my lips have kissed, and where, and why." From *Collected Poems* by Edna St. Vincent Millay, HarperCollins. Copyright 1917, 1923, 1945, 1951 by Edna St. Vincent Millay and Norma Millay Ellis. Reprinted by permission of Elizabeth Barnett, literary executor.

Vassar Miller, "Subterfuge" from *If I Had Wheels of Love: Collected Poems* by Vassar Miller. Reprinted by permission of Southern Methodist University Press.

Marianne Moore, "Poetry" and "Silence." Reprinted with permission of Macmillan Publishing Company from *Complete Poems of Marianne Moore*. Copyright 1935 by Marianne Moore, renewed 1963 by Marianne Moore and T.S. Eliot.

Robert Morgan, the poem "Mountain Bride" by Robert Morgan from his book *Groundwork* (1979) is reprinted by permission of Gnomon Press.

Howard Nemerov, "The Goose Fish" and "A Primer of the Daily Round" from *New and Selected Poems* by Howard Nemerov, copyright © 1960 by Howard Nemerov (University of Chicago Press). Reprinted by permission of Margaret Nemerov.

Naomi Shihab Nye, "The Traveling Onion." Reprinted by permission of Naomi Shihab Nye from *Yellow Glove*, Breitenbush Books, Portland, OR. Copyright ©1986 by Naomi Shihab Nye.

Frank O'Hara, "The Day Lady Died" from *Lunch Poems* by Frank O'Hara. Copyright ©1964 by Frank O'Hara. Reprinted by permission of City Lights Books.

Sharon Olds, "The One Girl at the Boys Party." From *The Dead and the Living* by Sharon Olds. Copyright ©1983 by Sharon Olds. Reprinted by permission of Alfred A. Knopf, Inc.

Mary Oliver, "The Black Walnut Tree" from *Twelve Moons: Poems* by Mary Oliver. Copyright © 1978 by Mary Oliver. First appeared in *The Ohio Review*. By permission of Little, Brown and Company.

Wilfred Owen, "Dulce et Decorum Est" from Wilfred Owen: *Collected Poems of Wilfred Owen*. Copyright © 1963 by Chatto & Windus Ltd. Reprinted by permission of New Directions Publishing Corporation.

Dorothy Parker, "One Perfect Rose", copyright 1929, renewed ©1957 by Dorothy Parker, "Résumé", copyright 1926, 1928, renewed 1954, © 1956 by Dorothy Parker, from *The Portable Dorothy Parker* by Dorothy Parker, Introduction by Brendan Gill. Used by permission of Viking Penguin, a division of Penguin Books USA Inc.

Linda Pastan, "Crocuses" is reprinted from *Heroes in Disguise*, Poems by Linda Pastan, by permission of W. W. Norton & Company, Inc. Copyright © 1991 by Linda Pastan.

Donald Petersen, "The Ballad of Dead Yankees" from *The Spectral Boy*. Copyright © 1964 by Donald Petersen. Reprinted by permission of the author.

Marge Piercy, "Barbie Doll." From *Circles on the Water* by Marge Piercy. Copyright © 1982 by Marge Piercy. Reprinted by permission of Alfred A. Knopf, Inc.

Sylvia Plath, "Daddy" and "Edge" by Sylvia Plath. Copyright ©1963 by Ted Hughes. "Metaphors" by Sylvia Plath. Copyright © 1960 by Ted Hughes. From *The Collected Poems of Sylvia Plath*, Edited by Ted Hughes. Reprinted by permission of HarperCollins Publishers and Faber and Faber Ltd.

Ezra Pound, "The River Merchant's Wife: A Letter" and "Sestina: Altaforte" from Ezra Pound: *Personae*. Copyright 1926 by Ezra Pound. Reprinted by permission of New Directions Publishing Corporation.

Craig Raine, "A Martian Sends a Postcard Home." © Craig Raine 1979. Reprinted from *A Martian Sends a Postcard Home* by Craig Raine (1979) by permission of Oxford University Press.

Dudley Randall, "Ballard of Birmingham" from *Cities Burning* by Dudley Randall. Copyright © 1966 by Dudley Randall. Reprinted by permission of Broadside Press.

John Crowe Ransom, "Bells for John Whiteside's Daughter" (Copyright 1924 by Alfred A. Knopf, Inc. and renewed 1952 by John Crowe Ransom) and "Piazza Piece" (Copyright 1927 by Alfred A. Knopf, Inc. and renewed 1955 by John Crowe Ransom). From *Selected Poems* by John Crowe Ransom. Reprinted by permission of the publisher.

Adrienne Rich, "Aunt Jennifer's Tigers," "Diving into the Wreck," and "Rape." Reprinted from *The Fact of a Doorframe*, Poems Selected and New, 1950-1984, by Adrienne Rich, by permission of W.W. Norton & Company, Inc. Copyright © 1984 by Adrienne Rich. Copyright ©1975, 1978 by W. W. Norton & Company, Inc. Copyright © 1981 by Adrienne Rich.

Alberto Rios, "The Purpose of Altar Boys" from *Whispering to Fool the Wind* (Sheep Meadow Press). Copyright © 1982 by Alberto Rios. Reprinted by permission of the author.

Edwin Arlington Robinson, "Firelight" and "The Mill." Copyright 1920 by Edwin Arlington Robinson, renewed 1948 by Ruth Nivison. Reprinted with permission of Macmillan Publishing Company from *Collected Poems of Edwin Arlington Robinson*.

Theodore Roethke, "Dolor", copyright 1943 by Modern Poetry Association, Inc. "My Papa's Waltz", copyright 1942 by Hearst Magazines, Inc. From *Collected Poems of Theodore Roethke* by Theodore Roethke. Used by permission of Doubleday, a division of Bantam Doubleday Dell Publishing Group., Inc.

Pattiann Rogers, "Concepts and Their Bodies (The Boy in the Field Alone)" from Rogers, Pattiann; *The Expectations of Light*. Copyright © 1981 by

Princeton University Press. Reprinted by permission of Princeton University Press.

Gibbons Ruark, "The Visitor" from A Program for Survival. Copyright © 1971 by the Rector and Visitors of the University of Virginia. Originally appeared in Poetry Magazine. Reprinted by permission of The University Press of Virginia.

Carl Sandburg, "Grass" from Cornhuskers by Carl Sandburg, copyright 1918 by Holt, Rinehart and Winston, Inc. and renewed 1946 by Carl Sandburg, reprinted by permission Harcourt Brace & Company.

Siegfried Sassoon, "The Hero" from Collected Poems 1908-1956 by Siegfried Sassoon. Copyright 1947, 1961 by Siegfried Sassoon. By permission of George Sassoon.

Anne Sexton, "The Truth the Dead Know", from All My Pretty Ones by Anne Sexton. Copyright © 1962 by Anne Sexton. "Wanting to Die", from Live or Die by Anne Sexton. Copyright ©1966 by Anne Sexton. Reprinted by permission of Houghton Mifflin Company. All rights reserved.

Enid Shomer, "Women Bathing at Bergen-Belsen" from Stalking the Florida Panther, published by The Word Works. Copyright ©1987 by Enid Shomer. Reprinted by permission of the author.

Charles Simic, "My Shoes" from Selected Poems 1963-1983. Copyright © 1971 by Charles Simic. Reprinted by permission of George Braziller, Inc.

Louis Simpson, "American Classic" from Caviare at the Funeral by Louis Simpson. Copyright © 1980 by Louis Simpson. Used with permission of the publisher Franklin Watts, Inc., New York. "My Father in the Night Commanding No" from At the End of the Open Road by Louis Simpson, copyright 1963 by Louis Simpson, Wesleyan University Press by permission of University Press of New England.

W.D. Snodgrass, "Mementos, I" reprinted by permission of Soho Press Inc. from W.D. Snodgrass, Selected Poems 1957-1987, © 1968, 1987 by W.D. Snodgrass.

Gary Snyder, "A Walk" from Gary Snyder: The Back Country. Copyright ©1968 by Gary Snyder. Reprinted by permission of New Directions Publishing Corporation.

Cathy Song, "Stamp Collecting" is reprinted from Frameless Windows. Squares of Light, Poems by Cathy Song, by permission of W.W. Norton & Company, Inc. Copyright © 1988 by Cathy Song.

Gary Soto, "How Things Work." Reprinted from Black Hair, by Gary Soto, by permission of the University of Pittsburgh Press. © 1985 by Gary Soto.

William Stafford, "Traveling through the Dark." Copyright © 1960 by William Stafford. Reprinted from Stories That Could Be True by permission of the author.

Timothy Steele, "Sapphics Against Anger" from Sapphics Against Anger and Other Poems (Random House, 1986). Copyright © 1986 by Timothy Steele. Reprinted by permission of the author.

Wallace Stevens, "The Snow Man," "Anecdote of the Jar," "Disillusionment of Ten O'Clock," and "Sunday Morning." From Collected Poems by Wallace Stevens. Copyright 1923 and renewed 1951 by Wallace Stevens. Reprinted by permission of Alfred A. Knopf, Inc.

Leon Stokesbury, "Day Begins at Governor's Square Mall." Reprinted by permission of the University of Arkansas Press from The Drifting Away by Leon Stokesbury, copyright 1986.

Mark Strand, "The Marriage". From Selected Poems by Mark Strand. Copyright ©1979, 1980 by Mark Strand. Reprinted by permission of Alfred A. Knopf, Inc.

James Tate, "Teaching the Ape to Write Poems" from Selected Poems. Copyright © 1970, 1971, 1972 by James Tate. By permission of Carnegie Mellon University Press.

Dylan Thomas, "Do not go gentle into that good night" and "Fern Hill" from Dylan Thomas: Poems of Dylan Thomas. Copyright 1945 by the Trustees for the Copyrights of Dylan Thomas. Reprinted by permission of New Directions Publishing Corporation and David Higham Associates Ltd.

Jean Toomer, "Reapers" is reprinted from Cane by Jean Toomer by permission of Liveright Publishing Corporation. Copyright 1923 by Boni & Liveright. Copyright renewed 1951 by Jean Toomer.

Ellen Bryant Voigt, "Daughter" is reprinted from The Forces of Plenty by Ellen Bryant Voigt, by permission of W.W. Norton & Company, Inc. Copyright © 1983 by Ellen Bryant Voigt.

Derek Walcott, "Central America" from The Arkansas Testament by Derek Walcott. Copyright © 1987 by Derek Walcott. "Sea Canes" from Collected Poems 1948-1984 by Derek Walcott. Copyright © 1986 by Derek Walcott. Reprinted by permission of Farrar, Straus & Giroux, Inc.

Alice Walker, "Even as I Hold You" from Good Night. Willie Lee. I'll See You in the Morning by Alice Walker. Copyright © 1979 by Alice Walker. Used by permission of Bantam Doubleday Dell Publishing Group, Inc.

Margaret Walker, "For Malcolm X" from This Is My Century: New and Collected Poems by Margaret Walker. Copyright © 1989 by Margaret Walker Alexander. Reprinted by permission of The University of Georgia Press.

Marilyn Nelson Waniek, "The Ballad of Aunt Geneva" reprinted by permission of Louisiana State University Press from The Home Place by Marilyn Nelson Waniek. Copyright © 1990 by Marilyn Nelson Waniek.

James Welch, "Christmas Comes to Moccasin Flat" from Riding the Earthboy 40 (Harper & Row, 1976). Reprinted by permission of James Welch. Copyright 1971 by James Welch.

Richard Wilbur, "Playboy" from Walking to Sleep: New Poems and Translations, copyright © 1968 by Richard Wilbur, reprinted by permission of Harcourt Brace & Company. "The Writer" from The Mind Reader, © 1971 by Richard Wilbur, reprinted by permission of Harcourt Brace Jovanovich, Inc. "Year's End" from Ceremony and Other Poems, copyright 1949 and renewed 1977 by Richard Wilbur, reprinted by permission of Harcourt Brace & Company. This poem first appeared in The New Yorker.

Nancy Willard, "A Hardware Store as Proof of the Existence of God." From Water Walker by Nancy Willard. Copyright © 1989 by Nancy Willard. Reprinted by permission of Alfred A. Knopf, Inc.

Miller Williams, "The Book" reprinted by permission of Louisiana State University Press from Living on the Surface by Miller Williams. Copyright © 1989 by Miller Williams.

William Carlos Williams, "The Red Wheelbarrow," "Spring and All," and "The Last Words of My English Grandmother" from William Carlos Williams: The Collected Poems of William Carlos Williams 1909-1939, Vol. I. Copyright 1938 by New Directions Publishing Corporation. Reprinted by permission of the publisher.

James Wright, "Autumn Begins in Martin's Ferry, Ohio" from The Branch Will Not Break by James Wright, copyright 1963 by James Wright. "Saint Judas" from Saint Judas by James Wright, copyright 1959 by James Wright, Wesleyan University Press by permission of University Press of New England.

William Butler Yeats, "Leda and the Swan" and "Sailing to Byzantium." Copyright 1928 by Macmillan Publishing Company, renewed 1956 by Bertha Georgie Yeats. "The Second Coming." Copyright 1924 by Macmillan Publishing Company, renewed 1952 by Bertha Georgie Yeats. Reprinted with permission of Macmillan Publishing Company from from The Poems of W.B. Yeats: A New Edition, edited by Richard J. Finneran.